wont we be happy together once more?
for I think we will be married soon
next year. I am really most anxious
to marry now – more than ever. Things
that have been in the way here tofore
can now be overcome. I think my
mind (is) better settled and really
wants some one to call wife. It is not
2 months now to Christmas

Wednesday night Oct. 30th Your
sweet letter came to hand to day
and made my heart leap for joy
for it always makes me happy to hear
from you. And I have been hoping
for that dear letter ever since Monday
but I got it now. So you really tried
to scold me + what for I dont know.
I assure you I did not go on a
spreeing with any one at al (all) for
I have not even been up to see Arthur
3 times since I was up home. I went
to see the girls 5 or 6 times while they
was here only for old acquaintance
?   Sara and I bought 3 tickets to go
and carry them to a party.

I Can't Wait to Call You My Wife

AFRICAN AMERICAN LETTERS OF LOVE AND FAMILY IN THE CIVIL WAR ERA

By Rita Roberts

CHRONICLE BOOKS

SAN FRANCISCO

For Angie and Becki

Library of Congress Cataloging-in-Publication Data

Names: Roberts, Rita, author.
Title: I can't wait to call you my wife : African American letters of love, marriage, and family in the Civil War era / Rita Roberts.
Other titles: African American letters of love, marriage, and family in the Civil War era
Description: San Francisco, California : Chronicle Books, [2022] | Includes bibliographical references and index. | Summary: "A collection of letters exchanged between African Americans during the Civil War era"-- Provided by publisher.
Identifiers: LCCN 2022012379 (print) | LCCN 2022012380 (ebook) | ISBN 9781797213729 (hardcover) | ISBN 9781797216379 (ebook)
Subjects: LCSH: United States--History--Civil War, 1861-1865--African Americans. | United States--History--Civil War, 1861-1865--Biography. | African Americans--Correspondence. | Slaves--United States--Correspondence. | Love-letters--United States--History--19th century. | United States--History--Civil War, 1861-1865--Social aspects. | African Americans--Family relationships--United States--History--19th century. | African Americans--Marriage--History--19th century.
Classification: LCC E540.B53 R63 2022 (print) | LCC E540.B53 (ebook) | DDC 973.7089/96073--dc23/eng/20220331
LC record available at https://lccn.loc.gov/2022012379
LC ebook record available at https://lccn.loc.gov/2022012380

ISBN 978-1-7972-1372-9

Manufactured in China.

Design by Jon Glick

JACKET: Unidentified African American soldier in uniform with his wife and two daughters, ca. 1863–1865

ENDPAPERS: Letter from John M. Washington to Annie E. Gordon dated October 27, 1861

10 9 8 7 6 5 4 3 2 1

Chronicle books and gifts are available at special quantity discounts to corporations, professional associations, literacy programs, and other organizations. For details and discount information, please contact our premiums department at corporatesales@chroniclebooks.com or at 1-800-759-0190.

Chronicle Books LLC
680 Second Street
San Francisco, California 94107
www.chroniclebooks.com

CONTENTS:

PROLOGUE

ON FRIDAY MORNING, APRIL 18, 1862, twenty-four-year-old Virginia slave John M. Washington woke up to the welcome sounds of gunfire. The Union army was only a mile away upriver and moving steadily toward Fredericksburg, his hometown. Now it would be only a matter of time, but he had to plan his escape carefully. There could be no misstep, and no white person must suspect.

A hired-out slave working at the Shakespeare Hotel as both steward and barkeeper, John had to keep his employers and his widowed slave owner completely in the dark. They all must believe that he would follow their orders explicitly. One employer, now an officer for the Thirtieth Virginia Confederate Infantry, told John to accompany him on his assignment in North Carolina as his servant while Mrs. Taliaferro, his slave owner, told John to flee with her to the countryside, away from the encroaching Yankee soldiers.

This Friday morning the hotel was in an absolute frenzy. Boarders were crowded in the dining room while a Rebel cavalryman started shouting, "The Yankees is in Falmouth," a city only a mile from Fredericksburg. As whites ran frantically about in the streets, gathering up their belongings to flee the city, blacks stood on the rooftops watching gleefully for Union soldiers. Hurriedly leaving their hotel, John's employers gave him a roll of banknotes, telling him to pay off the servants, close the hotel, and take the keys to a safe place. John followed these instructions diligently. But instead of catching up with his employer on his way to North Carolina, or escaping with his slave owner to the countryside, John, his cousin, and a friend fled northward one mile, to the Union line encamped on the other side of the Rappahannock River, a river he knew well. He had fond memories of fishing in its waters and playing on its banks with other children while his slave owner believed he was in church. And, most importantly, John Washington had been baptized in that very river only seven years before.

Now, just across the river, the river that had symbolized degrees of freedom, lay real, actual freedom—the freedom he had sought since childhood. So, when a few Union soldiers yelled across, asking if John and his companions wanted to cross, they responded without hesitation. Within minutes he and the others were free. They were safe, never to be owned by anyone again.[1]

Relying mostly upon the correspondence of ordinary individuals like John Washington, this book allows those whose voices have been largely muted to speak their truth. Though mainly enslaved until 1865, people of African descent lived complex, diverse, and yes, at times, rich but incredibly confined lives in all regions of the United States. In the years between the 1840s to the 1870s, African American letters provide a glimpse of just how complicated and

The position of the Union and Rebel armies at Fredericksburg, December 1, 1862

Position of Union and Rebel Armies at Fredericksburg
Decr 1st. 1862.

118

KELLYS FORD

Mt HOLLY
Church
Morrisville

Ruins Potomac Church

STAFFORD C·H·

FIELDS Ford

Shady Grove Church

Supply camp
BELLE PLAIN

RAPPAHANNOCK

Mountain Run

Barnetts Ford

Hartwood Church

Potomac Creek

Richards Ford

RIVER

Genl HOOKER

RR to AQUIA

RICHARDSVILLE

RAPIDAN RIV

United States Ford

Elys Ford

Scotts Run

BANKS Ford

Maries House

FALMOUTH

Germania Ford

Salem CHURCH

Dr Taylors

Maries

Mill

FREDERICKSBURG

Wilderness Run

Aldrichs

PLANK

MARIES HEIGHTS

Stansbury Hill

ROAD

Hazel Run

Ely's

CHANCELLORSVILLE

Dowdalls Tav

Salem Heights

HAZEL RUN

FREDERICKSBURG

Wilderness Tavern

The Wilderness

TA RIVER

SPOTTSYLVANIA C·H·

Bridge

Massaponax CR

RICHMOND and FREDERICKSBURG

MATTAPONI

PO RIVER

Bridge

Guiney Station

Union Army — — •   Rebel Army. ———   Houses ▪

Breastworks ∿   Batteries ⌂   Cavalry

diverse the black American experience had come to be. Indeed, this diversity has too often been ignored. The letters disabuse us of imagining a one-dimensional black experience, although they show us that African Americans did share one common element: family. Family was central to African Americans, whether enslaved or free, and sustained resistance to family separation was integral to the formation of family and community.

When read closely, letters tell stories. Although the majority of black people could not read or write until after the Civil War, we are still able to learn much of African American life from the letters that survive today. We come to know children, young adults, mothers, fathers, sisters, and brothers who worked, loved, married, worshipped, fought, resisted, protested, and created communities. The stories embedded in the letters reveal how enslaved, free, and freedpeople of African descent found meaning, purpose, and even joy in their individual and collective lives. It is an important part of the American story and fills significant gaps in our understanding of the American past.

To quote historian Lawrence Levine regarding black culture—"even in the midst of the brutalities and injustices of the antebellum and postbellum racial systems black men and women were able to find the means to sustain a far greater degree of self-pride and group cohesion than the system they lived under ever intended."[2] Many African Americans lived full lives with substance and meaning in spite of proscriptions. Rather than merely react to slavery and racism, they organized their lives as best they could around family and community. Like other Americans, they loved, worked, and developed friendships within community. Their stories are uniquely American and often universally human. Their letters tell these stories in their own words, mostly in conversation with one another, during the greatest crisis the United States has ever known.

African Americans cultivated family amidst a precarious existence. As historian James Oakes reminds us, pre–Civil War Southern laws disavowed families of slaves: "Slaves had no formal powers to exercise over anyone else—they were utterly powerless. They could make none of the commonplace claims on family and community for economic support or physical protection."[3] To support the financial interests of the slaveholding society, and all who benefitted from slavery, slavery legally meant kinlessness. Enslaved men, women, and children had no wives, husbands, or parents. Yet "kinship is the basis from which human beings normally establish their ties to the larger society."[4] Thus, when John Washington explains in a letter to his fiancée, Annie Gordon, in late 1861 that "I just want someone to call wife," he addresses what Oakes calls the heart of what it means to be human in most societies. In expressing not only his desire to marry, to have a wife, Washington also reveals his desire to be free of a system that denies his sense of personhood, that denies his legal right to be a husband in the nineteenth-century sense of that word: to be a provider and protector.

It is in this sense that John Washington's yearning for a wife reflects the values of the majority of slaves in the United States. So much so that, in spite of the laws, most enslaved adults "married" without a legal sanction, regarded their precarious unions as permanent, and tried to establish monogamous relationships as far as was possible. Enslaved people consistently

challenged the notion that they were kinless and tried to keep their kin together, challenging the law that said they were more property than human beings. As we will see, slave owners recognized enslaved kin when it suited their interest. This recognition did not translate to legitimization of slave spouses and families. The letters reveal how protest as well as family was embedded in the formation of African American culture, family, and community, overtly among Northern free blacks and covertly among slaves and Southern free blacks.

This book focuses on African American private lives. The few private letters extant among family members reveal the most about the diversity of African American thought. Some letters written to relatives discuss ordinary family matters—telling of personal health, material or educational achievements or losses, and how to manage particular situations—while others reflect intimate expressions of love.

This book is divided into three parts. Each part corresponds roughly with the decades of the Civil War era, so that the reader is able to grasp the impact particular moments had on African Americans leading up to the war, during the war, and following the war. Fortunately, in a few cases, we can observe a few individual and familial experiences throughout the entire era. Each part begins with a brief introduction that provides context for the letters, explaining the relevant political and social events of the period. In addition, each chapter includes descriptions of individual letters and their writers. While I have kept the political, economic, and social historical context to a minimum, so that the letters speak for themselves, the reader may desire to skip directly to the letters and read the contextual information later. I have mostly avoided using the term "sic" after errors in order to avoid disrupting the flow of the letters, and I have made only minor corrections to the punctuation, spelling, and grammar in the letters except when necessary for clarity. It's important to note that there was no standardized spelling and punctuation at the time, thus misspelled words and erratic punctuation were common among writers of all classes.

Also, African American writers followed the writing customs of the time. Many used "traditional epistolary frameworks."[5] Letter writing guides proliferated in the mid-nineteenth century to help writers learn the proper format. Guides provided templates that taught the writer how to begin the letter and what to include. Writers were taught to write the salutation, date their letter, and include the place from which they were writing. Instructions also encouraged writers to describe their own state of health and inquire about the health of the recipient, all this before explaining the reason for writing. For example, "Dear _____, I take this opportunity to write you a few lines to let you know that I am well." In following conventional American letter writing customs, African American writers revealed they were part of the American experience, although the content of their letters usually and decidedly distanced them significantly from white writers.

The letters in this book, then, provide an expanded understanding of the meaning of the American experience. We come to realize not only that there is no one American experience, but also that individuals who are placed within our ethnic and racial groupings represent much more diverse and complex lives than we have generally acknowledged.

Memory was given to man for some wise purpose. The past is . . . the mirror in which we may discern the dim outlines of the future and by which we make them more symmetrical.

FREDERICK DOUGLASS, 1884[6]

PART ONE:

Antebellum

BY 1862, THE YEAR JOHN M. WASHINGTON ESCAPED TO FREEDOM, people of African descent had been in the Americas for more than three centuries. Early on, a few Africans, voluntarily and involuntarily, were part of the Portuguese and Spanish expeditions to the Americas as soldiers, settlers, servants, and slaves. Soon most Africans arriving in the Americas and the Caribbean were enslaved persons through the highly profitable slave trade. Slavery increased exponentially from 1600 to 1800, making Africans integral to the economic success of European colonization of the western hemisphere. Indeed, the economic, social, and political life of all the Americas and their islands depended heavily on slavery. This slavery was of a particular kind. Slavery in the western hemisphere, especially the United States, constituted racial slavery and relied for its justification on a system of beliefs that argued for the moral and intellectual superiority of individuals of European descent and the inferiority of those of sub-Saharan African descent.

When the British North American colonies united to form the first modern republic, its founders, slaveholders and non-slaveholders alike, believed slavery would soon decline. In 1776, they thought that they could self-righteously blame Britain for African bondage even though their very break with the empire ensured slavery's expansion beyond the Appalachian Mountains, where the British had determined colonial incursion would end, at least temporarily. By 1787, thousands of citizens of, and recent immigrants to, the new republic had already pushed into Tennessee and Kentucky. They benefited from the Constitutional provision allowing for the further importation of Africans through the Atlantic slave trade for at least two more decades, assuring slavery's expansion rather than its decline in the Southern region. The cotton gin, invented in 1793, only six years after founders met in that historic Constitutional Convention, reduced the time needed for processing cotton while simultaneously increasing the demand for slaves to work on farms and plantations. Recent immigrants and others poured into the south-western region of the new country to profit from growing the cotton plants

needed to make the more available and cheaper cloth. Consequently, many migrants arriving in the Southern region in the early nineteenth century mimicked the quick spiral to wealth, prestige, and political power of former colonists in the southeastern seaboard.

Cotton could now be planted everywhere and satisfy the growing demand of British manufacturers, especially after the Louisiana Purchase in 1803 gave planters all the benefits of the Mississippi River. In the decades before the Civil War, the Mississippi Valley developed into a "Cotton Kingdom," giving new life to slavery in the United States. The United States provided most of the cotton imported by British manufacturers. Between 85 and 90 percent of the American cotton crop was sent to Liverpool annually to be sold in the global market. By 1860, there were more millionaires per capita in the Mississippi Valley than anywhere else in the nation. Indeed, the cotton trade represented the largest single sector of the global economy in the first half of the nineteenth century. Dependent on the labor of enslaved people, the South provided two-thirds of the nation's exports as planters invested heavily in land and slaves.[7] Besides cotton, slave labor provided for the planting, cultivating, and harvesting of tobacco, sugar, and rice for the regional, national, and international market.

Slave men, women, and children also worked in cities and towns. They were domestics, they worked in stores and warehouses, they worked on the docks, and they practiced various trades. Because slavery was so profitable, investors targeted the bodies of enslaved people early on. Thomas Jefferson recognized the great profitability simply in owning slaves. He advised a friend who had suffered financial losses that, if he had any cash left, "every farthing of it [should be] laid out in land and negroes, which besides a present support bring a silent profit of from 5. to 10. per cent in this country by the increase in their value."[8] Economic historians long ago documented the truth of Jefferson's and other slaveholders' successful financial strategy. On the eve of the Civil War, enslaved people in the aggregate formed the second most valuable capital asset in the United States. In a summary of these findings, historian David Brion Davis notes that "the value of Southern slaves was about three times the amount invested in manufacturing or railroads nationwide."[9] The only asset more valuable than enslaved black people was the land itself.

Jefferson's financial strategy became central to the finances not only of the slaveholding South but also of Northern industries, shippers, banks, insurers, and investors who weighed risk against returns and invested in slavery. Demonstrating the centrality of slavery in the establishment of the new republic, historian Edward Baptist argues that the "interlinked expansion of both slavery and financial capitalism was now the driving force in an

"$1200 to 1250! for Negroes!!" July 2, 1853

$1200 TO 1250 DOLLARS! FOR NEGROES!!

THE undersigned wishes to purchase a large lot of NEGROES for the New Orleans market. I will pay $1200 to $1250 for No. 1 young men, and $850 to $1000 for No. 1 young women. In fact I will pay more for likely

NEGROES,

Than any other trader in Kentucky. My office is adjoining the Broadway Hotel, on Broadway, Lexington, Ky., where I or my Agent can always be found.

WM. F. TALBOTT.

LEXINGTON, JULY 2, 1853.

Presented by W.H. Mussey.

emerging national economic system that benefited elites and others up and down the Atlantic coast as well as throughout the backcountry."

But we must return to Jefferson's language to get the full import of his meaning. The term "increase" has a double meaning, referring not only to the accrual of well-invested property, but also, and particularly, to the reproductive capacity of enslaved women. Jefferson noted in a letter to George Washington that he found that the "losses" by the death of slaves was more than made up for by "their increase." Enslaved people kept up "over and above . . . their own numbers." In other words, slave owners and other investors in slavery, and those connected to it directly or indirectly, depended heavily upon enslaved women having children to increase their financial gains. Enslaved women who bore children increased slaveholders' investments no matter who the fathers of the progeny were. As historian Tera Hunter notes regarding children of enslaved mothers and white slaveholding fathers, the "consequences of the sexual economy of slavery" meant that "black women gave birth to the capital that helped forge the nation's wealth, typically under the duress of coerced sex with the very men who sired biracial progeny and turned them into commodities."[12] These human assets, then, were inexhaustible as long as the market demanded the cheapest labor for the highest profits.

Most enslaved people worked in the fields of the rural South. They labored from "sunup to sundown" and, unlike John Washington or Frederick Douglass, almost all were illiterate. As property, enslaved people were bought, sold, inherited, auctioned, traded, and hired out to other slaveholders and non-slaveholders, especially if they had particular skills. By the antebellum period, the "hired-out system" was an integral part of slavery. The slaveholder allowed other slaveholders or non-slaveholders to hire enslaved people for wages that were given to the slave owner, not the slave. Hired-out slaves often worked in urban businesses and generally experienced greater autonomy than field or domestic slaves. They often lived away from their owners, sometimes in an urban boarding house, paying for their room and board out of their wages, with the remaining wages going to the slaveholder. Many slaveholders, particularly widows, relied heavily upon the wages of hired-out slaves.

Laws protecting slavery were established in the colonial era, and they were continually revised and expanded into the Civil War. All thirteen colonies established slave status as permanent and inherited through the mother. Colonial Slave Codes generally controlled enslaved people's movements— requiring written permission for slaves to leave the plantation—and denied legitimization of their marriages, forbade enslaved people to meet together in groups of three or more, forbade ownership of guns, and determined types of punishment for slaves who broke the laws. Antebellum Slave Codes, like

colonial codes, continued to protect slaveholders' interest in these valuable assets to ensure a stable, profitable, and docile labor force. Laws were fairly consistent throughout the slave states. Slave marriages were not legitimized, and the majority of slaves were forbidden to learn to read and write, leave the plantation without a pass, meet in groups of three or more without a white person present, or carry guns or other weapons. The records show that the lash was the main means of control, but slaveholders and their overseers were never without their guns and used them as blunt instruments or to shoot their own slaves. The laws against such deadly force generally protected slave owners, not the enslaved. Violence, therefore, was the central element in this labor system. Without it, slavery would not have existed.

Indeed, the consistent degree to which slave codes were passed and continually revised, even into the early 1860s, reveals how much Africans and African Americans resisted enslavement. Enslaved men, women, and children constantly challenged their status as the property of other human beings, a commodity to be bought, sold, inherited, traded, and auctioned. Insurrections and rumors of slave revolts were common. Other forms of violent resistance included physically resisting a slaveowner or overseer, arson, poisoning, and self-mutilation. The few slaves who engaged in this latter act did so to diminish the value of their slaveholder's investment. Running away, slowing down work, and feigning illness were also means of resisting.

Other nonviolent means countered slaveholders' insistence that according to the law, certain human beings were more property than human. One way that enslaved people demonstrated their determination to live lives with meaning and purpose was by consistently attempting to become literate. Enslaved people learned to read and write more than most scholars had previously thought. Recent scholarship reveals that while the majority of slaveholders tried to make slave literacy nearly impossible, not all Southern state legislatures passed laws prohibiting enslaved people from learning to read and write, though even without laws slaveholder attitudes generally held sway. Laws against slave literacy—that is, allowing slaves to learn rudimentary reading and writing skills—depended upon individual states and they waxed and waned. Antebellum laws were vague, inconsistent, and often ineffective in preventing slaves from becoming literate. Thus, scholars now believe that 5 to 10 percent of the slave population was semiliterate by 1860. In urban areas, a few slaves attended schools taught by free black men and women with their owner's knowledge, while most attended clandestine schools. Some enslaved men and women who were literate held school out of sight of whites, at night and in the woods or swamps. Others learned to read and write on an individual basis from adults or older children.

Scholars have found that measuring literacy, even among the non-enslaved population, during the nineteenth century is extremely difficult. New studies now estimate that by 1860 most white Americans were able to read and write, some on a rudimentary level, and about half of the free black American population was literate to some degree. The growing literacy of the entire American population in part explains why African Americans desired to understand and use the written word for their own purposes.[13]

African American slave families owned by Mrs. Barnwell, ca. 1860–1865

Family was another key means of resistance, whether on large or small plantations or in urban areas. From the 1840s to 1860s, in spite of the dominant culture's notion of white superiority, slaves denied black inferiority and insisted upon engaging, however tenuously, in universal human activities such as courtship, marriage, and rearing children. Most slave couples viewed their marriages as monogamous and permanent. Parents and other members of the slave community taught their children that slaveholders were immoral, that

slavery was evil, and that resistance was essential. Christianity reinforced these values when a large number of enslaved people became Christians in the decades before the war. Enslaved Christians' interpretation of Christianity even reinforced their willingness to use violence as a means of resistance, as black Christianity stressed God's wrath against injustice and greed. Slaveholding was, in the minds of African Americans, not only the greatest sin but also a system that God would end, perhaps violently.

Around four million individuals were enslaved in the Southern states on the eve of the Civil War. As commodities, slaves were subjected to the prevailing threat of being separated from their family members. The slave economy fueled regional and national economic growth by expanding into Alabama, Mississippi, Louisiana, Texas, Arkansas, and Missouri. At the same time that southeastern planters were moving into the Mississippi Valley to plant highly profitable cotton crops, slaveholders in Virginia and Maryland had exhausted the soil in their region and were switching from the labor-intensive tobacco crop to crops requiring less labor, such as wheat and corn. Contributing to the expansion of the domestic slave trade, Virginia and Maryland slaveholders sold "surplus" enslaved men, women, and some children to slave traders who then sold them to owners of cotton and sugar plantations in the Mississippi Valley.

This acceleration of the domestic slave trade coincided with the legal end of the Atlantic slave trade in 1808 and perpetuated many of slavery's horrors. Families were torn apart, auction blocks and slave pens existed throughout the mid-Atlantic region, including across the street from the United States capitol building, and slave coffles moved throughout the region on former Native American trails or via ships traveling down the East Coast to the mouth of the Mississippi and from there into the surrounding valley.

Thus, the profitability of cotton ensured the constant instability and vulnerability of most black lives. Even when the price of cotton fell, planters often went bankrupt, leading to mass breakups of slave families and communities. The threat of being sold hung over the head of every enslaved person. Women of childbearing age were as likely to be sold as men. Between 1820 and 1860 as many as one million people were sold into the Deep South, and 50 percent of the slave sales during the antebellum period resulted in breaking up families.[15] As historian Walter Johnson reminds us, we cannot distinguish between the work that slaves did, the economy that placed them there, and the way in which they lived their lives. Most black men, women, and children's lives on the eve of the Civil War were integrally linked to their labor.[16]

The British and American demand for cotton was not the only reason enslaved people were sold. Slaveholders' wills, debts, and desires to purchase any number or type of products also forced apart some members of enslaved

families throughout the South. Too often, children were separated from their parents, as were spouses and siblings, never to see or hear from one another again. Their last memory of a wife, husband, brother, sister, or child might be of that person being surreptitiously or overtly taken from the plantation by a slave trader, or when members of a family were sold separately on the auction block.

In the North, while slavery had never been the dominant form of labor, colonists did use slave laborers along with indentured or non-indentured white laborers in the region's diversified agricultural economies. These economies required less intensive, and more seasonal, labor. Yet, enslaved people were a significant part of colonial Northern labor, especially in the first half of the eighteenth century. They worked mostly on farms or in urban areas as domestics, and increasingly in the booming maritime industry into the early nineteenth century.

In addition to the perverse and pervasive presence of slavery, there had always been a small but significant population of free black individuals over the centuries. In the colonial era this population was mainly a mixture of people of African, European, and Native American ancestry and was generally the progeny of white or Native American mothers and black fathers. During the Revolutionary War era, the free black population grew incrementally in the North and Chesapeake Bay region as ideas of universal human freedom spread on both sides of the Atlantic, causing some slaveholders, especially Quakers, to free their slaves. Slavery declined not only because of humanitarian ideas but also because European immigration increased, providing labor for farmers and merchants. Also, white workers resented competing with the cheaper slave labor for certain jobs. In the newly established Northern states, then, economics, not humanitarian ideals, contributed significantly to the abolition of slavery. At the turn of the nineteenth century, abolition laws were passed in Northern states, resulting in a mostly free black population by the 1840s.

But it's important to note that the system of Northern abolition was so prolonged that scholars argue that emancipation in the United States was "far more protracted than anywhere else in the Americas."[17] By the first decade of the nineteenth century, most Northern states had provided for "gradual abolition," defined as "freeing" the children of enslaved women born after the "gradual abolition" acts were passed. In other words, gradual abolition freed no one, ensuring that, though declining, to a certain degree slavery continued in the North into the 1840s. The children born after the passage of the abolition laws were "apprenticed" to individuals, usually the slaveholder of the mother, to work until adulthood or beyond as a means to compensate the slaveholder's initial investment in slavery. These children and young adults could be sold or traded just as their parents were.[18]

The persistence of slavery in New Jersey into the 1840s was particularly egregious. There, slave owners, with the help of judges and others, engaged in slave rings in which they used legal loopholes to transport to the South enslaved mothers with their infants who had been freed under the gradual abolition law. Not only that, but they also continued to sell, trade, and auction enslaved people. Rather than follow New York in completely abolishing slavery in the late 1820s, New Jersey renamed the status of those who were still enslaved. They were "apprentices for life" according to New Jersey law.[19]

Slavery would have lasted much longer in most of the North if not for specific eventualities. Some Northern enslaved men gained freedom as soldiers fighting for the patriotic cause in the Revolutionary War. Others, like Richard Allen, who would go on to establish the African Methodist Episcopal Church, purchased their freedom from their slave owners and worked to purchase the freedom of their wives and children. By the early nineteenth century, a large number of Northern slaves had gained their freedom and lived in cities like New York City, Philadelphia, and Boston, where they founded institutions for free black communities.[20] By 1860, the free black population in the United States constituted about 490,000 persons, more or less evenly divided between the North and South. But free blacks existed in a kind of quasi-freedom. Antebellum free black status varied by time and place. Most states denied free black men the right to vote or serve on a jury. Nor could free blacks testify in court. If a crime was committed against them, they could not protect themselves unless a white person was present and willing to testify on their behalf. With echoes of U.S. society today, free blacks were imprisoned more than whites in both sections of the country and more than slaves in the South.

Northern free blacks generally lacked access to education. Many African American men and women, however, gained some degree of elementary education and a few had higher-education degrees. In urban areas like New York City, Philadelphia, and Boston, African Americans and white benevolent or abolitionist societies ran private schools for black children starting in the late eighteenth century. The New-York Manumission Society established the New York African Free School for black children beginning in 1787, before New York passed a gradual abolition law. Some students from that institution became prominent abolitionists and professionals, including Henry Highland Garnet, James McCune Smith, and Alexander Crummell. In Philadelphia, beginning in 1804, schools for black children were often connected with black churches. Some Northern cities eventually, and often reluctantly, established separate, largely inferior, public schools for black children in the early 1800s. By then African Americans who had obtained an education (because of the financial ability of their parents or through schools like the New York African

Free School) established black private schools in Northern cities. By the 1850s, several young African American men and women had been able to attend Oberlin College in Ohio. Founded in 1833, the innovative coed Ohio institution, with its strong abolitionist principles, admitted several black students. Even before Oberlin admitted black students, however, at least one black man had graduated from Bowdoin College in Maine and a few had attended that institution's medical school before the Civil War. In the 1850s, two other colleges joined Oberlin in admitting black students: Antioch College in Ohio and Wilberforce University, the first college specifically for black students, also located in Ohio and founded through a collaboration between the Methodist Episcopal Church and the African Methodist Episcopal Church. After falling on hard times, Wilberforce was purchased in 1863 by the African Methodist Episcopal Church and is still operating today.

While a minority of African Americans benefitted from strong or middling primary education, and a few went on to attend college, enroll in graduate studies, attend professional schools, or the equivalent, many Northern blacks were illiterate and worked as day laborers or domestics.[21] Most Northern blacks only had access to menial jobs. When European immigrants arrived in the 1840s and 1850s, mainly from Ireland and Germany, many black men, women, and children lost even those menial jobs, which they had counted on in the earlier decades. Northern blacks competed with European immigrants not only for jobs but also for housing. Although not yet forced to live in one area of cities, most African Americans in the North increasingly lived in crowded neighborhoods with the newly arrived immigrants. In New York City, where most Northern urban blacks lived, African Americans resided in every ward, but as real estate prices rose, they were forced to move into small basement apartments or hovels in the back alleys of poor neighborhoods.[22] Blacks were also generally denied access to public spaces and public transportation.

Besides political, economic, and social discrimination, Northern blacks routinely experienced white violence. White mobs, resenting the presence of blacks, regularly attacked men, women, and children, and black institutions. In fact, riots by white mobs were common throughout the nation. As early as 1837, young Illinois legislator Abraham Lincoln said that mob rule was becoming commonplace.[23]

SOUTHERN STATES NOT ONLY ESTABLISHED LAWS for controlling and containing slaves, they also passed laws that severely limited the freedom of "free people of color." Alabama's state statute, for example, forbade the teaching of free blacks "to spell, read, or write," under the threat of a fine of $500. Besides denying them the right to an education, Alabama forbade "free colored persons" from

buying "spirituous liquors," playing any game of cards or dice, "or substitute for the same," or from visiting slaves. "Any free person of color, found in company with any slave, in any kitchen, out house, or negro quarter without written permission from the owner, must receive fifteen lashes . . . and for every subsequent offense, thirty-nine lashes."[24] Alabama, like other Southern states, taxed African Americans for their freedom. Alabama required free black men to pay a two-dollar capitation tax and free black women and children a one-dollar tax per person. And "any free Negroes aiding a slave to escape" would be sentenced to a seven-year prison term.[25]

New Orleans, Louisiana, and Charleston, South Carolina, had significant urban free black populations, and laws controlling these populations became increasingly onerous in the decades before the Civil War. For example, South Carolina free blacks who left the state were prohibited from returning upon penalty of enslavement. Every black male over 15 years of age in South Carolina and other Southern states was required to have a "respectable free-holder," or white guardian, listed in the local court record and living in the same district as his ward. Any person not on the list was not free. Like slaves, free blacks in most Southern states could be whipped, placed in stocks, and hung for capital offenses.[26] In addition, free blacks in the South had to demonstrate consistent deference to all whites even when confronted with violence. A free black person in South Carolina and elsewhere was forbidden to strike a white person under any circumstance. "They cannot repel force by force; that is, they cannot strike a white man, who may strike any of them," Justice John B. O'Neall explained in 1848.[27]

Most Southern free blacks lived lives not unlike those of slaves: They resided and worked on farms and plantations as farmhands alongside slaves and were consistently threatened with enslavement. A significant number, though, lived and worked in cities with urban slaves, as menial laborers or as artisans, barbers, or seamstresses. A few were teachers in schools for free black children, and a small number of free blacks owned slaves themselves. Determined to keep their families together, these slave owners owned mostly family members, because state laws prohibited manumission. But a few of the free "mulatto" elite (a term used in that era) enslaved dark-skin color non-family members to work on their plantations or in their businesses. Skin color mattered not only in white society but also among the mulatto elite.

These latter individuals of African and European ancestry relied heavily upon a precarious white patronage for their protection and success. The free mulatto elite viewed themselves, and were often viewed by whites in South Carolina, Georgia, Alabama, Mississippi, and Louisiana or the Deep South, as distinct from those designated black. Many were far more European than

African, a fact that contributed to a kind of legal gymnastics as state and local courts determined what constituted whiteness. In South Carolina, for example, if the local community recognized a person as white, the person was white. What counted was acceptance by the white community. South Carolina Judge William Harper recommended that "a man of worth . . . should have the rank of a white man, while a vagabond" who looked white but had some degree of African ancestry "should be confined to the inferior caste."[28] Even those mulattoes who did not qualify as "white," however, stood apart from other blacks, enslaved or free.

By the 1850s, there were a few private schools operated by Southern free black teachers who provided black children with a strong elementary education. Some parents were financially able to send their children outside the South for higher education. (The South had few public schools, even for white children.) South Carolina prohibited free black schools after the 1822 Denmark Vesey slave insurrection conspiracy, but when tensions died down officials ignored the existence of the schools. South Carolina, Tennessee, and other slave states allowed free black schools and churches at some points in the years before the Civil War. The Charleston African Methodist Episcopal Church was established in 1818 but was closed even before the Vesey conspiracy.[29] Southern free black schools and churches existed in precarious circumstances.

Antebellum Southern free blacks (including slaveholders) were, like most Northern free blacks, denied political, economic, and social rights. Although the particulars varied in each state, most free blacks not only lacked the right to protest but were also consistently subjected to intense surveillance. Based on the assumption that all blacks were slaves, several Southern state laws required free blacks to register and carry papers certifying their free status. If freed by an individual owner, they were required to leave the state, meaning they were forced to leave family members behind. Manumitted men or women could petition to remain in the state, but this required having a white sponsor willing to attest to their character, essentially assuring that the newly freed person would not threaten the slave system. Nevertheless, many manumitted men and women, especially mulattoes, ignored the law and remained. Deep South states usually assumed mulattoes were free.[30]

Whenever a rumor of a slave revolt spread, or when an actual slave insurrection occurred, local officials subjected free blacks to the search of their homes and businesses, treating them as possible collaborators. In South Carolina, every white adult male or his substitute was required to participate in policing the activities of black people, enslaved and free, several times a month. Southern states had "no-knock" policies that allowed slave patrols to enter any free black person's home to learn if they were harboring slaves.[31]

Laws limiting black freedom in the North, South, and West were integral to the legal system of racial subordination. They preserved the fiction that people of African descent were morally and intellectually inferior to Europeans and European Americans. To admit free blacks into the body politic would be to remove the justification for slavery. The ideology of white superiority justified inequality, asserting that black people had no right to become equal citizens and benefit economically, politically, or socially from the rights and privileges defined in the Constitution. The very idea of a free black person challenged not only racial ideology but also slavery itself, contradicting slaveholders' insistence that all blacks must be controlled and contained. As one Virginia legislator explained, "If blacks see all their color as slaves, it will seem to them a disposition of Providence, and they will be content. But if they see others like themselves free, and enjoying the rights they are deprived of, they will repine."[32]

Free people of color not only gave the lie to the belief that blacks were physically and intellectually fit only for slavery, but also to the idea that, because of their supposed deficient intelligence, black men and women could not survive independently of whites. Black dependency was a critical element in the racial justification for slavery. If freed, according to racial ideology, African Americans would starve because they could not take care of themselves; they would return to savagery because of their innate licentious natures. Thus, to be free and black was antithetical to pro-slavery propaganda. State laws and racial ideology contained multiple paradoxes. If people of African descent were intellectually inferior, it would have been unnecessary to deny them access to education and jobs requiring skills beyond menial labor. Instead, as in the North, either laws or policies prevented most Southern free blacks from becoming literate.

Racial ideology and the laws, policies, and customs enforcing it protected the economic interests of all those who benefitted from slavery, including merchants, investors, banks, insurers, the maritime industry, domestic slave traders, the illegal transatlantic slave trade centered in New York City, and all the middlemen, such as textile owners and factory workers in the Northeast and Britain. Discriminatory laws also benefitted ordinary white Americans and the immigrants pouring into the country in the 1840s and 1850s. European immigrants quickly learned the extent to which race determined basic rights and embraced the idea of white superiority as integral to assimilating into the new nation. Popularized by the 1850s, racial ideology was now supported through "scientific" evidence "proving" the natural superiority of all those of European descent and the innate inferiority of all others.[33]

Although their rights were circumscribed in multiple ways, Northern free blacks, sometimes at the risk of their lives, could and did exercise the

The July 23, 1859, edition of *The Weekly Anglo-African*

The Weekly Anglo-African.

1. NEW YORK, JULY 23, 1859. PRICE FOUR

Anglo-African
ED
URDAY,
MILTON,
EET, NEW YORK.
RIPTION.
Four Cents per copy,
RTISING.
first insertion, and
quent insertion.
ages, Deaths, Public
wenty-five Cents, pro-
d five lines; if more
h additional line.
e paper must be ad-
HAMILTON,
t, [P. O. Box 1212.]

Magazine for July.]

NGTON RESCUE.

LANGSTON.

tember 1858 is at
e brightest day in
It is the darkest
, that heartless and
ecrated the sanctity
heir shameless pre-
one of those black
render the kidnap-
picable. The foul
into the hands of
Davis, Mitchell, and
lled through the
oynton, a fast young
s of age, the son of
of Russia Town-
rly distinguished for
and honesty. It
the son of such a
ced and hired, for
ty dollars, to assist
d of *kidnapping* a
opinion of every
licious persons, that
"aid and comfort,"
, to these traitors to
positively asserted,
the father of this
knew nothing of his
oyed to betray John
s after the deed had
Anderson Jennings,
Shakespeare, very
der oath, when un-
witness, that he gave
ermation in regard to
the services of his
n be truthful in his
false, or Jennings
Boynton fake, it
determine. For the
is to be hoped, that
g of this collusion
r its development.
base, who can allow
thing for hire. The
d and his want of
l lead us to excuse
though calamitous
e father, intelligent
observation and ex-
forgiveness at our
of aiding in this ne-

of September, 1858,
in the Calendar of
at day the noble and
by their brave and
escue of John Price,
mination not to allow
ing "to be deprived
operty, without due
in their power to
hat day, too, Oberlin,
another and more
of her purpose to
Justice and Christi-
and the Constitution,
gainst Injustice and
d Slavery, Mob-vio-
Indeed, that day and
guish it shall never
ity shall regard it as
day in the history
Freedom," and shall
ong most sacred re-

ich John Price was
this connection, but
s already well under-
mpting the slightest
then, it is enough to
ared by the huge and
of young Boynton,
h a friendly appear-
bent upon his ruin.
or fugitive belonged
ergetic, the industri-
He knew, too, that
st Price had suffered
most excruciating
at, in consequence of
s he had been driven
e of want; and, now
cing, he was anxious
nt, that he might re-
revenue. Therefore,
man—poor in body
, "My father has sent
hat he wants you to
otatoes for him, and
for your services one
ive cents per day."
n such feeble health
dertake such laborious
ting anything wrong
evil that lurked in the
l but arch deceiver—
kind and neighborly
the dwelling-place of
and faithful fugitive.
oynton could secure.
t two miles from the
d to reach his house
pass over an unfre-
d rode along in their
ble-seated carriage. They were armed with Bowie-knives and revolvers. As soon as they overtook young Boynton and Price, seizing Price, they dragged him from the buggy in which he was riding, and forced him into the carriage in which they rode. This they did without making exhibition of the process, or giving any account of the authority in accordance with which they acted. Thus, having secured their prey, by an untravelled route, in the most expeditious manner, they hurried off towards Wellington. Meantime, Shakspeare Boynton returned to Oberlin to find Anderson Jennings, of whom he was to receive compensation for his dirty work. He found Jennings, reported that the negro had been captured, and received his reward. This ended his connection with this black and infamous drama. After having learned of this miscreant what had been done, Jennings left Oberlin, and joined his comrades and co-workers in iniquity at Wellington.

But before these ruffian negro-catchers arrived at Wellington, fortunately for the kidnapped man and for the Anti-Slavery cause, the report of their doings reached Oberlin, and thrilled and aroused our community, already intensely agitated by villainous deeds done within a few days prior to this time by these hunters of men, under the cover of night. Now one purpose only animated the hearts of the people. Old men and young men, old women and maidens, all expressed in looks and voice their determination to rescue this stolen man. At once, men of strong heart and moral nerve—men of stalwart arms and prowess such as knows no fear—with wondrous determination pictured in their faces, were seen hurrying off in buggies, carriages, wagons, and some on horse-back, and others on foot, towards Wellington, a place yet to be celebrated in story and in verse, in forensic address and judicial record, as the scene of the rescue of John Price, a stolen and kidnapped man, from his cowardly and brutal captors.

It is not fit that this rescue be dwelt upon with too great particularity at this time. Names must not be mentioned. The conduct of particular individuals must not be described. It is enough for us to know, just now, that the brave men who came together in hot haste, but with well-defined intention, returned as the shades of night came on bringing silence and rest to the world, bearing in triumph to freedom the man who, but an hour before, was on the road to the fearful doom of Slavery. To-day John Price walks abroad in his freedom, or reposes under his own vine and fig-tree, with no one to molest him or make him afraid. But for this boon—this glorious boon—he must be ever grateful to the courageous men who jeopardized their lives, their property, and their liberty to secure his release; for, according to the Fugitive Slave Law of 1850, those who rescue a man under such circumstances, or who aid, assist, and abet in the rescue, are to be indicted, convicted, imprisoned, and fined. It matters not if its victim be born in freedom and reared under its benign influences, and it be thus distinctly understood that he is a free man. It matters not if he be kidnapped. In this sense the law is no respecter of persons. Nor does it make any complexional discriminations. And still it subjects to pains and penalties most severe and cruel all who oppose its execution, whether the opposition be violent, legal, or only such as find an expression in prayerful ejaculations in behalf of the captured. If this statement be doubted, let the incredulous peruse with thoughtfulness and care, the unreasonable, the blasphemous, and the atheistic charge delivered by Judge Wilson to the Grand Jury that found bills of indictment against thirty-seven citizens of Lorain county, charging some with rescuing, and others with aiding and abetting in the rescue of John Price. If the incredulous are still unmoved in their unbelief, they would read with edification and profit the charges of the same Judge delivered to the traverse Jurors before whom Bushnell and Langston were tried and convicted. All these charges harmonize with, and strikingly illustrate this Fugitive Slave Law. It is under such a Congressional enactment—an enactment whose soul is not unreasonableness, but injustice and wrong—an enactment whose horrid features are seen in its unconstitutionality, in its denial of the free exercise of religion, in its subversion of State Sovereignty and individual rights, and in its overthrow of all the ancient bulwarks of liberty and law—that the philanthropic and Christian men who are now confined in the jail of Cuyahoga county, together with those of the noble thirty-seven who have been already released from their confinement, were indicted by a packed and partizan Grand Jury, of which Lewis D. Boynton was an influential member.

Of the persons thus indicted, only two have as yet been tried. Both were found guilty and sentenced. Mr. Simeon M. Bushnell, the first one tried, is a man of true nobility of soul and Christian fortitude. A man of very small physical endurance, he has a heart capable of the boldest endeavor and the most unshrinking purpose in the discharge of duty. After his conviction, when ordered to stand up and receive his sentence, Judge Wilson, seeking to extort some word of humiliation and contrition, asked him if he had anything to say why sentence should not be pronounced upon him. In a clear and manly voice, he answered, "I have not." But the Judge was not satisfied with this stern reply; so he asked him if he had no regrets to offer for his conduct. To this, Mr. Bushnell, conscious of the rectitude of his intentions and and courage, and none of the disposition of the poltroon and the coward, he was sentenced by this unjust Judge to sixty days' confinement in the county jail, and to pay a fine of six hundred dollars and the costs of the prosecution. And to-day, he, a white man, an American citizen, is in the common jail, serving out his time, for doing nothing other than giving succor to an oppressed and outraged brother.

Mr. Charles H. Langston, the other person who has been tried, convicted, and sentenced, needs no eulogistic words from my humble pen. He is widely known as a devoted and laborious advocate of the claims of the negro to liberty and its attendant blessings. Indeed, his entire life has been a free offering to the Anti-Slavery cause. Discreet and far-seeing, uncompromising and able, he has labored most efficiently in behalf of the slave and the disfranchised American. But in no position has he demeaned himself with greater propriety and wisdom, with greater decision and courage, and with greater efficiency, than when he stood before Judge Wilson, and, as the representative of the Negro Race, in the most beautiful and powerful tones, told him why sentence should not be pronounced upon him. He spoke as follows:—

MR. LANGSTON'S SPEECH.

"I am for the first time in my life before a court of Justice, charged with the violation of law, and am now about to be sentenced. But before receiving that sentence, I propose to say one or two words in regard to the mitigation of that sentence, if it may be so construed. I cannot of course, and do not expect, that which I may say will, in any way, change your predetermined line of action. I ask no such favor at your hands.

"I know that the courts of this country, that the laws of this country, that the governmental machinery of this country, are so constituted as to oppress and outrage colored men, men of my complexion. I cannot then, of course, expect, judging from the past history of the country, any mercy from the laws, from the constitution, or from the courts of the country.

"Some days prior to the 13th day of September, 1858, happening to be in Oberlin on a visit, I found the country round about there, and the village itself, filled with alarming rumors as to the fact that slave-catchers, kidnappers, negro-stealers were lying hidden and skulking about, waiting some opportunity to get their bloody hands on some helpless creature to drag him back—or for the first time, into helpless and life-long bondage. These reports becoming current all over that neighborhood, old men and innocent women and children became exceedingly alarmed for their safety. It was not uncommon to hear mothers say that they dare not send their children to school, for fear they would be caught up and carried off by the way. Some of these people had become free by long and patient toil at night, after working the long, long day for cruel masters, and thus at length getting money enough to buy their liberty. Others had become free by means of the good will of their masters. And there were others who had become free—to their everlasting honor I say it—by the intensest exercise of their own God-given powers;—by escaping from the plantations of their masters, eluding the blood-thirsty patrols and sentinels so thickly scattered all along their path, outrunning blood-hounds and horses, swimming rivers and fording swamps, and reaching at last, through incredible difficulties, what they, in their delusion, supposed to be free soil. These three classes were in Oberlin, trembling alike for their safety, because they well knew their fate, should those men-hunters get their hands on them.

"In the midst of such excitement the 13th day of September was ushered in—a day ever to be remembered in the history of that place, and I presume no less in the history of this Court—on which those men, by lying devices, decoyed into a place where they could get their hands on him—I will not say a slave, for I do not know that—but a *man*, a *brother*, who had a right to his liberty under the laws of God, under the laws of Nature, and under the Declaration of American Independence.

"In the midst of all this excitement, the news came to us like a flash of lightning that an actual seizure under and by means of fraudulent pretences had been made!

"Being identified with that man by color, by race, by manhood, by sympathies, such as God had implanted in us all, I felt it my duty to go and do what I could toward liberating him. I had been taught by my Revolutionary father—and I say this with all due respect to him—and by his honored associates, that the fundamental doctrine of this government was that *all* men have a right to life and liberty, and coming from the Old Dominion I brought into Ohio these sentiments, deeply impressed upon my heart; I went to Wellington, and hearing from the parties themselves by what authority the boy was held in custody, I conceived from what little knowledge I had of law, that they had no right to hold him. And as your Honor has repeatedly laid down the law in this Court, a man is free until he is proven to be legally restrained of his liberty, and I believed that upon that principle of law those men were bound to take their prisoner before the very first magistrate they found, and there establish the facts set forth in their warrant, and that until they did this, every man should presume that their claim was unfounded, and to institute been misled both by your Honor, and by the prevalent received opinion.

"It is said that they had a warrant. Why then should they not establish its validity before the proper officers? And I stand here to-day, sir, to say that with an exception of which I shall soon speak, *to procure such a lawful investigation of the authority under which they claimed to act, was the part I took in that day's proceedings, and the only part.* I supposed it to be my duty as a citizen of Ohio—excuse me for saying that, sir—as an *outlaw of the United States* (much sensation), to do what I could to secure at least this form of Justice to my brother whose liberty was in peril.—*Whatever more than that has been sworn to on this trial, as an act of mine, is false, ridiculously false.* When I found these men refusing to go, according to the law, as I apprehended it, and subject their claim to an official inspection, and that nothing short of a *habeas corpus* would oblige such an inspection, I was willing to go even thus far, supposing in that county a Sheriff, might, perhaps, be found with nerve enough to serve it. In this I again failed.—Nothing then was left to me, nothing to the boy in custody, but the confirmation of my first belief that the pretended authority was worthless, and the employment of those means of liberation which belong to us. With regard to the part I took in the forcible rescue, which followed, I have nothing to say, further than I have already said. The evidence is before you. It is alleged that I said, '*We will have him anyhow.*' *This I NEVER said.* I did say to Mr. Lowe, what I honestly believed to be the truth, that the crowd were very much excited, many of them averse to longer delay, and bent upon a rescue at all hazards; and that he being an old acquaintance and friend of mine, I was anxious to extricate him from the dangerous position he occupied, and therefore advised that he urge Jennings to give the boy up. Further than this I did not say, either to him or any one else.

"The law under which I am arraigned is an unjust one, one made to crush the colored man, and one that outrages every feeling of humanity, as well as every rule of right. I have nothing to do with its constitutionality; about that I care but little. I have often heard it said by learned and good men that it was unconstitutional; I remember the excitement that prevailed throughout all the free States when it was passed; and I remember how often it has been said by individuals, conventions, legislatures, and even *Judges*,* that it never could be, never should be, and never was meant to be enforced. I had always believed, until the contrary appeared in the actual institution of proceedings, that the provisions of this odious statute would never be enforced within the bounds of this State.

"But I have another reason to offer why I should not be sentenced, and one that I think pertinent to the case. I have not had a trial before a jury of my peers. The common law of England—and you will excuse me for referring to that, since I am but a private citizen—was that every man should be tried before a jury of men occupying the same position in the social scale with himself. That lords should be tried before a jury of lords; that peers of the realm should be tried before peers of the realm; vassals before vassals, and *aliens before aliens*, and they must not come from the district where the crime was committed, lest the prejudices of either personal friends or foes should affect the accused. The Constitution of the United States guarantees, not merely to its citizens, but to *all persons*, a trial before an *impartial* jury. I have had no such trial.

"The colored man is oppressed by certain universal and deeply fixed *prejudices*. Those jurors are well known to have shared largely in these prejudices, and I therefore consider that they were neither impartial, nor were they a jury of my peers. And the prejudices which white people have against colored men, grow out of the facts that we have as a people *consented* for two hundred years to be *slaves* of the whites. We have been scourged, crushed, and cruelly oppressed, and have submitted to it all tamely, meekly, peaceably; I mean as a people, and with rare individual exceptions,—and to-day you see us thus, meekly submitting to the penalties of an infamous law. Now the Americans have this feeling, and it is an honorable one, that they will respect those who will rebel at oppression, but despise those who tamely submit to outrage and wrong; and while our people, as people, submit, they will as a people be despised. Why, they will hardly meet on terms of equality with us in a whiskey shop, in a car, at a table, or even at the altar of God—so thorough and hearty a contempt have they for those who will meekly *lie still* under the heel of the oppressor. The jury came into the box with that feeling. They knew they had that feeling, and so the Court knows now, and knew then. The gentleman who prosecuted me, the Court itself, and even the counsel who defended me, have that feeling.

"I was tried by a jury who were prejudiced; before a Court that was prejudiced; prosecuted by an officer who was prejudiced, and defended, though ably, by counsel that were prejudiced. And therefore it is, your Honor, that I urge by all that is good and great in manhood, that I should not be subjected to the pains and penalties of this oppressive law, when I have *not* been tried, either by a jury of my peers, or by a jury that were impartial.

"One more word, sir, and I have done. I went to Wellington, knowing that colored men have no rights in the United States, which white men are bound to respect; that the Courts had so decided; that Congress had so enacted; that the people had so decreed.

"There is not a spot in this wide country, not even by the altars of God, nor in the shadow of the shafts that tell the imperishable fame and glory of the heroes of the Revolution; no, nor in the old Philadelphia Hall, where any colored man may dare to ask a mercy of a white man. Let me stand in that Hall and tell a United States Marshal that my father was a Revolutionary soldier; that he served under Lafayette, and fought through the whole war, and that he fought for *my* freedom as much as for his own; and he would sneer at me, and clutch me with his bloody fingers, and say he has a *right* to make me a slave! And when I appeal to Congress, they say he has a right to make me a slave; when I appeal to the people, they say he has a right to make me a slave, and when I appeal to your Honor, *your Honor* says he has a right to make me a slave, and if any man, white or black, seeks an investigation of that claim, they make themselves amenable to the pains and penalties of the Fugitive Slave Act, for BLACK MEN HAVE NO RIGHTS WHICH WHITE MEN ARE BOUND TO RESPECT. (Great Applause.) I, going to Wellington with the full knowledge of all this, knew that if that man was taken to Columbus, he was hopelessly gone, no matter whether he had ever been in slavery before or not. I knew that I was in the same situation myself, and that by the decision of your Honor, if any man whatever were to claim me as his slave and seize me, and my brother, being a lawyer, should seek to get out a writ of *habeas corpus* to expose the falsity of the claim, he would be thrust into prison under one provision of the Fugitive Slave Law, for interfering with the man claiming to be in pursuit of a fugitive, and I, by the perjury of a solitary wretch, would by another of its provisions be helplessly doomed to life-long bondage, without the possibility of escape.

"Some may say that there is no danger of free persons being seized and carried off as slaves. No one need labor under such a delusion. Sir, *four* of the eight persons who were first carried back under the act of 1850, were afterwards proved to be *free men*. They were free persons, but wholly at the mercy of the oath of one man. And but last Sabbath afternoon, a letter came to me from a gentleman in St. Louis, informing me that a young lady who was formerly under my instructions at Columbus, a free person, is now lying in the jail at that place, claimed as the slave of some wretch who never saw her before, and waiting for testimony from relatives at Columbus to establish her freedom. I could stand here by the hour and relate such instances. In the very nature of the case they must be constantly occurring. A letter was not long since found upon the person of a counterfeiter when arrested, addressed to him by some Southern gentleman, in which the writer says:

"'Go among the niggers; find out their marks and scars; make good descriptions and send to me, and I'll find masters for 'em.'

"That is the way men are carried 'back' to slavery.

"But in view of all the facts, I say that if ever again a man is seized near me, and is about to be carried southward as a slave, before any legal investigation has been had, I shall hold it to be my duty, as I held it that day, to secure for him, if possible, a legal inquiry into the character of the claim by which he is held. And I go further: I say that if it is adjudged illegal to procure even such an investigation, then we are thrown back upon those last defences of our rights which cannot be taken from us, and which God gave us that we need not be slaves. I ask your Honor, while I say this, to place yourself in my situation, and you will say with me that if your brother, if your friend, if your wife, if your child, had been seized by men who claimed them as fugitives, and the law of the land forbade you to ask any investigation, and precluded the possibility of any legal protection or redress, then you will say with me, that you would not only demand the protection of the law, but you would call in your neighbors and your friends, and would ask them to say with you that these, your friends, *could not* be taken into slavery.

"And now I thank you for this leniency, this indulgence, in giving a man unjustly condemned by a tribunal before which he is declared to have no rights the for it. I shall submit to the penalty, be it what it may. But I stand here to say, that if, for doing what I did on that day at Wellington, I am to go in jail six months and pay a fine of a thousand dollars, according to the Fugitive Slave Law—and such is the protection the laws of this country afford me—I must take upon myself the responsibility of self-protection; when I come to be claimed by some perjured wretch as his slave, I shall never be taken into slavery. And as in that trying hour I would have others do to me, as I would call upon my friends to help me, as I would call upon you, your Honor, to help me, as I would call upon you (to the District Attorney) to help me, and upon you (to Judge Bliss,) and upon you (to his counsel,) *so help me God!* I stand here to say that I will do all I can for any man thus seized and held, though the inevitable penalty of six months imprisonment and one thousand dollars fine for each offence hangs over me! We have all a common humanity, and you all would do that; your manhood would require it, and no matter what the laws might be, you would honor yourself for doing it, while your friends and your children to all generations would honor you for doing it, and every good and honest man would say you had done *right!*" (Great and prolonged applause, in spite of the efforts of Court and Marshal.)

This terse, argumentative and eloquent speech so touched the sensibility of the Judge that he sentenced Mr. Langston to confinement in the county jail for but twenty days, to pay a fine of one hundred dollars and costs of the prosecution. He has already served out his time, and is now in his office in Cleveland, discharging his duties as Recording Secretary of the Ohio State Anti-Slavery Society.

How the United States officials will collect the fines imposed upon these men it is impossible to tell. They are said to be destitute of lands, and all manner of personal property. It is reported that they are very poor. Then blessed be nothing!

There still remain in jail awaiting their trial, Prof. Henry E. Peck, John Watson, Henry Evans, J. M. Fitch, David L. Watson, Ralph Plumb, Wilson Evans, A. W. Lyman, John H. Scott, Robert Winsor, and William E. Lincoln. These are all men of indomitable purpose. The terrible penalties of the Fugitive Slave Law cannot drive them from their firm position in favor of Liberty and Right. Nor are they men who will fear and tremble before a tyrannical Judge. The ruffian threats of a Government Prosecutor cannot deter them. These are men, too, whose lives are marked by acts of selfishness, but by deeds of benevolence and charity. Some of them are distinguished by their scholarly attainments; all of them are distinguished by their deep and consistent devotion to the welfare of humanity. The large circle of friends and acquaintances who daily and hourly express their sympathy for these good and noble men, feel confident that they will conduct themselves in such manner while they remain in jail and when they are brought before the Court for trial, as to further the interests of the Anti-Slavery cause.

It is a fact worthy of particular mention, that in this rescue the colored men played an important and conspicuous part. Twelve of them were indicted; four of them have not yet been taken into custody; two have been discharged; one is now at large upon his own recognizance, and five are still in jail. For the heroic conduct of these worthy men and their white co-laborers, they deserve and shall receive our hearty thanks and lasting gratitude.

Upon the conduct of the Court before which Bushnell and Langston have been tried, and before which the rest of the indicted are to be tried—upon the behavior of the Prosecutor, who has shown himself so anxious and determined to convict these men—upon the character of the Jurors called in the cases already tried, and upon the testimony of the witnesses on the part of the Government, it is needless to say a single word. The Court, the Prosecutor, the Jurors, and the witnesses, with one or two exceptions, are Pro-Slavery and Democratic in their connections and associations. It is well known, then, what we may expect. And, so far, we have not been disappointed.

But the object of this prosecution can never be accomplished. The free spirit of the Western Reserve cannot be "crushed out." Our deep love of liberty, our intelligent veneration for the precepts of Christianity, and our abiding determination to obey God rather than man, no prosecution, however oppressive, no irksome confinement in gloomy dungeons, no illegal and unjust confiscation of our property, can ever overthrow and destroy. And this prosecution, so far, has only tended to deepen and strengthen this conviction.

* The following resolutions were reported to and adopted by an indignation meeting, held in Cleveland soon after the passage of the Fugitive Slave Law, Judge Hiram V. Wilson being on the Committee on Resolutions:

1. *Resolved*, That the passage of the Fugitive Law was an act unauthorized by the Constitution, hostile to every principle of justice and humanity, and, if persevered in, fatal to Human Freedom.

2. *Resolved*, That the law strikes down some of the dearest principles upon which our fathers predicated their right to assert and maintain their independence, and is characterized by the most tyrannical exercise of power; and that it cannot be sustained without repudiating the doctrines of the Declaration of Independence, and the principles upon which all free governments rest.

3. *Resolved*, That tyranny consists in the wilfully violating, by those in power, of man's natural right to his personal security, personal liberty, and private property; and it matters not whether the act is exercised by one man or a million of men, it is equally unjust, unrighteous, and destructive of the ends of all just governments.

4. *Resolved*, That regarding some portions of the Fugitive Law as unconstitutional, and the whole of it as oppressive, unjust and unrighteous we deem it the duty of every good citizen to de-

AN INCIDENT IN OUR HONEYMOON.

I do not know if any one else will think the story I am going to try to write down as interesting as we—that is, John and I—did. I will try to tell it in the simple words in which it was told to us. But first I must say that we heard it during our honeymoon, which we were spending at a cottage in the beautiful park of Lord ——; I shall call him Dinsdale. The cottage was situated in a wild and lonely part of it, and the deer used to come up close to the door and lie under the fine old oaks, through whose branches the sun glimmered on the soft warm turf and clumps of young fern. And how the birds sang! for it was the beginning of May, and fine hot weather. But to come at once to the story

gave one the idea of perfec
peace. He asked us to dr
in his vicarage, to which w
and he led us through path
all bordered with primrose
to a small house covered w
in front having a garden a
can imagine a garden to l
old-fashioned flowers, such
rials, starch hyacinths, a
and sweet with southern
entering the house, I perc
parlor was full of children'
baskets, and I expected ev
a whole flock of grandchil
rushing in; but none appe
I suppose Mr. Morton o
prise, for while we were a
open window, he said: "
see you looking at those t
ing what little children co
ven an old man's loneline
comes here. The little g
fingers last dressed that
would have been an old w
the merry boys who laugh
at play with those hors
been elderly, care-worn m
were mine, and in one w
me."
I uttered some exclama
he went on in a dreamy w
to himself than to us, lo
window all the time.
"Yes, thank you, my d
in one week wife and child
and I became the solitary
ever since. * * * *
a fever," he continued, aft
fever brought here by s
who came one night to a l
lage, where one died, and
infection spread. The w
bad for it—burning l
dry. There was no rain
the flowers drooped and
ered with the summer su
all day long. There wer
me every day, and the
tolling for the passing of
ral. They brought the c
and he pointed to a gree
forest, "in the evening,
hardly see them and
against the dark green
dusk.
"I went to the sick as
But I took every pos
against infection to my w
We would have sent o
but we had no one to sen
were a mile and a half a
fested house. We had
Ellen, about eight years
quiet, loving little thing
years. How she used t
house after her mother, t
and looking up at her wi
eyes. Then there was l
rosy, boisterous boys, an
Ellen, Ellen! All that y
to you, Mr. Fairfield,
me."
He was silent, and loo
tice window into the swee
at the swallows darting a
shine, the young green
flowers, whose scent flo
open window, thinking
panion who had once w
in that sunshine, and t
with him.
"One evening," he w
liberty, and we took the
ting the breeze, what the
from us to the village.
from whence we could se
lage afar off. The boy
shouted in their glee, bu
and laid her golden head
looked in my face wit
eyes. She said: 'Papa
great many people sorro
the village. I would lik
wish we could comfort
like so much.' I told h
help them, by asking H
all our troubles to help u
tiently, knowing that the
and pity. Then we wal
sun was setting like a re
children gathered great
and honeysuckles, which
ter when we got home
honeysuckles always bri
again before me.
"My darling laid her
as it lies now, and wish
good-night; the boys a
play-things, and then t
them to bed, and I sat
now, looking into the da
heard them sing the even
and her mother softly an
with loud, eager, joyous
heart was very thankf
blessings vouchsafed to
"That night there wa
our house, as in Egypt
born was to die. The
Our frighted servants ra
at midnight, and we wer
our stricken child. The
The boys awoke, and w
themselves, and go and
Meanwhile, I went to M
est town, for the doctor
solved, on their arrival,
the boys away to the w
nice; I knew she would
But neither nurse no
spared from Marston, a
July day we watched b
listening to the distant
at play in the forest,
her ravings. Hardly
there was nothing frigh
ness and peace, as her s

right of free speech. They consistently protested from the late eighteenth century onward through speeches, petitions, newspapers, and various organizations, including black conventions. From the 1830s into the late nineteenth century, black activists held conventions to discuss strategies for developing black institutions and also gaining equal access to jobs, education, housing, the right to testify in court, and the franchise for black men. Most early conventions also focused on the need for a black press so that their views could be expressed in their own words. They were determined to live their lives with purpose and hope in spite of tremendous constraints.

Black newspapers, beginning with the New York City *Freedom's Journal* in 1827, struggled financially because most African Americans lacked the means to help keep a newspaper solvent. The *North Star*, Frederick Douglass's weekly newspaper printed in Rochester, New York, began publication in December 1847 and lasted longer than other black newspapers due to significant financial help from white abolitionists in the U.S. and Britain. In 1851 Douglass changed the name from the *North Star* to the *Frederick Douglass' Paper* and then, in 1858, to *Douglass' Monthly*. Douglass viewed his papers as the voice of African America, and most black activists apparently agreed. Activists' conviction that they needed their own newspaper was confirmed time and again as anti-black and pro-slavery propaganda monopolized much of the American press. In 1859, black activist and New York journalist Thomas Hamilton published a monthly magazine, the *Anglo-African Magazine,* that focused on black literature and social criticism. Hamilton's list of contributors included Dr. James McCune Smith, Frances Ellen Watkins Harper, Mary Ann Shadd Cary, and Frederick Douglass, with topics ranging from McCune Smith's analysis of racial ideology to Harper's poignant poetry. Around the same time, Hamilton published the *Weekly Anglo-African* newspaper which, with the help of his brother, the teacher Robert Hamilton, and funding from James McCune Smith, lasted until a few months after the end of the Civil War. Unfortunately, because Hamilton could not get sufficient financial support for his *Anglo-African Magazine*, this truly remarkable publishing achievement folded after a little more than a year. [34]

As they protested against local, state, and federal governments' inequities, African American activists established black institutions such as churches, schools, male and female literary societies, fraternal organizations, and other social organizations. Women were especially active in raising funds to support schools and churches, and several were critical to establishing and teaching at black schools. The Institute for Colored Youth in Philadelphia had a strong academic curriculum that included mathematics, natural philosophy, Latin,

Greek, higher algebra, trigonometry, natural sciences, and rhetoric. Grace Douglass (no relation to Frederick Douglass) headed the Female Department and her daughter Sarah Mapps Douglass headed the elementary school. In 1852, Sarah Mapps Douglass would become the first African American woman to attend the Female Medical College of Pennsylvania. African Americans not only established their own schools in the larger cities, such as Philadelphia, but in the early nineteenth century they also created two distinct Protestant denominations: African Methodist Episcopal Church and African Methodist Episcopal Zion Church.

Most of all, black activists—men and women—concentrated on the abolition of slavery in the years leading up to the Civil War. Abolition was the first step toward a stable and permanent place for individuals, families, and communities in American society. A minority of black and white individuals formed antislavery societies that petitioned individual Northern states and the federal government to end slavery. Yet anyone looking at the small group of black and white abolitionists who gathered in Philadelphia to form a national organization in 1833 would have predicted failure. The response to the idea of immediately abolishing slavery—the idea that Southerners must immediately begin the abolition process—was swift and hostile from most quarters of the country. The slaveholding South placed bounties on the heads of abolitionists who dared speak against slavery. Black abolitionist David Walker became the target of pro-slavery supporters when his 1829 pamphlet, *Appeal to the Coloured Citizens of the World,* was disseminated throughout the country. By the 1850s, however, the abolitionist movement had spread throughout the North. Through speeches, slave narratives, petitions, and evangelical-style recruiting efforts, abolitionists convinced many Northerners that slavery was immoral and had no place in the free republic.

In this endeavor, fugitive slaves were critical. Frederick Douglass and Jermain W. Loguen were just two of several (mostly men, often accompanied by white abolitionists) who traveled the lecture circuit hoping to persuade white Northerners to join the movement. Black women abolitionists formed their own abolitionist societies or joined white female antislavery societies. Some, like the former New York slave who named herself Sojourner Truth, were part of the lecture circuit. Whether male or female, white or black, abolitionists were regularly shouted down, ridiculed, and derided. Men not only suffered derision but were also beaten by white mobs, especially in the early years of the movement. William Lloyd Garrison, the passionate and influential antislavery editor of the *Liberator* newspaper, was often attacked. He and other white abolitionist newspaper editors published many black abolitionists' lectures and letters, and other antislavery information.

Abolitionists not only recruited white Northerners to their cause but also organized boycotts of products, like cotton, that depended upon the labor of slaves. Equally as important, many abolitionists were deeply involved in the Underground Railroad that helped transport thousands of fugitive slaves to the North or to Canada through "vigilance committees." The railroad, a series of interlocking local networks operating throughout the North and upper South, could not have functioned without the aid of local blacks—both slaves and free individuals.

Black abolitionist William Still, the "operator" of the Pennsylvania Anti-Slavery Society's Philadelphia Vigilance Committee, was a key agent who, with his wife, Letitia, sometimes hid fugitives in their home. Still's record of the individuals who escaped through Philadelphia provides an invaluable resource for understanding the multiple means fugitives used to escape enslavement. During the two decades before the war, they often took advantage of newer means of transportation and stowed away on coastal vessels, or found ship captains willing to transport them for a price. Aiding fugitives directly was only part of Underground Railroad activities; Still and other agents, black and white, were constantly raising funds to support their operations and to buy enslaved people out of slavery, a controversial strategy among abolitionists.

Abolitionists all agreed that slavery should be abolished immediately, but they disagreed on some of the means to attain their goal. For example, Bostonian William Lloyd Garrison and his followers were opposed to abolitionists participating in America's political system. The government, after all, supported and protected slavery. Others argued that abolitionists needed to place antislavery politicians in local, state, and, especially, the federal government. Abolitionists also disagreed on whether enslaved people should be purchased out of slavery. Opponents of this approach argued that the purchase of an enslaved person only reinforced the immoral argument that humans could be owned as property. Others believed that even though the numbers were incredibly small, purchasing people out of slavery would weaken the system.[35]

With the help of abolitionists and philanthropists, many fugitives settled near the Canadian border. The Canadian government had officially granted asylum to fugitives in the early nineteenth century, and it consistently rejected demands for extradition by slaveholders and the United States government. Fugitives became free when they arrived on Canadian soil and, depending upon the region, found less racism in law and custom than in the Northern states. Free Northern blacks joined them, settling mostly in parts of the Ontario province and some in the city of Montreal. Black Canadians from the United

States brought a diverse set of skills and included farmers, domestics, cooks, carpenters, dressmakers, and waiters. Many had been hired-out slaves. [36]

The fugitive population in Canada increased in the 1840s and, especially, in the 1850s after the passage of the Fugitive Slave Law. Just a few years before, abolitionists had watched with satisfaction as several Northern states demonstrated their resentment of the Fugitive Slave Act of 1793 by passing "personal liberty laws," signaling their official opposition to returning fugitives to slavery. The U.S. Supreme Court had ruled these laws unconstitutional in 1842 but determined that the return of slaves was a federal matter. Thus, several northern states enacted new personal liberty laws that prohibited state public officials from assisting in the recapture of fugitives.[37] Now the new Fugitive Slave Law of 1850 gave in to slaveholders' demands that Northern states help return fugitive slaves to their owners. Bending to slaveholder interests, and infuriating abolitionists, the law gave the slave-owning South a clear and legal right not only to retrieve enslaved people from the Northern and Western states, but it also rewarded commissioners who found in their favor. Federal commissioners determined the fate of the accused without giving them the benefit of a jury trial or court testimony, and they received $10 (about $342 today) if a claimed runaway was returned to slavery and $5 if the claimed runaway was set free. The law prohibited local authorities from interfering with federal action and required individual citizens to aid in the capture of alleged fugitives. This meant retrenchment to abolitionists and placed Northern black individuals, homes, and community in jeopardy even more.[38]

The Fugitive Slave Law and the Supreme Court's Dred Scott decision in 1857 left Northern blacks with a sense of despair. In the latter case, the Southern majority court, joined by a Pennsylvania justice, determined that only white persons could be citizens of the United States and that historically blacks "had no rights which the white man was bound to respect." Therefore, African Americans could never become part of the nation's "political family." Some African Americans gave up on the possibility of a positive future in the United States and made plans to emigrate to Canada and, later, West Africa. Others dug in their heels and refused to leave the land of their birth, where enslaved relatives remained and where they and other blacks had helped build the nation "with their blood, sweat, and tears." These activists experienced hope and despair throughout the 1850s. Black abolitionists, as well as some white abolitionists, were as dedicated to obtaining the rights of citizenship for African Americans as they were to eliminating slavery.

The Fugitive Slave Law and the Dred Scott decision also increased support among abolitionists for using violent means to end slavery. When, in 1859, white abolitionist John Brown devised a plan to seize the federal

arsenal at Harpers Ferry, Virginia, and start an armed slave revolt, several activists were not so much opposed to the idea of an insurrection as they were to the method to achieve it. "I believe in insurrections," declared John S. Rock, a black Boston abolitionist who practiced as a dentist, physician, and lawyer. He and others held that only armed resistance would topple the institution of slavery.[39] Frederick Douglass, however, thought Brown's plan would fail. Brown didn't understand, Douglass believed, how well the various institutions of government protected slavery, especially in 1850s Virginia. Nor did Brown understand that most slaves were unwilling to engage in rebellion without some possibility of success. Brown did succeed in recruiting five free black men for the raid at Harpers Ferry. Two of them, Dangerfield Newby and Lewis S. Leary, were killed in the raid; Osborne P. Anderson escaped to the Ontario province; and Shields Green and John Copeland Jr. were captured and indicted for treason and for inciting slaves to revolt. They were executed on December 16, 1859, two months after the raid.[40] Even abolitionists who disagreed with using violent means to end slavery viewed Brown's failed attempt as courageous. Brown quickly became a martyr among many Northerners after he was executed on December 2, 1859.

On the eve of the Civil War, Southern free blacks were in greater peril from Southern laws than ever before. While the Upper South and Lower South differed in their attitudes toward free blacks, and often in their treatment of free blacks, they were nonetheless still threatened with extinction. Many free blacks had benefitted from the economically prosperous 1850s, and material success was evident in almost every Southern free black community. The number of free black property holders increased, and they often rented to whites. Free black wage earners easily found jobs, making it unlikely that they would sign yearlong contracts with a slaveholding planter. Some free blacks had nice homes and carriages, and attended new churches—all clear signs that the racial order was "under siege." Free blacks in several areas petitioned for the removal of black codes that placed their status close to slavery, and many appeared to help fugitive slaves escape. To whites, free blacks were eroding the color line; they were acting like whites, as if they were really free. The justification for the enslavement of inferior beings was being challenged forcefully in the years leading up to the war. White dominance was threatened.

Thus, Southern states revised existing laws and passed new laws for controlling free blacks while kidnappings and white vigilantism increased. State legislatures gave in to white workers' demands that slave and free black artisans be prohibited from certain jobs. Surveillance increased and most state legislatures considered laws requiring that free blacks leave the state or be enslaved. Arkansas, a state with one of the smallest free black populations,

successfully passed one such expulsion law. The funds from the sale of free blacks would go to the Arkansas school fund.[41] In return for acquiescing to white workers' demands, the politically dominant slaveholding minority hoped to gain support for secession, and possibly war, to protect slavery. Many free blacks who could fled the South.

In the North, more and more abolitionists believed that slavery would end violently. A political solution seemed weak and vacuous—it required too many compromises with the evil system. Most Northern blacks held out hope that emancipation was inevitable if the South was foolish enough to incite a war.[42]

CLEARLY, AFRICAN AMERICAN LIFE in the decade before the Civil War was more complicated than the simple categories of enslaved or free. In the following correspondence, status, class, and regional distinctions are evident, as are urban and rural differences. Even coastal versus inland experiences, and types of labor within these varied distinctions, reveal the incredible complexity of African American lives in this period. Reflecting different degrees of literacy, these letters illustrate this diversity of black life. Letters written by enslaved people and Southern free blacks were generally surreptitiously sent via trusted white couriers who might carry a letter to the North and then mail it to its destination. Or, in the case of the Underground Railroad, agents often used black sailors to deliver messages from fugitives to family members.[43] Some slaveholding families wrote letters for their slaves. These letters must be read with the understanding that enslaved people who used their owners as their amanuenses were unable to express all they may have wished, but through them we do learn much of the emotional trauma of enslavement.

Whether enslaved or free, black people developed values and ideals that enabled them to come to terms with one of the darkest of human experiences: existing in a society that allowed human ownership and all the horrors that it entailed. Family, the letters show, was central to their sense of self and community. It enabled them to transcend complete hopelessness and work to transform their circumstances and, therefore, the nation.

"I Can Ashore You I Think Highly of Freedom and Would Not Exchange It for Nothing."

LETTERS BETWEEN PARENTS AND CHILDREN, between husbands and wives, and between lovers provide a glimpse of the experience and values of African Americans in the immediate decades before the war.

There are very few letters extant written or dictated by enslaved men and women in the antebellum era, but the majority involve family, mainly the desire to be united with family members or to learn of their welfare. Letters between free blacks cover, unsurprisingly, more topics and are more numerous. Free blacks had much more control over their time and where they directed their energy. Besides their lack of access to writing materials, most enslaved people were under constant surveillance. Slaveholders were not only concerned about potential rebellions but also restricted slaves to activities that profited them. Yet the centrality of familial connections is evident in the private letters among both slaves and free blacks, revealing the importance, resilience, and strength of familial ties. These relationships are linked to African Americans' determination to live lives of purpose and meaning. At the same time, family responsibilities were also a constant source of both anguish and joy, especially for slaves.

Through these letters, we also learn the degree to which African Americans valued literacy. They used whatever means available to remain in contact. While the majority of slaves lost all contact with family members when they were separated after being sold, a small number who were literate, semiliterate, or had access to someone willing to write and serve as a courier

for them, kept in contact. Because of the obvious risks, slave letters lack condemnations of slavery, but the pleas for a family member to purchase them, or for news of the impending sale of a family member, speak volumes about their view of the system. In the letters that follow, we meet specific families living in the North and South who reveal the important role that literacy played in maintaining family bonds throughout this critical time in their history and that of the nation.

Correspondence of the Plummer family of Maryland illustrates the fortitude of enslaved families' affections and the central role literacy played in their ability to stay connected. Unlike the vast majority of slaves, Emily Saunders, born in 1816, and Adam Plummer, born in 1819, obtained a marriage license and married in a church on Sunday, May 30, 1841. But like many other enslaved couples, the Plummers were owned by two different slave owners. Fortunately, Adam was enslaved on an extraordinarily financially stable plantation, and Emily experienced a degree of stability as well, meaning she was not threatened with being sold, or by the death of her slave owner, until she was an adult. The young couple lived close enough to see one another regularly on the weekend, when Adam was allowed to visit his wife. He walked eight miles from the Calvert Riversdale plantation and returned to his owner for work on Monday mornings. Adam's slaveholder, Charles B. Calvert, considered him a trusted and dependable slave. Calvert loaned him the use of a mule and gave him permission to cultivate, plant, and profit from three to four acres on the Calvert Riversdale plantation. By the 1850s, Adam successfully sold fruit from the small plot, enabling him to supplement his growing family's needs. According to his daughter, Adam loved to farm and could build anything—a house, barn, or stable. He built or rebuilt and expanded Emily's and their children's cabin on the Three Sisters Plantation during his visits, adding windows, doors, and a loft to the cabin.

Even though Adam and Emily Plummer's enslaved experience was exceptional—Adam's limited degree of autonomy and Emily's owner's willingness to allow her to benefit from it—the couple resented a system that owned them and denied them control over their lives and those of their children. Like all enslaved people, they never knew when their circumstances would change, when one family member might be sold. Being owned meant not only the constant fear of being separated and placed in a crueler living situation, but also the inability to choose what they did, when they did it, and where they went. They were also robbed of the ability to express themselves honestly, and the chance to live up to their potential.

As a young man, Adam became marginally literate when he convinced "a colored preacher" to teach him to read and write. Although the state of

Maryland did not legislate against slave literacy, if a slaveholder objected to an enslaved person learning to read and write, their decision had the force of law. Even so, as we know, Frederick Douglass and other slaves became literate through various means.[44] For Adam Plummer, literacy was another means of autonomy. By the antebellum period, Maryland's large free black population had formed viable communities in Baltimore and nearby Georgetown and Washington, D.C., that included churches and schools.[45] Adam and other enslaved Marylanders participated in the life of African American communities near them.

Ultimately, the young couple decided that escaping was the only solution to protect themselves and their children. In 1845 Adam and Emily made plans to leave for a free state, or Canada, with their two children, Sarah Miranda, born in 1842, and Henry Vinton, born in 1844. To his dying day, Adam could not forget that one of Emily's relatives informed on the couple, placing the entire family in serious jeopardy. After discovering the failed escape, Emily's slaveholders talked of selling her, but instead she was banished to back-breaking fieldwork with much less opportunity to see her children. Evidently, however, Emily's cooking skills saved her, and she returned to laboring in the slaveholding household not long after the failed escape.

Working in the household, however, had its own drawbacks. Enslaved children generally worked in slaveholders' households, or in areas surrounding the house, until they were old enough to work in the field, constantly exposing them to the eyes and demands of the slaveholding household. The Plummer children were no different. They ran errands, helped in the kitchen and yard, and performed other duties that may have included babysitting, even though they were quite young themselves. When the Plummer children didn't meet the satisfaction of their slaveholding family members, they were whipped, slapped, or shouted at. Emily intervened constantly to protect her children, expressing anger that anyone would dare correct them. Adam urged Emily not to convey her resentment of enslavement to slaveholders so strongly, even when their children were abused. He continued his visits, bringing food and other goods purchased with the proceeds he earned by selling his prized fruit. This arrangement came to an end when Emily's elderly female slave owner became ill and eventually died in 1851. Three years before, in 1849, Emily and the four children had been for sale, but because Emily was recovering from the birth of six-day-old Julia Ann, the sale was postponed until November 1851. This time, the fact that Emily had given birth to Nicholas Saunders the previous month did not result in another postponement; Emily and three of the children were sold at a public auction. To the utter dismay of Adam and Emily, the heir to the Three Sisters Plantation decided to hire out two

children, nine-year-old Sarah Miranda and five-year-old Elias, instead of selling them with their mother and siblings. According to Emily and Adam's daughter Nellie Arnold Plummer, her parents' primary focus had been to keep the family together; now they would be separated not only from one another but also from two of their children. Nellie explained that the sale and separation of her mother from two of the children was "the beginning of separation, sorrows and unrequited labor" for the family.[46]

Still, for the next four years, Adam and Emily were able to see each other, and their children, though not as often as before. Adam, who remained at the Calvert Riversdale Plantation, now walked 15 miles to see his wife and the three children at Meridian Hill in Washington, D.C., every two weeks, and sometimes weekly, for the next four years. The Plummer family saw one another fairly regularly, and they also remained in contact with other family members and friends with letters (Sarah Miranda was somehow learning to read and write) and through a communication network of slaves who passed along news between plantations. Enslaved coach drivers, artisans, hired-out slaves, and others whose work required them to leave the plantation of their owner often traveled between plantations, acting as messengers. Throughout the South, enslaved people were leased or hired out to other slaveholders or non-slaveholding employers, including colleges, on a short-term basis to perform various types of labor. This system enabled the original slaveholders to profit from their slaves' labor, while those who hired the slaves benefitted because they did not have to produce the capital required to invest in the increasingly high cost of owning enslaved persons. In May 1852, six months after her mother and siblings were sold, Sarah Miranda joined her mother in Washington. Emily's slave owner, perhaps at Emily's urging, hired out Sarah Miranda for $1 a month. Emily and Adam's family continued to increase with the birth of Marjory Ellen Rose in 1853, and Margaret Jane in 1854, following Marjory Rose's death in that same year. However, Elias, their third child, remained at Three Sisters Plantation, where Emily's mother, siblings, other relatives, and friends lived until many were sold.

The death of Emily's original slaveowner continued to plague the family with greater instability as Emily and the children were moved, then moved again, because of complicated inheritance matters. In December 1855, Emily and the children, except Elias, were moved to Mount Hebron, Maryland, about twenty miles west of Baltimore. Then, within several months, Emily and four of the children were moved again, this time to Woodlawn Plantation. Though still in Maryland, the plantation was too far for Adam to walk to and also far away from other family members and friends. Now, Adam saw his immediate family only on Easter and Christmas, when his slaveholder gave

him a pass to take the B&O Railroad to Relay, where he would change trains to go to Ellicott's Mills and from there walk to Woodlawn. Fourteen-year-old Sarah Miranda was again separated from her parents, hired out, this time to a Washington, D.C., clergyman.[47]

On the eve of the Civil War, most of the children remained with Emily, including the twins, Nellie and Robert, born in September 1860. But the event everyone dreaded most came in November 1860, when Sarah Miranda's slave owner sold her to a New Orleans slave owner. This event became a historical marker for the family, even after Sarah Miranda's death in the early twentieth century. The Plummer family would continue to mourn the sale of Sarah Miranda but may have gained some comfort from being able to remain in touch with most of their family members, not only through letters but also from reports from various visiting enslaved family and friends. The ability to maintain contact became the indispensable link for the Plummer family even as they lived apart. With Adam and Sarah Miranda writing in their own hands, and Emily relying upon others', the family maintained contact into the Civil War.

The Plummer family's attitudes about the importance of familial relationships were representative of most enslaved people. Though we do not have an abundance of letters by enslaved people in the antebellum period, freedpeople immediately began searching for family members during and after the war, testifying to the centrality of family. Kin mattered, perhaps even more to enslaved people because of the horrors of a system that denied them a legal family.

Correspondence was particularly important among slaves when their relatives escaped to the North or Canada. Parents, spouses, and children sent letters via Underground Railroad operators to get news of the fugitive's safe arrival. As one of the most important Underground Railroad operators, William Still received many letters from fugitives in various places of the North and Canada expressing their gratitude and requesting that he help them free family members.

In addition to letters inquiring about a fugitive slave's safety, Northern black correspondence, especially among family members, sometimes blended activism and intimate issues in one letter. Frederick Douglass and Anna Murray Douglass corresponded regularly with their children. Even though Anna never learned to read and write, the children often wrote to both parents and received messages from their mother through literate family members. In 1838, free Baltimorean and laundress Anna Murray had contributed money to help pay for her twenty-year-old fiancé's escape from slavery. She then quickly followed Frederick to New York City, where they married. They soon settled in New Bedford, Massachusetts, with the expectation that Frederick would find

work as a ship's caulker, a trade he had learned in slavery. Anna and Frederick soon found that Northern whites were as racist as Southern whites when white caulkers refused to work alongside a person of African descent. As a result, he worked at various jobs while Anna continued to work as a laundress and later mended shoes to support them and their growing family. Eventually settling in Rochester, New York, the Douglasses had five children, Rosetta (1839), Lewis Henry (1840), Frederick Jr. (1842), Charles Remond (1844), and Annie (1849).[48]

In the next three years, Frederick became a member of the abolitionist movement, joining the lecture circuit and, in 1845, publishing his narrative. He was a prolific writer. Besides numerous letters, he wrote three autobiographies and published and edited four newspapers: *The North Star*, *Frederick Douglass' Paper*, *Douglass' Monthly*, *New Era*, and *New National Era*. The Douglass family, like many Northern blacks, fought inequality on a personal level and as part of organizations engaged in demanding that the nation live up to its founding principles.

Unlike Northern free blacks, free people of color living in the South corresponded cautiously, mostly through friends who carried mail secretly to its destination. Like enslaved people, they valued freedom and family above all else. Alabama barber John H. Rapier Sr. obtained his freedom when he was twenty-one-years old, thanks to the strategic maneuverings of his enslaved mother, Sally Thomas. Removed with her two sons to Nashville from Albemarle County, Virginia, sometime after the death in 1814 of their slave owner, Charles Thomas, thirty-year-old Sally chose the surname Thomas and gained permission from the Thomas Estate to hire herself out as a cleaning woman. She rented a frame house in the central business district of the city and soon established a laundry business caring for fine clothes. The front room of the house was the laundry room, where she made her own soap, while the rest housed her small but growing family. Recognizing that her position and that of her now three sons could change at any moment, Thomas concentrated on gaining freedom for herself and her family.

Even though she managed to save some money from her income, it was inadequate to meet the rising value of slaves. All three boys could be sold for a high price in the antebellum era. Thus Thomas, who was labeled mulatto and whose sons all had white fathers, planned for the freedom of her two eldest, John and Henry. She convinced a barge captain who transported tobacco to New Orleans via the Cumberland and Mississippi Rivers to hire John to work as a waiter and "pole boy." As per Sally Thomas's wishes, Captain Rapier left $1000 to his executors for purchasing the freedom of "mulatto boy John" from the Thomas Estate. In 1829, the Alabama General Assembly, the only legal emancipator of slaves in antebellum Alabama, granted John his freedom.

Not finding an arrangement for Henry, Sally Thomas made the difficult decision to encourage him to run away to the North. At twenty-five, Henry's value was beyond Sally's financial ability to buy his freedom. Though he was caught, arrested, and jailed in Louisville, Kentucky, he successfully escaped from jail and crossed the Ohio River into Indiana, ultimately settling in Buffalo, New York, as Henry K. Thomas. Some months later, Sally, who could not read or write, learned of Henry's safe arrival, but she never saw her second son again. She gained comfort, though, in knowing not only that Henry was no longer a slave, but also that he would remain in contact with the family. Though she was illiterate, Sally Thomas corresponded with her children. John, who took the name Rapier, regularly visited his mother in Nashville and carried letters between her and Henry. Southern literate free blacks like John smuggled letters through friends, white and black, throughout the antebellum era.[49]

By the 1840s, John Rapier Sr. and Henry Thomas were fathers of growing families. Unfortunately, John's wife Susan, a free person of color from Baltimore, died, leaving him with four sons to raise. Like other states, Alabama provided that the boys follow the status of their mother, meaning John Rapier's sons were born free. At the same time, Alabama prohibited both slaves and free blacks from becoming literate. John Sr. sent John Jr. and James to live with their grandmother, Sally Thomas, in Nashville, so that they could attend the school established for free children of color by a free black man. His other sons, Richard and Henry, went to school in Buffalo, New York, where their uncle lived, and in the Elgin Settlement, a Canadian fugitive community often called Buxton, Canada West or Ontario. By the 1850s, John Rapier's thriving barbering business earned sufficient money to help send all four of his free sons to college and to buy real estate in Alabama, Minnesota, and Ontario, Canada.

Like the Rapier family's, the Ellison family's correspondence provides a glimpse through their own words of how free blacks maneuvered within a slave society. Twenty-six-year-old April Ellison, probably the son of a white South Carolina slaveholder and his slave, purchased his freedom in 1816. He moved to Stateburg, South Carolina, and went into business repairing cotton gins, a trade he had learned while still in bondage. Soon after he gained his freedom, Ellison purchased his wife, Matilda, and daughter, Eliza Ann, out of slavery. In 1820, eschewing the symbols of slavery even more, April legally changed his slave name to William, the name of his former slaveholder. By then William Ellison himself owned two adult male slaves.

Surrounded by wealthy white planters, Ellison bought an acre of land in a strategic location and established a gin–making and gin-repairing business

that became a great success with the cotton boom. He became wealthier than nine out of ten Southern whites, enabling him to purchase the home of a former South Carolina governor, which he rechristened "Wisdom Hall." Ellison added carpentry and blacksmithing to his business, with slave labor and that of his three sons when they became old enough to help. By 1860 he was also a successful planter, with sixty-three enslaved men, women, and children who produced hundreds of bales of cotton on over eight hundred acres of land.

Ironically, Ellison financially benefitted from the very machine that contributed to the expansion of slavery and, therefore, the tremendous growth in the slave populations of Alabama, Mississippi, Arkansas, and Texas. As the wealthiest free black person in South Carolina, and the owner of more slaves than any other black slaveholder outside of Louisiana, Ellison practiced and taught his children the habits of deference, tact, and circumspection to elicit the respect and patronage of the white elite. He consistently demonstrated his support for slaveholding, believing that "the route to security lay through accommodation and sweat."[50] Ellison embraced the slave system and, at least superficially, the doctrine of white superiority.

According to Ellison's biographers, Michael Johnson and James Roark, he and other mulatto elite lived in a kind of "middle ground." They had to keep their distance from slaves as much as possible to avoid the associated degradation. At the same time, that distance placed them dangerously close to white status, implying an unimaginable and illegal equality. Thus, their concessions to white prejudice involved deference, to reassure whites that they knew their place. "But every concession," write Johnson and Roark, "every failure to assert their freedom to the full, not only kept them safely below whites but also narrowed their distance from slaves."[51]

Above all else, Ellison and the other mulatto slaveholding elite prioritized their freedom and that of their families. Living in slave societies that considered all free people of color suspect, to be watched at all cost, the mulatto elite considered freedom their most prized possession; preserving themselves and their families was utmost.[52] All the while William Ellison Sr. had been enlarging his family and fortune, he and his family had become part of the Charleston mulatto elite, engaging in social activities such as courtship, weddings, revivals, and travel, especially over the hundred miles between Charleston and Stateburg. Their letters show how Ellison kept a tight control of his business and also kept his large and growing family close. When they married, all the children lived on his large estate with their spouses. The critical moment for the Ellisons came, as it did for all Southern free blacks, in the 1850s' when Southern states discussed and began enacting laws to further protect slavery by expelling or enslaving all free blacks. In response,

free blacks began leaving the South by the hundreds, some to the North and others to Canada and Haiti. In South Carolina, many slaveholders had illegally manumitted their slaves in defiance of 1820 law. Although they lived as free people, these individuals were vulnerable to the enforcement of the law.

In contrast to their Southern counterparts, most African Americans and European Americans in the North lived in distinct geographical worlds; worlds that overlapped, often to the point of intimacy, but that enabled most whites to avoid thinking about the horrors of slavery and the blatant inequities free African Americans experienced in their daily lives. Most Northern whites did not imagine equality with the growing but comparatively small black population living in the region. And the majority of white abolitionists held various degrees of racial prejudice against African Americans of all classes, including black abolitionists. Even though they often worked together to end slavery, only a few black and white abolitionists seem to have developed true friendships. This handful of relationships evolved into a kind of extended family. The relationships between schoolteachers Emma V. Brown and Emily Howland, on the one hand, and Sarah Mapps Douglass and Sarah Grimke, on the other, transcended the racial divide and may have given the correspondents hope for a future where race would not determine social relationships.

Emma V. Brown was the daughter of a widowed free black Georgetown seamstress, Emmeline Brown. Emma attended the School for Colored Girls in Washington, D.C., founded in 1851 by Myrtilla Miner, a white woman from upstate New York. When Miner returned to the North to recuperate from mental exhaustion about six years after opening the school, her young fourteen-year-old student Emma Brown assisted her replacement, the thirty-year-old Quaker teacher Emily Howland. Emma Brown and Emily Howland corresponded with each other into the post–Civil War decade. Brown's letters suggest that her relationship with Howland had evolved from that of a protégé and mentor to a friendship between women with a shared interest in abolition and the education of African American children.

It seems that two of teacher and abolitionist Sarah Mapps Douglass's closest friends were Sarah and Angelina Grimke. The Grimke sisters, part of a prominent South Carolina white slaveholding family, had left the South and became noted Quaker abolitionists and feminists. Sarah Mapps Douglass and Sarah Grimke corresponded with each other for nearly forty years, sharing not only their experiences as teachers and abolitionists, but also their personal lives as friends.

The majority of the letters in this chapter, however, reflect intimate relationships among African Americans. This correspondence illustrates that, whether enslaved or free, Northern or Southern, African Americans worked

hard to create and maintain viable social relationships that enhanced their lives and the lives of their children. The letters also show the diverse and varied ways in which those relationships took shape. We begin with Lucy Tucker, an enslaved woman in Alabama, writing to her mother in Virginia about news of family members and friends, and end with Frederick Douglass's eldest son Lewis Douglass expressing his romantic interest in a letter to Helen Amelia Loguen, the daughter of prominent minister and fugitive slave, Jermain Loguen. The letters help us see how, in spite of enslavement or quasi-freedom, many black Americans lived lives that contributed to the richness of black families and communities.

Letters between enslaved people in this era often reflect the sale and transport of slaves to cotton planters in the Mississippi Valley from the Upper South. Separated from her mother for more than ten years when she and several others were sold into Alabama, Lucy Tucker dictates a letter, probably via a member of the slaveholding family, to her mother in Virginia. She asks about the family she left behind and informs her mother of her health and that of the others with her in Alabama. In spite of her inability to comment directly on the slave system, Tucker, who hires out her time as a washerwoman, implicitly protests against the slave system when she expresses her grief at familial loss and frustration about her inability to keep abreast of her family's welfare.

Huntsville, Alabama, May 20, 1845

Dear Mother:

I have never heard from you but once since I lef . . . for I know not whether you all still live or whether many have not since passed. . . . . My son Burrel . . . has been absent from me nine years. He is now grown but I have not seen him since he was a boy though I hear from him now & then. Mary Ann the child which I brought with me died as also Susanna who was born after I came to this country in their fifth year. I have seen a great deal of trouble since I came to Alabama. . . . Moses was drowened some years ago in Kentucky drunk as usual. Scipio is in Nashville doing very well. All he desires is to hear from his wife & children.

I have been very sick for the las two or three years. But now am doing well. Have a good husband & give the white people 25cts a day. I follow washing ironing &c . . . This is from your daughter

Lucy Tucker[53]

Enslaved letter writers wrote as often to learn about the welfare of family members as they did to ask a free relative to purchase them out of slavery. Emily Russell was held in an Alexandria, Virginia, slave pen with her grandmother, her aunts, and their children, waiting to be sold to the highest bidder. Although she does not directly ask, Emily's one hope is that her free mother, Nancy Cartwright, who bought her own freedom and was now living and working in New York as a washerwoman, would be able to purchase her. Some owners of slave pens permitted their prisoners to write to relatives about purchasing them. Cartwright, with the help of abolitionists in Washington, D.C., and New York, learned that the slave traders were asking $1,800 for Emily, whom the traders explained, "is said to be the finest-looking woman in the country," and $5,300 for her sisters and their children. When Cartwright was unable to pay the cost of her daughter, Emily was sold for the New Orleans "fancy girl" market. This term was used for young girls and women of African and mostly European descent who were placed in the city's brothels and patronized by wealthy white men. In the letter below, Emily pleads with her mother to rescue her.

Alexandria, [Virginia] January 22 1850

My Dear Mother:

I take this opportunity of writing you a few lines, to inform you that I am in Bruin's Jail, and Aunt Sally and all of her children, and Aunt Hagar and all her children, and grandmother is almost crazy. My dear mother, will you please to come on as soon as you can? I expect to go away very shortly. O mother! My dear mother! Come now and see your distressed and heart-broken daughter once more. Mother! My dear mother! Do not forsake me, for I feel desolate! Please to come now.

Your daughter,
Emily Russell

P.S. If you do not come as far as Alexandria, come to Washington, and do what you can.[54]

Interior view of a slave pen in Alexandria, Virginia, ca. 1861–1869

Within days of writing her letter, Emily Russell died during the overland trip to New Orleans.

Louisa Picquet's story ends better for at least one family member. Separated from her mother for twenty-two years, Louisa, who now lives in Ohio, learned that her mother, Elizabeth Ramsey, was the slave of Colonel A.C. Horton in Wharton County, Texas. Louisa and her husband tried to raise the purchase price Horton demanded. In the meantime, mother and daughter corresponded. In a letter dated March 8, 1859, Ramsey explains to her daughter that it would take $2,500 to buy both her and John, Louisa's fifteen-year-old brother. Within a year the slaveholder changed his mind; he would not sell John at any price.

Matagorda [Texas], April 21, 1860

Dear Daughter:

I received your kind & affectionate letter, & was glad to hear that you was well, & getting along very well. I was sorry to learn that you were disappointed in raising the amount of money required to purchase me. In conversation with my master he says he is willing to take a woman in exchange for me, of my age, and capasity or he will under the circumstances take nine hundred dollars in *cash* for me. He also says that money cannot buy John. He is a training John to take charge of one of his Plantations & will not part with him untel death parts them. I should be very happy to see you My Dear Daughter as well as my Grandchildren. I hope there will be a way provided for us to meet on earth once more before we die. Cant you come and see us. Your Brother John is well and desires to be very kindly remembered to you. Farewell My Dear Daughter. May God protect you from All evil, is the prayer of you affectionate Mother.

Elizabeth Ramsey[55]

An Alexandria, Virginia, slave pen operated by Price, Birch & Co. dealers in slaves ca. 1861–1869

Eventually abolitionists in Ohio and elsewhere were able to help Louisa Picquet raise the $900 to purchase her mother's freedom. Elizabeth Ramsey finally saw her daughter and met her grandchildren in October 1860.

Letters from Harriet Newby to her husband, Dangerfield Newby, begging him to buy her freedom, are representative of a number of letters between husbands and enslaved wives in this era. Dangerfield, the son of a white slave owner and an enslaved woman, had moved from Virginia to Bridgeport, Ohio, in 1858 with his father, mother, and siblings, thereby becoming free. He had to leave Harriet and their six children behind but immediately set to work to raise the money to buy their freedom.

Brentville April 11 1859

Dear Husband

I mus now write you apology for not writing you before this but I know you will excuse me when tell you Mrs. gennings has been very sick she has a baby a little girl ben a grate suffere her breast raised and she has had it lanced and I have had to stay with her day and night so you know I had no time to write but she is now better and one of her own servent is now sick I am well that is of the grates importance to you I have no newes to write you only the chrilden are all well I want to see you very much but are looking fordard to the promest time of your coming oh Dear Dangerfield com this fall with out fail monny or no money I want to see you so much that is one bright hope I have before me nothing more at present but remain

your affectionate wife
Harriet Newby

P S write soon if you please

Brentville April 22 1859

Dear Husband

I received your letter to day and it give much pleasure to here from you but was sorry to [hear] of your sickeness hope you may be well when you receive this I wrote to you several weeks a go and directed my letter to Bridge Port but I fear you did not receive it as you said nothing about it in yours you must give my love to Brother Gabial and tell him I would like to see him very much I wrote in my last letter that Miss Virginia had a baby a little girl I had to nerse her day and night Dear Dangerfield you Can not amagine how much I want to see you Com as soon as you can for nothing would give more pleasure than to see you it is the grates Comfort I have is thinking of the promist time when you will be here oh that bless hour when I shall see you once more my baby commenced to Crall to day it is very delicate nothing more at present but remain your affectionate wife.

Harriet Newby

P s write soon

Brentville [Virginia] August 16, 1859

Dear Husband.

your kind letter came duly to hand and it gave me much pleasure to here from you and especely to hear you are better of your rhumatism and hope when I here from you again you may be entirely well. I want you to buy me as soon as possible for if you do not get me somebody else will. . . . Dear Husband you [know] not the trouble I see the last two years has ben like a trouble dream it is said Master is in want of monney if so I know not what time he may sell me an then all my bright hops of the futer are blasted for there has ben one bright hope to cheer me in all my troubles that is to be with you for if I thought I shoul never see you this earth would have no charms for me do all you Can for me witch I have no doubt you will I want to see you so much the Chrildren are all well the baby cannot walk yet all it can step around enny thing by holding on it is very much like Agnes I mus bring my letter to Close as I have no newes to write you mus write soon and say when you think you Can Come.

Your affectionate Wife

Harriet Newby[56]

Dangerfield Newby raised nearly $742 toward the $1,000 price for Harriet and one child but was unable to free his family. Utterly disappointed, he joined John Brown, John A. Copeland Jr., and others in the futile October 1859 raid on Harpers Ferry. When Dangerfield was shot and killed in the short battle, Harriet's letters were found on his body.

Dangerfield Newby, who was killed during John
Brown's raid at Harpers Ferry, October 1859

John A. Copeland,
ca. 1850s

In his letter to his family on the eve of his execution for participating in John Brown's raid, twenty-five-year-old John A. Copeland, an Oberlin, Ohio, carpenter, abolitionist, and teacher, tells his family that he is at peace with God and explains why he was willing to sacrifice his life for the "holy cause."

Charlesto[w]n, V[irgini]a
Nov[ember] 26, [18]59

Dear father & mother:

I now take my pen to address you for the first time since I have been in the situation that I am now in. My silence has not been occasioned by my want of love for you but because I wished to wait & find what my doom would be. I am well at this time & as happy as it is possible to be under the circumstances. I received your kind and affectionate letter, which brought much consolation to me, & the advice that you have therein given me. I thank God I can say I have accepted, & I have found that consolation which can only be found by accepting & obeying such advice.

Dear father & mother, happy am I that I can now truthfully say that I have sought the Holy Bible & have found that everlasting Life in its holy advice which man can from no other source obtain. Yes, I have now in the eleventh hour sought for & obtained that forgiveness from my God, whose kindness I have outraged nearly all my life.

Dear Parents, my fate so far as man can seal it, is sealed, but let not this fact occasion you any misery; for remember the cause in which I was engaged: remember it was a holy cause, one in which men in every way better than I am, have suffered & died. Remember that if I must die, I die in trying to liberate a few of my poor & oppressed people from a condition of servitude against which God in his word has hurled his most bitter denunciations. . . . If die I must, I shall try to meet my fate as a man who can suffer in the glorious cause in which I have been engaged, without a groan, & meet my Maker in heaven as a christian man who through the saving grace of God has made his peace with Him.

Dear Parents, dear bros & sisters; miserable indeed would I be if I were confined in this jail awaiting the execution of the law for committing a foul crime; but this not being the case, I must say (though I know you all will feel deeply the

fate I am to meet), that I feel more deeply on acc't of the necessity of myself or any other man having to suffer by the existence of slavery, than from the mere fact of having to die. It is true I should like to see you all once more on the earth, but god wills otherwise. Therefore I am content, for most certainly do I believe that God wills everything for the best good, not only of those who have to suffer directly, but of all, & this being the case I beg of you not to grieve about me. Now dear Parents I beg your forgiveness for every wrong I have done you, for I know that I have not at all times treated you as I ought to have done. Remember me while I shall live & forget me not when I am no longer in this world. Give my love to all friends. . . . Now, dear father & mother, I will close this last—or at present I think last letter—I shall have the pleasure of writing to you.

Good-bye Mother & Father, Goodbye, brothers & sisters, & by the assistance of God, meet me in heaven. I remain your most affectionate son,

John A. Copeland[57]

Though illiterate, Maryland slave Emily Saunders Plummer is able to write to her husband, Adam, through her elderly slaveholder. In the letter below, Emily expresses concern about the status of their marriage and the welfare of their two children, who were left behind when she and their other children were moved to a plantation far from family and friends. She could not see them as regularly as she had in the past.

Ellicott Mills, Maryland
April 20, 1856

My Dear Plummer:

I want you to let me know why you wrote me so troubled a letter. I was very sorry to hear that you should say you and I are parted for life, and am very troubled at it. I don't think I can stand it long. What do you mean? Does your master say he will not let you come any more? Or what is the reason you say we are parted for life? I can't think it is your wish to give me up for another wife. I should like to understand your difficulties very much.

I would not wish you to bring any trouble on yourself on my account. If you cannot get his consent to come to see me, I don't want you to do anything that would displease him for me, but I shall be sorely troubled. I cannot think we are parted forever. You have a good master and a good house, and I want you to do all you can to please him, but I hope he will let you come and see me and your children sometimes. It is heart-breaking to think we are parted. Write to me soon and tell me what your difficulty is. I can't think it is your wish to give me up for another wife.

I want you to write me about my two children, if they are well and comfortable, and how mother is. Saunders said today "My Pappy is coming to bring me a hat and a pair of boots to go to church with. . . ." I want to have the baby baptized and I want to know if you can come, when you will be able to do so, and I will wait until you come.

The baby has her chills come back on her now and then. The other children are all well, and Henry sends his love to his father. I have been quite well, and have no trouble but the one great trouble, the want to see you sometimes.
God bless and keep you!

Your affectionate wife,
Emily Plummer[58]

Evidently, Emily's fears about losing her husband's affection were unfounded. The two write consistently, especially after Adam is separated from his wife and most of the children by an even longer distance. He had to convince his slaveholder to allow him to visit his family at least twice a year, taking two trains and walking a short distance to her cabin. In this letter, Adam Plummer expresses his strong desire to be with and take care of his family. He explains to Emily that he, too, finds their separation hard and tells her of his long illness.

April 3th, 1859

My Dear Wife: I take this opertunity to answer your letter. and the same day in the moning I wish that I could see you in my haerte and in a few minutes after a littel boy came running to me at my House with a Letter . . . [dated] March 31 . . . I reseve it with open Hands and Joyfull Hear[t], and it Read thus. I am not well myself and the Childrens have ben sick [with] colds you are mistaken that I do not wish to here form you and the Childrens, for i have some things for you and your Childrens last Chrismus it is not my . . . wish that I cannot here form you or see but I am not satisfied in my mind with your care for three years or more I wish that I came to see you as . . . [was] before in time pas. but I think it is very [severe] on me and Hard that I cannot come. . . . I Exspect to came up in April 23 If I can to see you and your Chilldrens . . . .

        Your Son Elias plummer is well about a week for I go to see him. Miss Marandia [Sarah Miranda] plummer is the same from George Town D C Green St No 135 my Bother Henry plummer form Goodwood came up to my house Last sunday and saying that all is well there they all give thir love to you and your Chilldreans with greates care of my self is not well for I havethe Dierar verry bad I have it for a mounth for it makes me verry week and feblee. . . . I am your uncomfitable Husband sitill . . . Adam Plummer form Rivers Dale 'seity,[city?] Md[59]

Now hired out in Georgetown, Sarah Miranda writes to her father expressing concern about his health, asks how her little brother Elias is faring, and shares family news. Elias, like her, was also separated from the rest of the family. Sarah Miranda alludes to the impact of John Brown's raid on black mobility. Southern states passed laws to control slaves even more by limiting passes. Sarah Miranda reveals, too, how much the family's diet depends on Adam's garden.

Georgetown December 2 nd 1859

Dear Father

I will write to you the second time and I hope you will grant my request. I hope to see you shortly. I sent Mother a letter last night and told her I had not heard from you yet. I was afraid that you were sick or that you had not got my letter. I suppose that old Mr. John Brown has kept you in the house. I would have been down on Saturday last but as some of the family were sick I could not get off, so I will wait a while longer. I went out in the city Sunday to try to hear from you, Grandmother told me that she saw you at market on Saturday. Aunt Rachel has not answered my letter yet. Have you heard from them lately. Please inquire for my brother and let me know how he is. Mother say'es the children are crazy to see me. Sandies [Saunders] has gathered some chesnut'es for me. I write you this note to let you know that I have not forgotten you. I want a good slip of that grape vine I want it for a lady. Don't you eat all the Cellery up before I come down. Please save me some eggs. I have no news to write. Now I must close. From

your beloved daughter
Sarah Maranda Plummer[60]

Six months later, Adam Plummer's letter to Emily expresses dismay that he has not heard from or seen her for some time. He notes that Emily has not responded to his letter in care of her white seamstress friend, Sarah Nicholson, but that he has heard from Sarah Miranda. Adam also shares news of Emily's mother and friends. One friend apparently died in April and the other friend is well. Adam tells Emily to tell the two youngest children, Nicholas Saunders and Margaret Jane, that he will see them soon.

May 11 1860

My Dear Wife I take This oppertuneity of writing you a few lins a gane in answer as I have not herd form you, séance I seen you. I wrote to you in febuary, in the care of Mrs. Sarah I Nicholson and I have not heard form you yet I have a letter form Miss Marandare form Georgetown in May 2th she say all is well. She [has] a bundle for me but do not expect to go to see her untell June 01th for I have a wish to come up to see you all on the 26th of May. your Mother came to Riversdale on 5th of April and she was well and in good health and she stay three days and then Return home she came to visit her sick sister: Lucy Scott but she is better now the Dr say she have the Gravels [kidney stones]. The Death tarleton Brown Apirl 21th I seen henry Brooks on 22 at tarleton Bevring he say that all is well at home. Till sondis and Margarat to loock for me. For I come in to see them. I am your very Respecfully

Husband Adam Plummer[61]

The event that the couple most feared occurred in the fall. In her letter to Adam, Emily expresses anguish that Sarah Miranda is in the Alexandria, Virginia, slave pen to be auctioned. The next two letters may have been written in Emily's own hand.

Emily Plummer, ca. 1870s

Adam Plummer, undated

wodloun [Woodlawn] September 7 1860

my Deare husband

i have not received a leter from you saince you went home wither you rote or no i don't now i suppose you heard of merandys trubles plese rite and let me heare from you as for my self i am very porly the chrildon are all well let me know how my boy is marandy says mother is coming up the last of this month plese rite as sune as you recive this

from yur wife

Emily Plummer

the childon all send thare love to you and wont to se you.[62]

59

Two weeks later Emily informs Adam of the birth of their twins, Robert and Nellie.

September 18 1860

My Deare Husband i recived you kind leter and was very much oblige to you for what you sent me the fridy night after i rote to you i was confined with too babys one was a boy and the other a girl every body that se them says they are the fines chrilden that every sar when mother came and scene them she was delited i am as well as can bee expected the chrilden ar all well and join me in love to you from your wife

Emily Plummer[63]

Just across the Maryland border from the Plummer family, several southeastern Pennsylvania blacks and white Quakers were active in the Underground Railroad. Black abolitionist, teacher, and Quaker Joseph C. Bustill was the son of prominent black Philadelphia Quaker abolitionist David Bustill, and a cousin of Sarah Mapps Douglass. He had been active in Vigilance Committee work since he was seventeen. Educated in black Philadelphia private schools, Bustill moved to Harrisburg, Pennsylvania, where he taught in the segregated public schools and established the Fugitive Aid Society (later renamed the Harrisburg Vigilance Committee) to continue his commitment to helping slaves escape slavery. Bustill reportedly helped hundreds of fugitives escape to Reading and Philadelphia, Pennsylvania, and Auburn, New York.[64] In his letter to William Still, the preeminent Underground Railroad operator, Bustill illustrates the language and activities of underground workers and the necessity of being aware of slave catchers, slave owners, or their agents pursuing human property.

Harrisburg, [Pennsylvania]

March 24, [18]56

Friend Still: I suppose ere this you have seen those five large and three small packages I sent by way of Reading, consisting of three men and women and children. They arrived here this morning at $8^1/_2$ o'clock and left twenty minutes past three. You will please send me any information likely to prove interesting in relation to them.

Lately we have formed a Society here, called the Fugitive Aid Society. This is our first case, and I hope it will prove entirely successful.

When you write, please inform me what signs or symbols you make use of in your dispatches, and any other information in relation to operations of the Underground Rail Road.

Our reason for sending by the Reading Road, was to gain time; it is expected the owners will be in town this afternoon, and by this Road we gained five hours' time, which is a matter of much importance, and we may have occasion to use it sometimes in the future. In great haste,

Yours with great respect,

Jos. C. Bustill[65]

A month later Joseph Bustill sarcastically describes an encounter with the son of a slaveholder who said he was willing to free his fugitive slaves beginning the next year. The letter shows how abolitionists generally viewed laws protecting slavery as immoral and unworthy of respect.

Harrisburg, April 28, '56

Friend Still: Your last came to hand in due season, and I am happy to hear of the safe arrival of those gents.

I have before me the Power of Attorney of Mr. John S. Fiery, son of Mr. Henry Fiery, of Washington county, Md., the owner of those three men, two women and three children, who arrived in your town on the 24th or 25th of March. He graciously condescends to liberate the oldest in a year, and the remainder in proportional time, if they will come back; or to sell them their time for $1300. He is sick of the job, and is ready to make any conditions. Now, if you personally can get word to them and get them to send him a letter, in my charge, informing him of their whereabouts and prospects, I think it will be the best answer I can make him. He will return here in a week or two, to know what can be done. He offers $500 to see them.

Or if you can send me word where they are, I will endeavor to write to them for his special satisfaction; or if you cannot do either, send me your latest information, for I intend to make him spend a few more dollars, and if possible get a little sicker of this bad job. Do try and send him a few bitter pills for his weak nerves and disturbed mind.

Yours In great Haste, Jos. C. Bustill[66]

In May, Bustill reports that John Fiery "visited us again and much to his chagrin received the information of their being in Canada."[67]

Fugitive slave letters sent to family members through operators of the Underground Railroad reveal the important role Northern black abolitionists played in the railroad's functioning and success. Even though the Fugitive Slave Law increased the risks for underground operators, they persisted in aiding fugitives. William Still used black sailors to carry letters between fugitive slaves in Canada and their families still in bondage. After John Thompson, a fugitive who had been a hired-out slave from Virginia, arrived safely in Syracuse, New York, he asked Still to "Direct this Letter to Vergenia for me to my Mother" so that she would know he was safely in the North and had a job. Thompson assures his mother that nothing can replace freedom.

Syracuse, Jeny 6th [probably 1850s]

My Dear Mother: I have imbrace an opportunity of writing you these few lines (hoping) that they may fine you as they Leave me quite well I will now inform you how I am geting I am now a free man Living by the sweet of my own Brow not serving a nother man & giving him all I Earn But what I make is mine and iff one Plase do not sute me I am at Liberty to Leave and go some where elce & can ashore you I think highly of Freedom and would not exchange it for nothing. . . . I am waiting in a Hotel I suppose you Remember when I was in Jail I told you the time would Be Better and you see that the time has come when I leave you my heart was so full & yours But I new their was a Better Day a head, & I have Live to see it I hird when I was on the Underground R. Road that the Hounds was on my Track but it was no go I new I was too far out of their Reach where they would never smell my track when I Leave you I was carred to Richmond & sold & From their I was taken to North Carolina & sold & I Ran a way & went Back to Virginna Between Richmond & home & their I was caught & Put in Jail & their I Remain till the oner come for me then I was taken & carred Back to Richmond then I was sold to the man who I now Leave he is nothing But a Bit of a Feller Remember me to your Husband & all in quirin Friends & say to Miss Rosa that I am as Free as she is & more happier I no I am getting $12 per month for what Little work I am Doing. I hope to here from you a gain I your Son & ever By.

John Thompson[68]

Emma Brown, a forty-five-year-old fugitive from Petersburg, Virginia, notifies William Still of changing her name from Mary to Emma, reports her safe arrival in Toronto, and asks him to write to her husband, who was planning his escape after paying a ship captain $100 to take Mary to the Philadelphia Vigilance Committee offices. Mary had delivered fifteen children: four were sold away, one remained enslaved in Petersburg, and the rest were dead.

Toronto, [Canada,] March 14, 1855

Dear Mr. Still: I take this opportunity of addressing you with these lines to inform you that I arrived here to day, and hope that this may find yourself and Mrs. Still well, as this leaves me at the present. I will also say to you, that I had no difficulty in getting along. the two young men that was with me left me at Suspension Bridge [Niagara Falls] they went another way.

I cannot say much about the place as I have ben here but a short time but so far as I have seen I like very well. you will give my Respect to your lady, & Mr & Mrs Brown. If you have not written to Petersburg you will please to write as soon as can I have nothing More to Write at present but yours Respectfully

Emma Brown (old name Mary Epps)[69]

Rebecca Jones escaped from slavery six years after her husband. Her letter to Still shows that almost all the options for work for Northern blacks were limited to menial labor, even for those who were literate and had skills. Jones was probably a maid at the famous Parker House Hotel in Boston. In the 1850s, the newly established state of California afforded more job opportunities for the few free blacks who moved West. Jones's letter also reveals that some fugitives engaged in immediate "divorces" after their escape.

Parker House School Street, Boston, October 18th, 56. My Dear Sir: I can hardly express the pleasure I feel at the receipt of your kind letter; but allow me to thank you for the same.

And now I will tell you my reasons for going to California. Mrs. Tarrol, a cousin of my husband, has sent for me. She says I can do much better than in Boston. And as I have my children's welfare to look to, I have concluded to go. . . .

I should like to hear from my brothers and sisters once more, and let me hear every particular. You never can know how anxious I am to hear from them; do please impress this upon their minds. . . .

I suppose you think I am going to live with my husband again. Let me assure you 'tis no such thing. My mind is as firm as ever. And believe me, in going away from Boston, I am going away from him, for I have heard he is living somewhere near. He has been making inquiries about me, but that can make no difference in my feelings to him. I hope that yourself, wife and family are all quite well. Please remember me to them all . . . . I should be most happy to have any letters of introduction you may think me worthy of, and I trust I shall ever remain

Yours faithfully,

Rebecca Jones

P.S. I do not know if I shall go this Fall, or in the Spring. It will depend upon the letter I receive from California, but whichever it may be, I shall be happy to hear from you very soon.[70]

William Still, ca 1870s

Now safe in Toronto, twenty-three-year-old Isaac Forman escaped slavery probably in mid-to-late 1853 without his wife. A Norfolk, Virginia, hired-out slave who worked as a steward on a steamship, Forman left without informing his wife of his intention to flee bondage. In February 1854 he writes to Still, informing him of his address and thanking him "from the bottom of my heart, that the high heavens may bless you for your kindness." Forman then asks if his contacts had "heard anything from my brother" and whether one of Still's contacts had seen his wife, a slave in Richmond—had Still "thought of any way that he can get my wife away." Forman's next letter was more desperate. He appears to be planning to return for his wife if he does not get help immediately.

Toronto, May 7, 1854

Mr W. Still: *Dear Sir*—I take this opportunity of writing you these few lines and hope when they reach you they will find you well . . . .

My soul is vexed, my troubles are inexpressible. I often feel as if I were willing to die. I must see my wife in short, if not, I will die. What would I not give no tongue can utter. Just to gaze on her sweet lips one moment I would be willing to die in the next. I am determined to see her some time or other. The thought of being a slave again is miserable. I hope heaven will smile upon me again, before I am one again. I will leave Canada again shortly, but I don't name the place that I go, it may be in the bottom of the ocean. If I had known as much before I left, as I do now, I would never have left until I could have found means to have brought her with me. You have never suffered from being absent from a wife, as I have. I consider that to be nearly superior to death, and hope you will do all you can for me . . . . I am determined to see her, if I die the next moment, I can say I was once happy, but never will be again, until I see her; because what is freedom to me, when I know that my wife is in slavery? . . . .

I remain evermore your obedient servant,

I. Forman[71]

Apparently, Isaac Forman did not have to wait long for his family to be reunited. His wife and twenty-three-year-old brother, James, both fugitives, joined Isaac in the North. James Forman is now waiting for his fiancée, Mariah Moore, to follow.

Niagara Falls, June 5TH, 1856

Mr. Still: Sir—I take my pen in hand to write you theas few lines to let you know that I am well at present and hope theas few lines may find you the same. Sir my object in writing to you is that I expect a young Lady by the name of Miss Mariah Moore, from Norfolk, Virginia. She will leave Norfolk on the 13th of this month in the Steamship Virginia for Philadelphia you will oblige me very much by seeing her safely on the train of cars that leaves Philadelphia for the Suspension Bridge Niagara Falls pleas to tell the Lady to telegraph to me what time she will leave Philadelphia so *i* may know what time to meet her at the Suspension Bridge my Brother Isaac Forman send his love also his family to you and your family they are all well at present. . . .

I Remain Your Friend,

James H. Forman

When you telegraph to me direct to the International Hotel, Niagara Falls, N.Y.

Later, Forman, whose father is apparently already living in Canada, notifies William Still of Mariah Moore's safe arrival and their marriage.

Niagara Falls, July 24th, 1856

Dear Sir: I take this opportunity of writing these few lines to you hoping that they may find you enjoying good health as these few lines leave me at present. I thank you for your kindness. Miss Moore arrived here on the 30th of June and I was down to the cars to receive her. I thought I would

have written to you before, but I thought I would wait till I got married. I got married on the 22nd of July in the English Church Canada about 11 o'clock my wife sends all her love to you and your wife and all enquiring friends please to kiss your two children for her and she says she is done crying and I am glad to hear she enjoyed herself so well in Philadelphia give my respects to Miss Margaret Cunningham and I am glad to hear her sister arrived my father sends his respects to you no more at present but remain you friend,

James H. Forman[72]

Probably reflecting the views of most fugitives when they arrived safely, Virginia fugitive John Clayton calls Canada the "glorious land of liberty."

Toronto, March 6th, 1854

Dear Mr. Still: I take this method of informing you that I am well both in health and mind You may rest assured that I fells myself a free man and do not fell as I did when I was in Virginia thanks be to God I have no master into Canada but I am my own man. I arrived safe into Canada on friday last. I must request of you to write a few lines to my wife and jest state to her that her friend arrived safe into this glorious land of liberty and I am well and she will make very short her time in Virginia. tell her that I likes here very well and hope to like it better when I gets to work I don't meane for you to write the same words that are written above but I wish you give her a clear understanding where I am and Shall Remain here untel She comes or I hears from her.

Nothing more at present but remains your most respectfully,

John Clayton[73]

Underground Railroad operators and other abolitionists were in awe of Maryland fugitive Harriet Tubman, whom many called "the Moses of her people." Tubman, who escaped in 1849, returned to Maryland at least thirteen times to lead seventy men, women, and children, including several relatives, out of bondage. The Delaware Quaker and abolitionist Thomas Garrett wrote about Tubman in his letter to Presbyterian minister, abolitionist, and Underground Railroad operator in Philadelphia, J. Miller McKim. Garrett reports on her latest arrivals, who were on their way from Delaware to Philadelphia. Both men represent the many white abolitionists who worked tirelessly with black abolitionists in various and multiple capacities for the abolition of slavery.

Wilmington, 12 Mo. 29TH, 1854.

Esteemed Friend, J. Miller McKim: We made arrangements last night, and sent away Harriet Tubman, with six men and one woman to Allen Agnew's, to be forwarded across the country to the city. Harriet, and one of the men had worn their shoes off their feet, and I gave them two dollars to help fit them out, and directed a carriage to be hired at my expense, to take them out, but do not yet know the expense. I now have two more from the lowest county in Maryland, on the Peninsula, upwards of one hundred miles. I will try to get one of our trusty colored men to take them to-morrow morning to the Anti-slavery office. You can then pass them on.

Thomas Garrett[74]

Abolitionists consistently sought financial support nationally and internationally for their activities and found several individuals and organizations more than willing to offer what they could. Poet Frances Ellen Watkins, who was born free in Baltimore and became a teacher, abolitionist lecturer, and writer in the North, sent Still money regularly for his "underground" activities. He apparently helped sell her books, and she admonished him for his unwillingness to put the proceeds toward the Vigilance Committee. Watkins also wanted to keep abreast of the individual lives of fugitives the Philadelphia operators helped. In her letter below, probably written in 1856, Watkins may be referring to Ann Maria Weems, a fifteen-year-old who dressed as a boy to escape a Maryland slave trader. Ann Maria's parents succeeded, with the invaluable help of black and white abolitionists, in getting all of their children out of slavery, even three sons sold into Alabama. Watkins' letter shows how Christian principles guided many activists' work.

[n.d. or place]

How fared the girl who came robed in male attire? Do write me every time you write how many come to your house; and, my dear friend, if you have that much in hand from my books, will you please pay the Vigilance Committee two or three dollars to help carry on the glorious enterprise. Now, please do not write back that you are not going to do any such thing. Let me explain a few matters to you. In the first place, I am able to give something. In the second place, I am willing to do so. Oh, life is fading away, and we have but an hour of time! Should we not, therefore, endeavor to let its history gladden the earth? The nearer we ally ourselves to the wants and woes of humanity in the spirit of Christ, the closer we get to the great heart of God; the nearer we stand by the beating of the pulse of universal love.[75]

An old slave block in the St. Louis Hotel, New Orleans, Louisiana, ca. 1900–1910

"Unlimited Credit Sale of a Valuable Gang of Georgia and South Carolina field hands. And a washer and Ironer, and Dining Room Servant." By J.A. Beard & May, Saturday, February 23, 1856, New Orleans

Green Hill slave auction block, Campbell County, Virginia, 1933

The business of slavery: The slave market, Atlanta, Georgia, 1864

NEW ORLEANS
SLAVE DEPOT,
No. 15 Perdido street—near St. Charles.

J. W. BOAZMAN,

Will keep constantly on hand a large and well selected lot of SLAVES FOR SALE. Negroes also Bought and Sold on Commission.

☞I have on hand a number of NEGROES TO HIRE BY THE MONTH, among them are men, boys, house servants, cooks, washers and ironers, nurses, &c.

———o———

REFER TO { Wright, Williams & Co. | Moon, Titus & Co.
Williams, Phillips & Co. | S. O. Nelson & Co.
Moses Greenwood. | E. W. Diggs.

New Orleans slave depot. "Will keep constantly on hand a large and well selected lot of SLAVES FOR SALE," ca. 1840s–1850s

$100 REWARD!
RANAWAY

From the undersigned, living on Current River, about twelve miles above Doniphan, in Ripley County, Mo., on 2nd of March, 1860, A NEGRO MAN, about 30 years old, weighs about 160 pounds; high forehead, with a scar on it; had on brown pants and coat very much worn, and an old black wool hat; shoes size No. 11.

The above reward will be given to any person who may apprehend this said negro out of the State; and fifty dollars if apprehended in this State outside of Ripley county, or $25 if taken in Ripley county.

APOS TUCKER.

$100 Reward! Ranaway from Ripley, Mo., . . . 1860, a Negro Man

$20 Reward,

FOR the apprehension and delivery to the undersigned, or any of the city jails, of the BOY DAN, who ran away on Monday, the 8th inst. Age 40 years; 5 feet 6 inches high, stout built, thick lips, dark color, walks at a slow gait and slightly drooped, and acts polite and bashful when spoken to. Captains of steamboats and other trading vessels will please have a look-out, as he may cross the Lake. HENRY McGUINN,
aug11 tf Julia street, corner Magnolia and Basin.

ONE HUNDRED DOLLARS REWARD—Left my premises on the 24th of June last, my yellow woman FRANCES She is about 24 years old, 5 feet in height, stout, good looking, and has quite a round face. Her two front upper teeth are parted. I will give $50 for her delivery at either of the jails of this city or Lafayette, and $50 for such information as will convict the party who has harbored her, if a white person or free negro; or I will give $100 for the recovery of the girl alone if taken out of the State.
sep9—1m HENRY RENSHAW, 96 Camp st.

TWENTY DOLLARS REWARD—Ran away from the subscribers, on the 10th inst., a mulatto boy by the name of LUIS, alias SINNOT, about 22 years of age, stout built, speaks French and English; he is about 5 feet 7 inches in height Said boy is a good cook and steward; he may try to get employment on a steamboat in that capacity. The above reward will be paid to any person who will arrest him and lodge him in jail.
sep12—tf THAYER & CO. 74 Poydras street.

TWENTY-FIVE DOLLARS REWARD—Ran away from steamship Mexico, a bright mulatto boy named GREEN, about 24 years old and about 5 feet 9 inches high. The above reward will be paid for his apprehension and delivery to
au30—tf LUSK & CO, 20 Poydras st.

ONE HUNDRED DOLLARS REWARD—Will be paid for the apprehension and delivery to the subscriber of the slave named ROBERT REED, who ran away on Tuesday, the 5th instant. Robert is a light mulatto, between 30 and 35 years old, about 5 feet 6 inches in height, weighing about 140 lbs, and has a cross and dissatisfied look. He is supposed to be still in the city.
au18—1m F. FARRE & CO, 29 Magazine st.

TWENTY DOLLARS REWARD—Will be paid for the delivery of the yellow woman FANNY, who ran away from the subscriber on the 29th of last April. She is about 30 years of age, rather stout built, about 5 feet in height, very active when about her business, teeth very irregular and somewhat decayed. She has a black fellow for a husband called Aaron, who, it is believed, knows all about her, as they have lately been seen together. He may be seen about the corners of Common and Tchoupitoulas streets. They were both residents once of Holmes county, Miss. All persons are cautioned against harboring said slave Fanny, as they will be prosecuted to the extent of the law.
WILLIAM DUNCAN,
au16—tf corner Jackson and Prytania sts., Lafayette.

TWENTY-FIVE DOLLARS REWARD.—Ran away from the Battle-Ground plantation on Sunday, the 6th instant, the boy JOHN, aged 30 years Said boy was formerly from Maryland and recently belonged to Mr Nathalie Ballentin, known as Jim, who kept a coffee stand in the Port Market, Third Municipality Said boy attended the stand He is about 5 feet 9 or 10 inches high, is very light colored, and at a short distance might be mistaken for a white man. He has long, dark, wavy hair, gray eyes, a downcast look, speaks slowly and hesitatingly. His wife is living at the above named place, near the French market, Third Municipality, and it is thought that he may be lurking in that vicinity.
au5

ONE HUNDRED DOLLARS REWARD—Ran away from the subscriber on the 15th instant, a negro woman named BETSY, aged about 35 years, medium size, long nose, pop eyes, upper front teeth out except one; answers quick when spoken to. The above reward will be paid for her apprehension
my16—tf CHAS. PRIDE.

Runaway Apprehended.

There is a mulatto boy in ail in this place, who says he ran away from a man by the name of Copeland, in Louisiana. Said boy is of bright color, says he will be twenty one years old next March, has light eyes and kinky hair, is about six feet one inch high, very straight, and would weigh about 160 pounds. He has a scar on the upper point of the right shoulder, about an inch and a half long, and one on the outside of the left thigh, about the size of a dollar. Said boy calls himself THOM, and says he was raised near Danville, Va., and was sold to a man named Copeland, in Louisiana, somewhere below Vicksburg. The owner is requested to have him taken away.
WM. S EUBANKS,
Sheriff of White county, Illinois.
Carmi, Ill., August 25, 1855. s13—d&W1m

10/14/1855

TWENTY DOLLARS REWARD—Will be paid for the apprehension of slave ELLEN, belonging to H M Hyams. She absconded a few days since from No 46 Prytania street, is about 25 years of age stout and about 5 feet 5 inches in height, and nearly of griffe lor. Jy19—1taw4w

TWENTY DOLLARS REWARD—Ran away on the 27th June last, from Elder's Wood-yard, parish of Ascension, the griff boy WILLIAM, aged 22 years, 5 feet 7 or 8 inches high, with a small scar near one of his eyes. He is a smart boy and will no doubt attempt to go up the river. The above reward will be paid for the delivery of said boy to me, in Donaldsonville, or to Messrs. J. A. BRAUD & LANDRY, 14 Bienville street.
au10—6t H. L. DUFFEL.

TEN DOLLARS REWARD—Ran away from the subscriber, the mulatto girl JANE, about 26 years of age, about 5 feet in height; she has a scar on the inside of one of her hands; she is rather stupid in her manner She is perhaps harbored in the Third Municipality The above reward will be paid for her apprehension and lodgement in any jail of this city.
au7 tf JOHN SWILER, 110 Casacalvo st.

TWENTY-FIVE DOLLARS REWARD.—Ran away from the Battle Ground plantation on Sunday, the 6th instant, the boy JOHN, aged 30 years Said boy was formerly from Maryland and recently belonged to Mr Nathalie Ballentin, known as Jim, who kept a coffee stand in the Port Market, Third Municipality Said boy attended the stand He is about 5 feet 9 or 10 inches high, is very light colored, and at a short distance might be mistaken for a white man He has long, dark, wavy hair, gray eyes, a downcast look, speaks slowly and hesitatingly. His wife is living at the above named place, near the French market, Third Municipality, and it is thought that he may be lurking in that vicinity.
au5

FIFTY DOLLARS REWARD—Ran away from the subscriber, boy AUGUSTUS, about 23 years old, about 5 feet 6 inches high, yellow complexion, slender figure and rather sprightly disposition; formerly belonged to Rob't Jemison, of Tuscaloosa, Ala, and recently the property of Rufus Greene, of Mobile. He was raised at Nashville by Thomas Hill.
Jy22—tf SAMUEL B EWING, Mobile, Ala

ONE HUNDRED DOLLARS REWARD—Ran away from the subscriber on the 15th instant, a negro woman named BETSY, aged about 35 years, medium size, long nose, pop eyes, upper front teeth out except one; answers quick when spoken to. The above reward will be paid for her apprehension
CHAS PRIDE

SIXTY DOLLARS REWARD—Ran away on the evening of the 5th instant, the negro man ROBERT, and woman MARIA. Robert is 25 years old, 5 feet 5 inches high, bright mulatto, rather stout made; and Maria about 40 years old, very black, rock-marked and delicate frame, white and handsome teeth, large eyes, whites very conspicuous; has a startled look when spoken to. The above reward will be paid for the two, or $30 for either one of them delivered to us. W. R. NORCOM,
au9—6t F. FARRE & CO

TWO HUNDRED DOLLARS REWARD—Ran away on Saturday, the 5th July, the black boy GILBERT. Said boy is about 22 years old, 5 feet 7 or 8 inches high is knock-kneed; he is always genteelly dressed and is a smart, shrewd fellow; is a good looking boy, and can read and write; he has been in the habit of wearing a gold watch; he had money with him when he left. He is no doubt secreted in the city, and is probably harbored by white persons. The above reward will be paid for the apprehension and delivery of the said boy to me in the city.
au4—tf ROBT. H. BOWLES, 1 Royal st.

TWENTY FIVE DOLLARS REWARD.—Ran away from my plantation in the parish of Carroll, on the 10th of May last, SANDY, entirely black, rather stout make, about 5 feet 10 or 11 inches high, short thick neck, aged from 30 to 35 years; has formerly resided at Natchez, Miss, and for the last five or six years near Jackson, Hinds Co, and was purchased from Wm P and Thos O Owens, now residing on Red river in Bossier parish, in this State.
The above reward will be paid for the delivery of above named negro, or his confinement so that he may be obtained, on application to me, or to Jos H Moore, at 107 Poydras street, N. O.
WILLIAM GLOMAN.

ONE THOUSAND DOLLARS REWARD—Ran away from the plantation of Madam Dehommer, on the night of the 23d November last, the yellow man BOB. He is about 6 feet high, stout built, high, retreating forehead, full face, and has an impudent look; he has a mark on one or both arms, made with india ink; aged about 25 years
Also, the black boy CHARLOE, rather spare built, quick spoken and intelligent; speaks English and French, is about 5 feet 6 inches high, and about 18 years of age.
It is believed that these two boys have been decoyed off by a man who ran a trading boat up and down the coast, who went by the name of John It has been ascertained that he offered to run these negroes off to a free State for $150 each, and as the negroes stole a considerable amount of money the night they left, and as this man has not since been seen, it is thought that he has the negroes in charge, endeavoring to reach some of the free states, and we have reason to believe they are in the State of Ohio. The above reward will be paid for the recovery of the negroes, or $500 for either of them.
Jy29—d&Wtf CLARK & MOSBY.

PICAYUNE 5/14/1851

LIKELY SLAVES FOR SALE—
Received this day, TEN EXTRA LIKELY
Slaves.
Will be sold at private sale in block or separately. Apply at—
No. 161 GRAVIER STREET,
Opposite the Varieties Theater.
J. L. CARMAN,
R. W. LONG.
m5 tf

BY M. BARNETT, Sr.

WILL be sold on Monday 4th of April, at Hewlett's Exchange.

The negro woman Betsey, aged about 28 years in the country since her infancy, speaks Fuench and English, she is a good cook, washer and ironer, fully guaranteed.

Terms—6 and 12 months credit, for satisfactorily endorsed notes and mortgage.

Act of sale before Wm Boswell, notary public, at the expense of the purchaser.

Fanny, a mulatress, aged about 18 years, since her infancy in the country. She is a good cook, washer and ironer, fully guaranteed against the vices and maladies prescribed by law.

Terms—One half cash, the balance payable in six months credit, for an approved endorsed note with mortgage.

Acts of sale before Wm Y. Lewis, notary public, at the expense of purchasers.

The above slaves are sold on account of departure.
a 1-2t

Negroes for Sale.

ARRIVED on 15th inst. and may be seen on St. Philip street, Eighty Virginia Slaves, among them two or three mechanics. Application can be made where the slaves are, or at Elkins' Hotel, Canal street.
april 9 ABNER ROBINSON.

SLAVES FOR SALE.

Planters and citizens of the city wishing to purchase Slaves will find it to their interest to call at Nos. 260 and 262 Common street, corner of Tremé.
ANDREWS & HATCHER.
B. LITTLE.
N. B. Persons wishing to sell slaves may find it to their advantage to call as above.
dec 31 4m A. & H.

SLAVES FOR SALE.

Citizens wishing to purchase will find it to their interest to call at 152 Camp street, where they may find some valuable house servants and young negro boys. [feb 4 2m] M. GARRISON.

Succession of the late J. P. Foltz.
SALE ON ACCOUNT OF A FORMER PURCHASER
BY N. VIGNIE, Auctioneer.

BY virtue of an order from the Honorable the Second District Court of New Orleans, will be sold at public auction in the Rotunda of the St. Louis Hotel, on SATURDAY, 18th February, 1854, at 12 o'clock, M., for account of Matilda Bushey, who has not complied with the conditions of the adjudication made to her through Mr. Kendig, on the 17th December last, of the following described slave;

ADAM, a field hand, aged about 35 years.

Terms: One-fourth cash, and the balance on a credit of 6 and 12 months, for approved endorsed notes, on the slaves, and secured by mortgage on said slave.

Acts of sale before A. C. Bienvenu, Esq., notary public. jan 17

BY WEATHERS & WATERMAN
SALE OF NEGROES.

AT the City Exchange, St Louis st, on Tuesday 5th June, at 12 o'clock.

Negro **Ben,** aged about 38 years, a good field hand, and fully guaranteed except having absented himself.

Negress **Eliza**, aged 15 years, house servant, fully guaranteed and a good subject.

Negro man **John**, aged 28 years, good field hand and has worked several years at the tanners' trade—fully guaranteed.

Negro man **Sam**, aged 26 years, field hand, and has worked with the buildders making mortar, &c —fully guaranteed.

Terms at sale. J4

Newspaper clippings of slave runaway and auction notices, 1820s to 1850s

Fugitive slaves often wrote down or dictated their personal experiences in slavery. The many slave narratives include those of Frederick Douglass, William Wells Brown, Jermain Loguen, Harriet Jacobs, and William and Ellen Craft. They stressed the importance of family and were published broadly in abolitionist newspapers, mainly as a means to convince white Northerners to join the cause of freedom. The Crafts, who had escaped to England after the passage of the 1850 Fugitive Slave Law, quickly made sure that Ellen learn to read and write. When pro-slavery advocates circulated a rumor that she was dissatisfied with freedom, Ellen wrote a letter that was published in the *Liberator.* Abolitionists persistently countered pro-slavery propaganda that slaves were content.

Ockham School, near Ripley, Surrey [England]
Oct. 26th, 1852

Dear Sir, I feel very much obliged to you for informing me of the erroneous report which has been so extensively circulated in the American newspapers: 'That I had placed myself in the hands of an American gentleman in London, on condition that he would take me back to the family who held me as a slave in Georgia. So I write these few lines merely to say that the statement is entirely unfounded, for I have never had the slightest inclination what ever of returning to bondage; and God forbid that I should ever be so false to liberty as to prefer slavery in its stead. In fact, since my escape from slavery, I have got on much better in every respect than I could have possibly anticipated. Though, had it been to the contrary, my feelings in regard to this would have been just the same, for I had much rather starve in England, a free woman, than be a slave for the best man that ever breathed upon the American continent.

Yours very truly
Ellen Craft

William and
Ellen Craft, ca.
1850s–1860s

Before moving to England, the Crafts lectured widely about slavery and their extraordinary escape, which involved fair-skinned Ellen posing as William's male slaveowner and traveling by first-class railway. In the same issue of the *Liberator* that William Lloyd Garrison published Ellen's letter, William Craft's letter to the Massachusetts Anti-Slavery Society underscored the couple's hatred of slavery when he announced to his American friends the birth of their first child. The idea of bringing a child into slavery wrenched the hearts of enslaved parents.

My Dear Mr. May, You and "other friends" will heartily rejoice to hear that my wife has given birth to our first free born babe . . . . nothing can be more consoling to the hart of a fugitive slave, than to look upon his new-born infant, and feel that there are no chains and fetters waiting in readiness to grasp and stunt his physical structure, and no hell-born despotism like American slavery hanging over his head, ready to drop, and crush his intellectual faculties to the dust, should they dare to expand beyond the tyrant's will."[76]

In the antebellum decades some fugitive slaves published their letters from and to their legal owners in antislavery newspapers. This was part of abolitionists' strategy to underscore the barbaric nature of humans owning other humans. Abolitionists stressed the physical and emotional violence slaves suffered when they were separated from their family members. Not knowing she was writing on the eve of a war that would end slavery, Tennessee slave owner Sarah Logue addresses her slave, now the Rev. Jermain W. Loguen, who escaped bondage in the mid-1830s. She threatens to sell him if he does not pay for the loss of her profits from the ownership of his body.[77]

Maury Co., State of Tennessee

February 20th, 1860

To Jarm—I now take my pen to write you a few lines, to let you know how we all are. I am a cripple, but I am still able to get about. The rest of the family are all well. Cherry is as well as common. I write you these lines to let you know the situation we are in—partly in consequence of your running away and stealing Old Rock, our fine mare. Though we got the mare back, she was never worth much after you took her; and, as I now stand in need of some funds, I have determined to sell you; and I have had an offer for you, but did not see fit to take it. If you will send me one thousand dollars and pay for the old mare, I will give up all claim I have to you. Write to me as soon as you get these lines, and let me know if you will accept my proposition. In consequence of your running away, we had to sell Abe and Ann and twelve acres of land; and I want you to send me the money that I may be able to redeem the land that you was the cause of our selling, and on receipt of the above named sum of money, I will send you your bill of sale. If you do not comply with my request, I will sell you to some one else, and you may rest assured that the time is not far distant when things will be changed with you. . . . You had better comply with my request.

I understand that you are a preacher. . . . I would like to know if you read your Bible. If so, can you tell what will become of the thief if he does not repent? . . . You know that we reared you as we reared our own children; that you was never abused, and that shortly before you ran away, when your master asked you if you would like to be sold, you said you would not leave him to go with any body.

Sarah Logue[78]

Reverend Jermain Wesley Loguen, whose mother, Jane, was born free in Ohio but kidnapped and sold to Tennessee slaveholders at the age of seven, responds. By 1860, Loguen had escaped to Canada through the underground network, worked at odd jobs, gained an education, and then opened schools for black children in Utica and Syracuse, New York. He was now a prominent New York minister, abolitionist, and Underground Railroad operator.[79] By stressing the importance of family, Loguen clearly spells out the meaning of enslavement for individual lives and argues that the nature of slavery is antithetical to human-rights principles.

Syracuse, N.Y., March 28, 1860

Mrs. Sarah Logue: Yours of the 20th of February is duly received, and I thank you for it. It is a longtime since I heard from my poor old mother, and I am glad to know she is yet alive and as you say, "as well as common." What that means I don't know. I wish you had said more about her.

You are a woman; but had you a woman's heart you could never have insulted a brother by telling him you sold his only remaining brother and sister, because he put himself beyond your power to convert him into money.

You sold my brother and sister, Abe and Ann, and 12 acres of land, you say, because I ran away. Now you have the unutterable meanness to ask me to return and be your miserable chattel, or, in lieu thereof, send you $1000 to enable you to redeem the *land*, but not to redeem my poor brother and sister! If I were to send you money it would be to get my brother and sister and not that you should get land. You say you are a *cripple*, and doubtless you say it to stir my pity, for you know I was susceptible in that direction. I do pity you from the bottom of my heart. Nevertheless, I am indignant beyond the power of words to express, that you should be so sunken and cruel as to tear the hearts I love so much all in pieces, that you should be willing to impale and crucify us all, out of all compassion for your poor *foot* or

leg. Wretched woman! Be it known to you that I value my freedom, to say nothing of my mother, brothers and sisters more than your whole body; more, indeed than my own life; more than all the lives of all slaveholders and tyrants under heaven.

You say you have offers to buy me, and that you shall sell me if I do not send you $1000, and in the same breath and almost in the same sentence, you say, 'You know we raised you as we did our own children.' Woman did you raise your *own children* for the market? Did you raise them for the whipping post? Did you raise them to be drove off in a coffle in chains? Where are my poor bleeding brothers and sisters? Can you tell? Who was it that sent them off into sugar and cotton fields, to be kicked and cuffed, and whipped, and to groan and die; and where no kin can hear their groans, or attend and sympathize at their dying bed, or follow in their funeral? Wretched woman! Do you say *you* did not do it? Then I reply, your husband did, and *you* approved the deed— and the very letter you sent me shows that your heart approves it all. Shame on you!

But by the way, where is your husband? You don't speak of him. I infer, therefore, that he is dead; that he has gone to his great account, with all his sins against my poor family upon his head. Poor man! Gone to meet the spirits of my poor, outraged and murdered people, in a world where Liberty and Justice are *Masters*.

But you say I am a thief, because I took the old mare along with me. . . . Is it a greater sin for me to steal his horse, than it was for him to rob my mother's cradle, and steal me? . . . Have you got to learn that human rights are mutual and reciprocal, and if you take my liberty and life, you forfeit your own liberty and life? Before God and high heaven, is there a law for one man which is not a law for every other man?

If you or any other speculator on my body and rights, wish to know how I regard my rights, they need but come here and lay their hands on me to enslave me. Did you think to terrify me by presenting the alternative to give my money to you, or give my body to slavery? Then let me say to you, that I meet the proposition with unutterable

Jermain W. Loguen, ca. 1850s–1860s

scorn and contempt. The proposition is an outrage and an insult. I will not budge one hair's breadth. I stand among a free people, who, I thank God, sympathize with my rights, and the rights of mankind; and if your emissaries and venders come her to re-enslave me, and escape the unshrinking vigor of my own right arm, I trust my strong and brave friends in this City and State, will be my rescuers and avengers.

Yours, &c.,

J.W. Loguen[80]

John Rapier, a financially successful, free black Alabama barber, knew all too well the hardships of having a fugitive family member living far from home. He writes to his brother, Henry Thomas, a fugitive slave in Buffalo. Thomas, also a barber, had married and, at that time, the couple had two children. Rapier keeps his brother abreast of family news about their mother, Sally Thomas, and his sons, Richard (or Dick), John Jr., Henry, and James. Rapier reports that their younger brother James Thomas was learning the barbering business from a free black barber in Nashville. John also informs Henry of financial troubles during Alabama's depression and complains about the extra state tax free blacks were forced to pay to make up state losses. Finally, Rapier reveals how he smuggled letters to the North. A trusted white man, Mr. Fox, carried Rapier's letter to Cincinnati and then apparently mailed it to Buffalo.[81]

Florence, Alabama February 28, 1843

Dear Brother, yours of the date of Febuary 6th [arrived]. I am in hopes you are in good health. The Boys and myself are in good health at the present, and Mother, James, and My two Sons that are with Mother are all well when I Last heard from them. I entend to go up to Nashville in the course of ten days to See them all. I have not been to Nashville Since last April. I want to See them all very much. John and James are well please with thir grand Mother and Don't want to come home, So James writes. I have not wrote to Mothr as you request me as yet, but I Shall See her in the corse of ten or Twelve days and then I [will] Show your letter to her. James [Thomas is] Still with frank parrish and has the character of a good barber, So a Gentleman toald me and is well thought of by the Gentlemens. James has manners to please almost any one who do not let thir perdudice go to fair on account of color.

We never had Suth times in this country Since I have been in Alabama as we have now: produce is worth nothing . . . cotton is the only article that is made in this country . . . and . . . Men [enslaved men] will not bring more then four Hundred and fifty dillars; women three . . . fifty, not halft what they [slave owners] have been in the habbet of Getting

for ther cotton and Servants. . . . All the banks in this State have close doors for the pirpose to Settle up thir business . . . The Banks will take in two Hundread and fifty Thousands dollars of thir Sirculation. This is an Extra Tax [that] has been laid on us this winter. We color men pay one dollar and the white man pay 25 cents. After that, I will Not Say any more on that Subject.

I can not Say at this time when I shall leave home, But I Think on bout the first of May. I am not Sirtan wether I will bring Booth of the Boys with me on tell I go to Nashville. . . . This letter will be made By Mr Fox [sent by Mr. Fox] who is going on to that place, I meane to Cincinnati. . . . When you get this you can write what you think best.

I am yours Truly,

John H. Rapier[82]

John Rapier's four older sons from his first wife kept in touch with one another as well. To continue his education, twenty-year-old James lived with his Uncle Henry Thomas and his family in the Elgin black settlement, often called Buxton, Canada West in Ontario. Henry, concerned that he was in danger of being returned to slavery after the passage of the Fugitive Slave Law, had moved his family to the safety of Canada and took up farming. James writes to twenty-two-year-old John Jr., who was living in Minnesota Territory, expressing nostalgia for their childhood in Alabama, perhaps revealing how their father had protected them in the slave state.[83] (The term "instant" or "inst" included at the beginning of some letters usually refers to a letter received within the month.)

Buxton C' West Jany 27, 1857

Dear Brother your welcome letter came to hand of the date both instant. . . . I am getting along at school very well but you will perceive this at once from my writing grammar & spelling John this is Sunday morning and every thing looks gloomy the ground is covered with 12 inches of snow the trees are covered with sleet and very smoky this

Buxton C West Jan 21 1855,

Dear Brother

Your welcome letter came to hand of
the date 4th instant with the cheque
of Fifty dollars drawn up in your favor
and transferred to me i have delay
no time in answering your letter for I
considered it quite essential for you to
know all about that piece of land be
longing to you i sold the cheque for forty
eight dollars and a half I then went to
the Rev om King and asked him
what was behind and he told me that
five installments were due yet you
know they are twelve dollars and half
each with interest the whole amount

due 81 dollars and 25 cents so i did not
pay him any of the draught but
I have it reserved for him if you say
pay it the papers you spoke of i una
stood you to mean the deed which he tell
me will probably be a year before you
could get it after the money was all paid
I knew Fifty dollars were of no avail
to wards getting the deed that was the reason
i did not pay him until I had farther
orders from you you can rest assured of
that fact the money is all safe enough
if you say pay him what you sent
i will do so or wait until you send the

morning [I'm] inclined to be a little sorry and being ensconced in a neat little cottage by a log fire and being all a lone i have a little chance to write the church bells sound echoes through the woods summoning the people to assemble together to hear the word of god proclaimed all of these combined is enough to turn my thoughts back to the home of our boy hood where all four of us boys were together where we all breathed as one but are we not scattered abroad on face of Earth do you expect-ever to see us all together again I do not just look where we are at you in the west and myself in the north Henry & Dick in California Father in Alabama did you ever think how small our Family is and Sarah the only female among them out of eleven I think you and me might drive down stakes together and keep them down what says you John I would write more but I have not room to express my feeling [it is] unusual for me to write so long a letter . . . they all send their respects to you . . . you fare well until we meet in April if both live . . . I remain your Brother

James T Rapier[84]

John Rapier Sr. remained in close touch with his older sons, constantly advising them to live rewarding and virtuous lives based on hard work and frugality. In his letter to John Jr. in December 1858, John Sr., who had amassed property holdings in Alabama and Canada, advises his son, *"Settle debts"* and *"Save money"* and *"Stay away from liquor"* and *"Stick the closer to work. . . ."*[85]

Letter from James
T. Rapier to John
Rapier Jr., January
27, 1857

Correspondence between another financially successful free Southern black man and his family members reveals both the routine life of a slaveholding planter, white or black, and of the mulatto elite, especially how they navigated the precarious life of quasi-freedom. Having learned to read, write, and do arithmetic as an apprentice to a cotton gin maker when he was a slave, William Ellison Sr. instructs his eldest son about collecting payments for his business—making and repairing gins—and depositing his funds and funds he had borrowed, and purchasing farm equipment. Apparently, Henry, who like his brothers shows evidence of having benefitted from some formal education, was visiting Charleston for social and business reasons.

Stateburg, March 26th, 1857

Dear Henry,

Your letter of 23rd instant was duly received and I perceived by it that you had not received mine of the 22nd. . . . As you did not get my letter in due time and for fear that you may not as yet received it, I will mention a few items of importance that I attended to. At once, if you have not done so, leave three hundred dollars in Messers Adams and Frost hands, subject to my order, and also the money that I have borrowed from William. Mr Benbow wrote to me and I sent you a copy in the letter that I wrote you. Mr. E Murray's accounts and order was presented to him last Friday and he was to send his noted when he sent to the post office, but he failed to do so.

I want you to get me a half doz. Weeding hoes, No. 2; get two hand saws from Mr Adger for the shop. I want you to get me 8 bags of guano. The above articles and instructions was stated in the other letter. I mention the same in case you should not have received my other letter. We are all well as usual. Give my respects to all my friends.

Your Father

William Ellison[86]

William Ellison Jr. also asks Henry (his eldest brother) to take care of purchases for him while in Charleston and attend to some of his business affairs. All three sons worked in the gin shop with their father and planted cotton on small plots on their father's estate. They, too, owned slaves and, like other slaveholders, singled out domestic slaves for minor indulgences. In his letter of March 26, 1857, William Jr. asks Henry to buy small items for three slaves and have the brother of his brother-in-law make linen pants for his nephew. The Johnson family was part of the Charleston free mulatto elite, as were the others to whom William Jr. sends his good wishes in the letter.

Stateburg, [South Carolina] March 26

Dear Henry,

As I have repeted the instruction in fathers letter of 22nd, it is nessessary that I [s]hould repeat the same in mine of 22nd. I wish you to draw the amount of three hundred dollars that you will see in W. J. Elison Saving Bank Book with all the dividends and surplus dividends that it have drawn since deposited. Place it with the money that I gave you and my cotton money in the hands of Messers Adams an Frost subject to Fathers order. Reserve enough to pay for whatever expences you incur for me. Get Charles to make a pair of drabatee pants for John Buckner and pay him out of my money. I believe he is about to be married soon and he ask me for a present. I don't wish the pant to exceed 5 or 6 dollars. Get a hankerchief for Charlotte, one dallars worth of starch, 4 lbs of bird shot about this size.

Gabriel request me to say to you that the guatters [garters] that he spoke to you for is for his wife. No 7's lether booties is what he want.

Our hands is imployed. Give my respect to Mrs. Bonneau, Mrs Weston, Mr J D & C J Johnson and families, James Lege & Sister, and all my inquiring Friends. No more at present, but remain you affectionate Brother.

William Ellison, Jr[87]

During the secession crisis in 1860, Charleston white workers were more successful in their determination to eliminate competition with blacks for skilled and unskilled jobs. Now that they made up the majority of the city's population, they could insist that city officials enforce the Badge Law, requiring that hired-out slaves wear badges and that free people of color (who dominated the skilled jobs) be further taxed. Since free blacks were not required to wear badges or have other evidence of their free status as in other Southern cities, white workers often mistook them for slaves. This situation was complicated by the fact that numerous African Americans who worked as carpenters, tailors, barbers, masons, and seamstresses, and in other skilled jobs, were freed illegally after the state's 1820 ban on manumission. Although these individuals were technically slaves and subject to the city's badge law, they could evade the law by producing official receipts showing they had paid the city's tax on all free persons. Intending to take jobs of slaves and free blacks, white workers routinely perpetrated violence against free blacks in the 1850s. Throughout the South, slaveholders and others considered legislation to enslave free blacks if they did not leave the state. In Charleston, blacks who had evidence of free status ("bona fide") for a generation, and those freed after the 1820 ban on manumission, were arrested on a regular basis, not only if they lacked the appropriate papers but also for such charges as "insolence." In the letter below to his brother-in-law Henry, James M. Johnson, a tailor, describes the crisis to his Stateburg family. He explains how free blacks, some of whom were part of the "several" mulatto slaveholding elite, were emigrating on steamers and railroads.

Charleston Aug 20th 1860

Dear Henry,

Since my absence the agitation has been so great to cause many to leave who were liable to the law of 1822 & the panic has reached those whom that law cannot affect. I was at Mr Jos Dereef last night & he seems to be more oppressed than any one I have spoken with. He cites the case of a Female whose Grandmother he knew to be Bona fide & knew her Mother also, when she had this child. She came to him to identify her, he being the only

person that knew her origin that she could refer to & he could not reliever her & there are numbers in the same dilemma. It is such cases that awaken sympathy. There are cases of persons who for 30 yrs have been paying capitation Tax & one of 35 yrs that have to go back to bondage & take out their Badges, & for the consolation of those who are exempt we are told this is the beginning. The next [legislative] session will wind up the affairs of every free cold. Man & they will be made to leave. Those who are now hunted down have divined what is to be done with them & before their destiny is sealed by an amendment are wisely leaving by every Steamer & Railroad too. The Keystone State takes out several to day. Their [white] friends & counsellors tell them to leave. The time is at hand when none may remain but them & their slaves. . . .

A Cold. Lady now North left a servt at Home to take care of her place. Her friend a lawyer is applied to. He says the Servt must have a Badge & the Lady who he will do any thing for, must make up her mind to stay, as no mortal man will be allowed to return. The Dereefs have had to pay some $80 fines, for Servts without Badges. I saw Mr. Jon Lee going down to Stmr to get off Demar's wife & *Matthews children.* He says it is plain now all must go & his Brother is of the same opinion. *Great change.*

The higher class [elite slaveholding whites whom free blacks considered supporters and patrons] is quite incensed but it is too late. The power is into other hands. . . . I heard in the [railway] cars that Petitions are drawn & handed around for signature by Country Members to sell those [free blacks without papers] . . . who are considered worthless, prior to passing a Law for the removal of the Body. . . .

Mr Veree has made up his mind to leave. Do acquaint your Father of the state of feeling. It is a State law, & to use the expression of those who have the matter in hands "What is to come will be worse." When that comes every property holder will be glad to take what he can get (irrespective of value) for his property. . . . Give my Love to All at Wisdom Hall & accept for yourself the same. Yrs truly

J M Johnson[88]

Within three years, matters in South Carolina had changed so dramatically that William Ellison Jr. decided to remove his children from the South to protect them from draconian legislation that would severely limit or threaten the freedom of all free blacks. In his letter to his elder brother Henry, William Jr. describes his ordeal in trying to get his children, a boy fourteen years old, and two daughters, twelve and ten, to safety in the North via boat. William's letter shows that in late 1860, his identity as a member of the mulatto elite mattered little, even with the support of prominent white cotton agents, Adams and Frost, who tried to vouch for him and his children.[89]

Charleston So Ca Oct 31st

Dear Henry

This will inform you that I got my children off this morning by the Marrion. They left this morning at 7 o'clock. They are comfortable provide for, having a state room and I believe a kind apt which have promise to put them aboard of the cars for Philadelphia under the care of the conductor. The stewardess has promise to take good care of them. I gave her a trifle so as to incourage her. I hope God will be with them and protect them. I am quite worried down.

I tried every plan and made every effort to get them off on board of the Keystone State but the agents took a stand and would not deviate although Messrs Adams & Frost interested themselves much to effect a passage. They positively wont take any free colored person unless there are cleared out of the custom house by some white person as there slaves. Then of course they cannot get a state room. The captain of the Key Stone State very kindly offered to take care of them if I should send them as above but I would not agree to send them as slaves when they are not and besides they might not be taken care of.

I wrote Monday's night mail to Miss Forten and to Monsier Barguet in New York informing them that I would send them by the Marrion. If they get the letter they will be on the look out for them. Inform Father and Sister that they are gone....

I hope you and all are well. I expect to leave Saturday. You will send for me that day. Your affectionate brother

Wm Ellison Jr[90]

Had Charleston officials known that William was sending his children to black abolitionist Margaretta Forten's school in Philadelphia, he and his family might have been arrested and jailed. Fortunately, he sent the children before the start of the war. On April 12, 1861, Confederate troops fired on Union soldiers at the United States federal arsenal at Fort Sumter. Following that attack, it became nearly impossible for any person of color to leave Charleston. The school, which accepted boarders, was a safe place for William's young children. In South Carolina, the Ellisons and all other free blacks were in jeopardy of being enslaved. John Brown's failed attempt to incite a slave insurrection only quickened the pace of Southern state legislation to enslave all free blacks. White Southerners were particularly incensed that Brown was made a hero in much of the North.[91] In her letter below to her father, twenty-year-old Rosetta Douglass exemplifies Northern admiration of Brown. With the Virginia governor demanding the arrest of those he believed to be Brown's Northern allies, Frederick Douglass fled to England, and his friend Gerrit-Smith entered an asylum because of a mental breakdown. Rosetta's reference to attending a lecture on "Physical Culture" reflects the health-reform movement that advocated physical activity and a healthy diet.

Rochester December, 6th, 1859

My Dear Father

Nearly two weeks have past since I wrote you last. I think my letter will have reached you in a week from this date. . . .

The Virginia hyenas have murdered our Hero he met his fate like a brave and good man as he was. If anyone even doubted Capt. Brown's bravery they cannot help now in feeling assured that they were mistaken in their doubts. His last letter to his wife and family is touching and cannot fail to draw tears from the eyes of the reader. The letter is full of a Christians hope and wishes.

Corinthian Hall was draped in mourning last friday evening and a meeting in sympathy with Capt. Brown was held between two and three hundred assembled. . . .The flag, which was also draped in

mourning hung all day floating in the breeze and attracting the attention of the passers by. I felt certain that a full house would be the result. Mr Payne spoke ably . . . he thunders away quite loud and suddenly his voice lowers to an ordinary pitch. Parker Pillsbury spoke after Mr. Payne he was very sarcastic in his remarks and several left the hall, he thinks Brown a greater man than Washington, that idea did not please the reporters at all and the next day the city papers criticizes his speech severely. . . .

Lewis and I heard Dr. George B. Windship on "Physical Culture" last thursday evening, he performed the wonderful feat of lifting with his hands 954 pounds of nails in kegs, besides putting a barrel of 214 pounds on his shoulder, he is a strong man certainly very young and weighing himself 148 lbs. His lecture was not much.

Annie attends school regularly. She is the favorite of her German teacher he says she is the best student he has. . . . Annie will fill a part of the remaining page she writes daily in her English writing book and intends to astonish you with her advance in penmanship. The ground is white with snow around us and winter has come in grand earnest. Gerrit-Smith is improving fast and will soon be able to go to his family, if he has not already gone.

Very Affectionately Yours
Rosetta Douglass[92]

Frederick Douglass, ca. 1850s

Rosetta includes ten-year-old Annie's letter to her father. Within three months, Annie would die of an extended illness that "baffled" doctors."[93] Her heartbroken father was still out of the country as mother Anna and the rest of the family grieved their loss in Rochester.[94]

Rochester Dec 7th 1859

My Dear Father

I am proceeding in my German very well for my teacher says so. I am in the first reader and I can read. I expect that you will have a German letter from me in a very short time. I have learned another piece and it is about slavery. I am going to speak it in school. My piece is this.

> This is not the man for me
>
> Who buys or sells a slave
>
> For he who will not set him free
>
> But send him to his grave
>
> But he whose noble heart beats warm
>
> For all men's life and liberty
>
> Who loves alike each human form
>
> That's the man for me

It is in the Garland of Freedom and four verses of it. My letter will not be very long. Poor Mr. Brown is dead. That hard hearted man said he must die and they took him in an open field and about a half mile from the jail and hung him. The German children like me very much but I have gone a head of them and they have been there longer than me too.

They all send their love.

From your affectionate Daughter
Annie Douglass[95]

Frederick Douglass with
daughter Annie Douglass, c. 1854.
Daguerreotype

Anna Murray Douglass, ca. 1850s

Rosetta Douglass, undated

Lewis H. Douglass, undated

Charles R. Douglass, undated

Frederick Douglass Jr., undated

Like the Douglass family, Northern black women, men, and children continued to make decisions they hoped would improve their circumstances. While their immediate family remained central, some African Americans developed a kind of extended family with white friends. Sixteen-year-old Washingtonian Emma Brown shows the dedication many African Americans had for obtaining a higher education. Arriving at Oberlin College in February 1860 to begin the spring term, Emma began experiencing blinding headaches. She wrote to her abolitionist Quaker friend Emily Howland, a white teacher whom she had assisted at a school for free black girls in Washington, D.C. Brown describes a day at college and her commitment to learning, and refers to the Republican Party's presidential and vice-presidential candidates: Abraham Lincoln and Hannibal Hamlin.

Oberlin, [Ohio,] May 22, 1860

My dear friend,

I went to my Algebra recitation this morning. This term closes tomorrow. This week nearly all the classes are examined and each student is marked. Without feeling much elated (it is impossible for me not to feel a little pleased) I inform you that I received six marks. This is the very highest number. Philosophy & Elocution examinations will take place this afternoon & tomorrow morning. The directress advised me not to attend but rest until the beginning of the next term but I think I must go. While I am in the class my head does not ache but as soon as the excitement is over it throbs terribly. I am not at all alarmed—it is only the natural result of change of climate.

Yesterday we had Monthly Rhetoricals—they were very interesting. One mean young man who is I must confess a brilliant orator under took to define the position of the colored people in America. He advocated Colonization doctrine warmly. He was frequently applauded—a number of colored persons hissed—I felt ready to cry Shame! Shame! A colored young man spoke [against colonization] as well as any other—much better than many. I felt proud that he did so nobly. . . . His voice is clear and powerful.

There was a grand torchlight procession here last Saturday night. The names of Lincoln and Hamlin were heard all over the village. There were bonfires, music and much cheering.

Ever yours,
Emma[96]

In the 1850s, Reverend William Douglass, rector of the first African American Episcopal church, St. Thomas Episcopal in Philadelphia, began courting African American teacher and abolitionist Sarah Mapps Douglass. Douglass was in her fifties and unsure if she wanted to be married to a widower with nine children. She shared some of Douglass's letters with her white abolitionist, feminist friend Sarah Grimke, fourteen years her senior. Grimke, who never married, encourages Mapps to consider Douglass an acceptable suitor and ignore his foibles.

[1854-55]

Dearest Sarah—

So far as I can judge from the letters I think Mr. D must be a good man, a pleasant companion, an affectionate friend. I greatly admire too the sprightly mirthful tone of some of his letters, such as that about your age, and sadly was I surprised to find that you were displeased at the innocent raillery. Dear you need a guard here, you have lived so long without the animating influences of cheerful companionship, that you are morbidly sensitive to an innocent & right degree of sportiveness, it seems to you unbecoming; but try to overcome this prejudice, wear yourself the bridal robes of cheerfulness, yea of pleasant mirthfulness, & you will find it diffuses a charm over your own life & over all around you. Can you bring me acquainted with Mr. Douglass, I should greatly love to see him & with your permission to converse with him relative to your union.

Yours most affy S. M. G.[97]

Apparently, Douglass's sense of humor was not Mapps Douglass's only concern. In a later letter, she reveals her anxiety about physical intimacy in marriage. Grimke continues to encourage Mapps to consider marriage.

Newark, [New Jersey,] June 19 [1855]

Dear Sarah:

I am glad you can reciprocate Mr. Ds affection, and that you have told him so. Oh Sarah how earnestly I hope you may find in him a husband in spirit & in truth. I do not wonder you shrink from sexual intercourse, yet, I suppose in married life, it is as much the natural expression of affection as the warm embrace & ardent kiss. Time will familiarize you with the idea, and the more intimate your union with Mr. D the less you will turn from it. I am sorry you feel as if you could not marry until a certain time has elapsed, there is a right time to do right things, seek for that dear Sarah, be governed by the still small voice within.

Yours in haste affy S.M.G. [98]

Sarah Mapps Douglass's floral illustrations appeared in newspapers and books; here she illustrated a poem titled "I Love a Flower," ca. 1833.

Encouraged by her friend, Mapps Douglass married William Douglass a month later. Both friendships, that between Emma Brown and Emily Howland and between Sarah Mapps Douglass and Sarah Grimke, lasted for over forty years. As the letters above show, some abolitionists developed true friendships across the color line.

Whether exchanged between friends, family, or, as we see in the next correspondence, a couple involved in a budding romance, letters on the eve of the Civil War tell us much about the distinct, diverse, and complex experiences of African Americans. They reveal the universal human need for maintaining connections, perhaps even more so during the tumultuous time of war. Henry Lewis Douglass and Helen Amelia Loguen were children of two of the most prominent abolitionists in antebellum America: Frederick Douglass and Reverend Jermain Loguen, respectively.[99] Lewis and Amelia met before the war and benefitted not only from a significant formal education but also, as children of famous abolitionist fathers and members of the Northern black middle class, from a vibrant black abolitionist social network. Lewis, a resident of Rochester, and Amelia, who lived in Syracuse, began exchanging letters soon after they met in 1858. In an early letter, Lewis chastises Amelia for wearing what he called the "near approach to masculine unmentionable bloomers." In his letter below, Lewis, now twenty years old, indicates that the relationship has moved beyond friendship.

Rochester, Dec. 22 1860

Dear Amelia:

I wish merely to wish you a merry Christmas and a Happy New Year. I hope this may find you well. I am feeling extremely well. I do not know when I have enjoyed a winter so well as this. I am looking with great pleasure to bonnie May for the renewal of our, (to me) most happy correspondence, until then I enjoy myself in seeking what pleasure may be found in re-perusing your letters to me, especially the last one.

"Ever of thee I'm secretly dreaming."

Yours Lovingly
Lewis[100]

When first the rebel cannon shattered the walls of Sumter . . . I predicted that the war, then and there inaugurated would not be fought but entirely by white men. . . . Only a moderate share of sagacity was needed to see that the arm of the slave was the best defence against the arm of the slaveholder.

FREDERICK DOUGLASS, 1863[101]

PART TWO

Civil War

WHEN THE WAR CAME, MOST AFRICAN AMERICANS BELIEVED IT WOULD END SLAVERY. Whether in the North, South, or West, enslaved or free, African Americans were certain that the Civil War would spell doom for the hideous labor system. Some believed that the only way to root out the evil of slavery was with violence. In his editorial of April 13, 1861, George Lawrence, the temporary editor of the *Weekly Anglo-African*, joined the chorus of Northern men and women who argued that using violent means was the only solution. "Only through the Red Sea of civil war and insurrection can the sins of this demonized people be washed away." Two weeks later, Lawrence invoked the 1831 slave insurrection led by Nat Turner, "We Want Nat Turner not speeches. . . ."[102] Sectional conflict was about slavery, and a Union victory would end it, settling the issue once and for all.

Contrary to African Americans' straightforward interpretation of the conflict, President Lincoln's response was more politically nuanced. In 1860, facing a nation divided as never before, Lincoln and his Republican Party had expressed strong opposition to the expansion of slavery but supported Southern states' right to maintain the institution of slavery where it already existed. Seven Southern states ignored or disbelieved Lincoln and the party's assurances that the administration would not touch slavery and seceded from the Union by February 1, 1861. At that time, the lower South states—South Carolina, Georgia, Florida, Mississippi, Alabama, Louisiana, Texas—created their own government. Alexander H. Stephens, the vice president of the Confederate States of America, summed up the Southern states' reason for secession when he stated that the protection of slavery "was the immediate cause," and the new government was founded upon "the great truth that the negro is not equal to the white man; that slavery subordination to the superior race is his natural and normal condition."[103] Lincoln, in his March 1861 inaugural address, reconfirmed his commitment not to interfere with slavery where it was already established. He had no lawful right "to do so" nor was he inclined "to do so." In the same address, though, Lincoln warned that "fugitive slaves, now only partially surrendered would not be surrendered at all." He assured the nation

that his responsibility as president was the preservation of the Union. No state could "lawfully get out of the Union," he made clear. The seceded states were engaging in insurrection against the authority of the United States. When, in April, a Confederate artillery fired on Fort Sumter (the federal fort located in the Charleston, South Carolina, harbor), Lincoln called for a 75,000-strong militia to put down the insurrection. Union officials planned to repossess all federal property, including arsenals, forts, and post offices, that the newly established Confederate army and navy had seized. Whether Democrat or Republican, most white Northerners insisted, like the president did, that the war was to preserve the Union, not to end slavery. According to historian James Oakes, Lincoln and many other Republicans recognized that slavery was the cause of the war but they insisted that abolition could not be the purpose of the war. It was unconstitutional to wage a war purely to abolish slavery.[104]

Wishing to express their patriotism, some Northern black men joined white men in rushing to fight for the Union cause. Young men in Pittsburgh formed a local militia, the Hannibal Guards, even though they were "deprived of all our political rights, we yet wish the government of the United States to be sustained against the tyranny of slavery...."[105] Men in other Northern cities formed similar militias. Black women supported the volunteers. In Albany, women gave a black volunteer company a homemade flag. Boston's Twelfth Baptist Church resolved to defend the Union and send "colored women" as "nurses, seamstresses, and warriors if need be." But federal and state governments dismissed all black people's attempts to join in the Union effort. Black men were prevented from signing up and told plainly that this was a "white man's war."[106]

Unable to fight, Northern black activists and other abolitionists strategically and consistently challenged the pervasive notion that the war was only about restoring the Union. Fundamentally, slavery was the cause of the war and everybody knew it. Fugitive slave and Presbyterian clergyman James W. C. Pennington told a Canadian congregation that politicians who said slavery had nothing to do with the war need only look at president of the Confederacy Jefferson Davis's own words. Davis had asserted "frankly and boldly" that slavery was "the corner stone of the Confederacy."[107] Editor Lawrence of the *Weekly Anglo-African* argued that the two factions might claim "that it is this or that which lies at the basis of the difficulty; but *we know*, these liars and drivellers know—and history will indelibly prove, that it is slavery alone which has cast a thunder cloud of civil war over the land.... Out of this strife will come freedom, though the methods are not yet clearly apparent." Lawrence added that because the war was caused by "arrogance and treason of the slave power," African Americans in the North needed to focus on how they could "best aid the slave." He thought black volunteer companies were wasting energy in their efforts to join the Union army. They should instead

prepare to strike if the Union compromised on slavery. Black men must consider themselves "Minute Men"—organizing, drilling, and procuring arms *when the slave calls.* Those who "feel the desire to aid the bond, must strike such a blow as will render peace impossible until justice is done."[108]

President Lincoln seemed to ignore abolitionists' attempts to make the war about emancipation, and he angered them even more when he supported colonization, a program developed in the early nineteenth century by philanthropists, slaveholders, and clergymen to encourage free blacks and recently freed slaves to leave the United States and settle in West Africa, where colonizationists had established a colony in the 1820s. Believing that African Americans could never become part of American society and that the growing free black population threatened slavery, colonizationists sought their removal. Lincoln's interests were more militarily strategic. Concerned about keeping Maryland, Delaware, Kentucky, and Missouri—slave states that did not secede from the Union, known as "border states"—from joining the Confederacy, he proceeded cautiously. First, he began drafting abolition statutes for Delaware, expecting that it would be a model of emancipation for the other border states. Within a year of war breaking out, and with Lincoln's support, Congress ended slavery in the District of Columbia, offering an average of three hundred dollars each to loyal slave owners if they freed their slaves, and setting aside one hundred thousand dollars for distribution among "free persons of African Descent . . . as may desire to emigrate." Congress and the Lincoln administration also ended slavery in the U.S. territories two months later.[109] In the spring and summer of 1862, Lincoln urged Congress to pledge financial aid to any state that undertook the gradual abolition of slavery, with compensation promised to slave owners. He appealed to border state congressmen to support compensated gradual abolition and the colonization of freedpeople. If they didn't, Lincoln warned border state slaveholders, slavery would be "extinguished by mere incidents of the war."[110]

If abolitionists were furious about Lincoln's unwillingness to make slavery a war aim, they were elated about the abolition of slavery in the nation's capital. "I trust I am not dreaming," Frederick Douglass wrote to Massachusetts Republican senator Charles Sumner. The *Weekly Anglo-African* declared, "It was a fitting celebration of the anniversary of Fort Sumter, that Congress should pass a bill to emancipate the Capital from the thrall of slavery forever."[111] At the same time, black abolitionists were dismayed that Lincoln and Congress continued to support the colonization of African Americans outside the United States.

Meanwhile, enslaved people living near Union battle lines made sure that the war would mean emancipation. By escaping whenever the army was nearby,

Fugitive slaves fleeing to Union lines in 1863

Refugees at Harpers Ferry, 1862

they rendered "untenable every policy short of universal emancipation."[112] The few fugitives who fled slavery in May 1861 turned into thousands by 1865, countering yet again the blatantly false pro-slavery charge that enslaved people were content. The government had not provided Union generals in the field with a policy for handling refugees, so the generals made their own decisions. Some allowed slave owners to claim their human property, while others came to other decisions. General Benjamin F. Butler, for example, declared fugitives "contraband of war" and put them to work. The status of refugees was complicated by the Union policy of protecting slavery in the loyal border states. But enslaved people fled whenever the chance arose. George E. Stephens, personal servant and cook for a Union officer in the Army of the Potomac's 26th Pennsylvania Regiment, gleefully ended his November 1861 report to the *Weekly Anglo-African*, "It gives me great pleasure to announce that the tide of emigration Northward continues to flow, all barriers to the contrary notwithstanding."[113]

Determined not to acquiesce to rebel slaveholders and states, Congress officially addressed the status of slaves in Union controlled areas in early August 1861 with the First Confiscation Act, which authorized the seizure of rebel property and "any person claimed to be held to labor or service" used in the aid of the rebellion. The bill, declaring that rebel slaveowners forfeited their claim to slave labor, applied only to enslaved people who worked on any Confederate "fort, navy yard, dock, armory, ship, entrenchment, or in any military or naval service whatsoever...." A year later, Congress passed the Second Confiscation Act declaring "forever free" all slaves of rebels, including those who came into Union lines or were captured from or deserted by rebels. This act also gave the federal government the power to seize and sell all rebel property and authorized the president to use persons of African descent in any way necessary to put down the rebellion.[114] In South Carolina's Sea Islands, Union generals put newly freed adults to work on the plantations abandoned by their slave owners. Approximately 10,000 former slaves lived on small plots of land, growing their own food and working for the federal government. Eventually, freedpeople in various refugee camps or within the Union army lines were put to work as cooks, servants, laundresses, diggers, and dockworkers and given army rations or wages. Their children often attended the schools taught by black teachers already living in the area and the many northern teachers who traveled South to aid former slaves in their quest for literacy. In Washington, D.C., some refugees who were ill, displaced, or unable to work were placed in Camp Barker in 1862. From this small beginning, a medical facility, Freedmen's Hospital, was established in 1863.[115]

The Second Confiscation Act, passed in July 1862, also provided for $500,000 in funds, in addition to the $100,000 provided three months

earlier, to pay the cost of blacks "willing to emigrate." This infuriated black abolitionists. Rather than leading the country toward freedom and equality for all people, they believed Lincoln was pandering to racists. In April 1862, some Congressmen had debated the forced removal from the United States of slaves seeking refuge behind Union lines, while other Congressmen stressed voluntary emigration. After the passage of the Second Confiscation Act, Lincoln met with a few Washington, D.C., black leaders, urging them to support his colonization plan, which involved settling freed slaves and free blacks in a region in Central America near present-day Panama. During an anti-colonization rally in New York City, the Reverend William T. Catto, an African American clergyman, called the president "a genuine representative of American prejudice and Negro hatred."[116]

The summer of 1862 proved crucial as the Union moved toward full emancipation. In July, Lincoln told his cabinet that he intended to free all slaves under the control of rebels as a military strategy. Encouraging slaves to flee would significantly undermine the Confederacy's dependence on slave labor for building trenches and fortifications and for feeding the army. Additionally, Lincoln hoped emancipation would reinvigorate Northern support for the war, garner international humanitarian support, and prevent European countries from formally recognizing the Confederacy as legitimate. A cabinet member urged Lincoln to wait for a Union victory.[117] In late September, after the successful Union battle along the Antietam Creek in Sharpsburg, Maryland, the president signed the Preliminary Emancipation Proclamation, giving the Confederacy one hundred days to cease its rebellion. If the rebels did not return to the Union, all slaves in Confederate states and regions of states not under Union control would be free as of January 1, 1863. The late-December final draft of the Proclamation included a provision for accepting black men into the Union army and navy.

When it became effective on January 1, 1863, the Emancipation Proclamation transformed black abolitionists into strong supporters of the war. Now, slavery had to be destroyed in order to restore the Union. Abolitionists celebrated with parades, speeches, and prayers throughout the North and in Washington, D.C. While some complained that the Proclamation applied only to slaves in Confederate states, where the Union army had no control, and not to the border states that remained in the Union, most viewed it as the beginning of the end of slavery. An African Methodist Episcopal clergyman, the Reverend Henry McNeal Turner, captured the mood of many African Americans in his letter to his denomination's newspaper, *The Christian Recorder*: "The first day of January, 1863, is destined to form one of the most memorable epochs in the history of the world. . . . The seeds of

freedom . . . have now been scattered where despotism and tyranny ranked and ruled."[118] Maryland fugitive and Presbyterian minister James W. C. Pennington explained that God was guiding the direction of the war in spite of national leadership. African Americans should recognize that the "proclamation was purely a military necessity imposed upon this government by an all-wise God."[119] In late December, Frederick Douglass described January 1, 1863, as "a day for poetry and song, a new song." The "causes of human freedom and the cause of our common country . . . are now one and inseparable."[120] Southern blacks in Union-controlled areas also celebrated the government's emancipation policy.

The Proclamation meant that African American men could directly participate in bringing an end to slavery. When Massachusetts Governor John Andrew received permission to raise a regiment of African American soldiers in January 1863, the 54th Massachusetts Volunteer Infantry became the first black regiment organized in the North. Activists, including Frederick Douglass, Martin Delany, and Mary Ann Shadd, immediately began recruiting for the federal government. But the process was slow at first. Before they placed their lives on the line, Northern black men wanted the full rights of citizenship. Black leaders advised them that if they demonstrated loyalty to the government as soldiers, rights of citizenship would follow.[121] In a July speech, Douglass explained that when "the black man gets upon his person the brass letters U.S. . . . an eagle on his button, and a musket on his shoulder, and bullets in his pocket, there is no power on earth or under the earth which can deny that he has earned the right of citizenship in the United States."[122] The government's promise of equal pay and treatment supported Douglass's and other black abolitionists' hope that the war would transform the nation. Governor Andrew personally assured black leaders that "the position of colored men who may be enlisted and mustered into the volunteer service of the United States . . . will be precisely the same, in every particular, as that of any and all other volunteers."[123]

In the South, there were already black men serving in the Union army. General Benjamin F. Butler incorporated the Louisiana Native Guard into a Union Army regiment when the federal government gained control of New Orleans and nearby areas. The Native Guard had consisted of units of free black soldiers with their own officers, a few of whom had volunteered to serve the Confederacy but swore allegiance to the Union in the late summer of 1862. General Butler added more free blacks and ex-slaves for a full regiment. In South Carolina's Sea Islands, where the Union had gained control early on, black men served in the First South Carolina Infantry and participated in action along the coast in November 1862. Similarly, the First Kansas Colored

Infantry had seen action at Island Mound, Missouri, in October 1862. In May 1863, the federal government established the Bureau of Colored Troops to coordinate and organize black regiments from all parts of the country into the United States Colored Troops (USCT).

Black soldiers fought heroically in several battles in mid-1863, including the assault on Port Hudson, Louisiana, and the battle at Milliken's Bend, Louisiana. Most notably, in the battle at Fort Wagner, in South Carolina, in spite of heavy Union losses the 54th Massachusetts Volunteer Infantry showed incredible bravery, proving to Union officials and the white public in general that African American men would fight courageously.[124] For African Americans, the question was not whether they would fight—this had been proven in other wars and in slave insurrections—but whether the outcome of their sacrifices would be rewarded. Reports from generals in the field on the bravery of black troops contributed to the Union's commitment to enlist more black men into the army. The black press, specifically the Philadelphia-based African Methodist Episcopal *Christian Recorder* and the New York City *Weekly Anglo-African*, encouraged black men to join up. These papers also kept their readership informed of individual battles through firsthand reports from soldier correspondents. George E. Stephens, a Philadelphia artisan, mariner, activist, and correspondent for the *Weekly Anglo-African,* joined the 54th Massachusetts Volunteer Infantry Regiment in April 1863 and continued as a *Weekly Anglo-African* correspondent during his time in the war. At least one white Northern press published a 54th corporal's letters from the front lines. The New Bedford, Massachusetts, *Mercury* regularly published Corporal James Henry Gooding's letters on the 54th regiment's activities. Black soldier correspondents consistently reported on the bravery of the "colored troops."[125]

Yet though black soldiers exhibited not only a strong desire to fight but also the ability to defeat Confederate attacks, racial prejudice prevailed in Union camps and official Union policy. First, the government insisted that black soldiers have white officers, even though not all officers had military training and often reflected the racism of their society. Off-duty black soldiers were subjected to assaults by individuals and mobs in Ohio, Indiana, and elsewhere.[126] And though abolitionist officers and a few others allowed black soldiers in their regiment to be taught rudimentary reading and writing skills during their spare time in camps, black soldiers were disproportionately assigned fatigue duty, issued inferior equipment, or issued no equipment at all. Most egregious of all was that they did not receive the same pay as white soldiers of the same rank. Until June 15, 1864, the army paid white privates $13.00 per month, plus a clothing allowance of $3.50, and black soldiers $10.00

per month, $3.00 of which would be deducted for clothing. Being assigned to menial duty and being paid less than white soldiers undermined African American soldiers' belief that the war would be a turning point, that it would not only end slavery but also moderate racial discrimination. Black newspapers and leaders joined soldiers and their families in protesting against the blatantly racist pay policy. The 54th and 55th Massachusetts Volunteer Infantry Regiments famously refused their pay until Congress changed the law.

The law that passed in June 1864 called for equal pay for black soldiers and was made retroactive to January 1, 1864. Congress distinguished between enlistees who had been free on April 19, 1861 and fugitive slaves who had escaped slavery after that date, making the formers' pay retroactive to the time of their enlistment. In order to avoid any potential conflict, and boost morale, Colonel E. N. Hallowell of the 54th solved the problem with an oath in which the men "solemnly" swore that they "owed no man unrequited labor on or before the 19th of April, 1861. So help you God." Other officers followed Hallowell's example. Believing slavery was anathema to God's law, soldiers who had been slaves could take the oath in good conscience.

The unequal-pay policy created such resentment that mutiny became a problem for officers in black military camps.[127] Sergeant William Walker of the Third South Carolina Volunteers was court-martialed and executed for mutiny. The court found that he had marched his company to his captain's tent and ordered them to stack their arms and resign from an army that broke its contract. More than twenty soldiers of the Fourteenth Rhode Island Heavy Artillery were jailed for their protest against unequal pay, and officers of the 54th shot and wounded two soldiers who refused to obey orders. Equal pay was as much an issue of principle as necessity. Freedom without equality was a precarious and limited freedom.[128]

The government's refusal to commission African American officers was also a matter of principle. Initially, Secretary of War Edwin M. Stanton refused to entertain the idea of African American officers leading black troops—all regiments were to be commanded by white officers who reported directly to the Adjutant General's Office. This issue was exacerbated by practices of blatant racism among many officers. While a few officers were committed abolitionists, or began supporting the abolition cause as commanders of black troops, other officers viewed black soldiers under their command with contempt. This latter group accepted their positions as a means to a quick promotion, higher pay, and a higher rank. They resented commanding black troops and expressed their racism openly. These officers, a few of whom were former slaveholders, abused their authority particularly in matters of discipline.[129] Army regulations required absolute obedience

District of Columbia. Company E, 4th U.S. Colored
Infantry at Fort Lincoln, Washington, D.C.

to superior officers, meaning that all black men, including corporals and sergeants, were required to obey and defer to all white superiors whatever the orders. Military regulations provided that force, or the threat of force, under-gird soldiers' obligations to obey orders. Actions that challenged military authority included refusing to obey orders, desertion, using violence against a superior officer, and mutiny. The penalty for any of these actions could be imprisonment or death.

The army's procedures and etiquette reinforced officers' authority in numerous rituals of deference, including symbols of rank, modes of address, and forms of punishment to distinguish between superiors and inferiors. To the former slaves in the USCT, who made up the majority of the USCT regiments, service in the military felt much too close to slavery. And yet, not quite. The difference concerned a soldier's right to defend himself in court-martial cases and to invoke the regulation requiring obedience only to "lawful orders" of a superior. Officers were to exercise their military command with "kindness and justice to inferiors," and punishments were to be "strictly conformable to military law." The army forbade superiors "to injure those under them by tyrannical or capricious conduct, or by abusive language."[130] These clauses placed officers and soldiers alike under military law, giving all soldiers the right to appeal. Black soldiers found that the military accorded procedural rights, such as testifying against a white person, that were not available in civilian life. Whether they were former slaves or free men before the war, in the military black soldiers had rights that were nonexistent to them outside the military in most states. Consequently, literate black soldiers, trying to lessen military sentences of fellow soldiers, sent numerous petitions and letters to higher authorities, including the president of the United States.

Yet a soldier's ability to hold his military superiors accountable was more theoretical than practical. Military protections favored officers over soldiers. A private's complaint against a lieutenant in his regiment, for example, was adjudicated by other officers in the same regiment, making it unlikely that the lieutenant's fellow officers would find him guilty. The same was true for complaints against the regimental commander. According to historian Ira Berlin, the grievance procedure lacked the safeguards soldiers needed in cases that seemed particularly tinged with racism. These cases generally involved petty offenses in which "company officers enjoyed great latitude in dealing with violators of the rules."[131]

The range of punishments for all soldiers included, as Berlin explains, "ritualized exaggerations of a soldier's duties, such as walking a beat shoul-dering a log instead of a musket, standing at attention for hours on a barrel

head, wearing a sign describing the offense while being drummed out of camp, and riding a wooden horse (a rail perched several feet above ground)." More sadistic punishments included "kicking, cuffing, striking with swords, whipping, tying up by the thumbs, and bucking and gagging." Black soldiers viewed certain military punishments with particular disdain, likening them to the same means used to control slaves. While they were willing to accept other forms of punishment, they consistently challenged any punishments that resembled those used to discipline slaves. This led to some commanders instituting a ban on the more sadistic punishments. Congress had already prohibited whipping as a military punishment. The broad discretion officers had meant that violations of the bans continued, leading to soldiers' violations of orders, assaults on officers, and, at times, mutiny.[132]

Discipline and punishment were at the top of black soldiers' complaints against many white officers. Soldiers also resented officers treating them as servants, ridiculing them for their ignorance of military ways, and treating their wives as prostitutes. Too often, white officers were more sympathetic to former slave owners than to the formerly enslaved men in their charge. These officers undercut black soldiers' particular pride in liberating enslaved people after successful battles against the rebels.[133]

In response to these conditions and inspired by the principle of equality, black soldiers and civilians constantly demanded that black officers command black troops. After multiple requests and petitions, the government slightly eased its policy by accepting black officers as chaplains and surgeons. By the end of the war, there were about one hundred (excluding chaplains) African American officers in the Union army, including surgeon John H. Rapier Jr., formerly of Alabama, whose letter to his Uncle James follows. We learned in Chapter One that John Rapier got an early education in Nashville while living with his grandmother Sally Thomas.[134]

Black soldiers not only faced racism in and out of the army, but they also faced greater jeopardy on the battlefield than their white counterparts. Confederate president Jefferson Davis ordered that all black soldiers and their officers be treated according to state laws, meaning that the soldiers could be enslaved or executed as insurrectionists and their officers imprisoned or executed. Confederate commanders in the field were already determining the fate of captured black men by executing them on the spot.[135] A Confederate colonel indicated his attitude in a report to his superiors about capturing black soldiers from Louisiana. Using the well-worn excuse of "while attempting to escape," he wrote: "I then ordered every one shot, and with my Six Shooter I assisted in the execution of the order." With approval from their authorities, Confederate soldiers followed suit. Referring to a skirmish with a black

regiment, a North Carolina soldier wrote his mother that "several [were] taken prisoner & afterwards either bayoneted or burnt. The men . . . rushed at them like so many devils."[136]

Some Union generals retaliated swiftly to the slaughter of black troops by Confederates. General David Hunter, who had created one of the first unofficial black regiments in 1862 and had become famous for emancipating slaves, without Lincoln's approval, in Florida, Georgia, and South Carolina that same year, wrote to Jefferson Davis warning of Union retaliation in April 1863. "Every outrage of this kind against the laws of war and humanity . . . shall be followed by the immediate execution of the Rebel of highest rank in my possession; man for man, these executions will certainly take place, for everyone murdered, or sold into a slavery worse than death."[137] Frederick Douglass met with the president, urging him to send a strong response. Lincoln did so on July 30, 1863, promising retaliation if captured black soldiers were not taken as prisoners of war.

Despite Lincoln's and Congress's promises, the order was generally not enforced. However, after the official Union response, many captured black soldiers (former slaves and others) *were* taken as prisoners of war. But throughout the entire Civil War, Confederates murdered, beat, and enslaved many black soldiers, generally with impunity. The Union outpost at Fort Pillow, in Tennessee near the Mississippi River, is just one of many glaring examples of Confederate perniciousness. In the spring of 1864, the fort was manned by nearly equal numbers of black and white troops in separate regiments. In what is called the Fort Pillow Massacre, Confederate soldiers, led by General Nathan Bedford Forrest, captured the fort and murdered black soldiers after they surrendered. The *Christian Recorder* blamed the federal government, writing that the "massacre, at Fort Pillow, has been invited by the tardiness of the government, and the action of Congress." The government's professions of equality were not matched by their actions, enabling Confederates to take "advantage of this equivocation, to commit just such horrible butchery as that at Fort Pillow."[138]

The presence of brave black men bearing arms was the nightmare of the white South. After Fort Pillow, enlistment of black men, who carried with them the cost of defeat into every battle, increased so much that black soldiers played a critical role in the Union victory in April 1865. Liberating tens of thousands of slaves, black Union soldiers fought in almost every major battle since their entry into the war, including in Yazoo City, Mississippi, near Petersburg, Virginia, and elsewhere. In February 1865, when rebel troops fled Charleston, the first Union troops to march into the city were the men of the 21st U.S. Colored Infantry, followed by detachments of the two black regiments, the 54th and 55th Massachusetts Volunteer Infantry Regiments.

According to Colonel Charles B. Fox, officer of the 55th, black Charlestonians met the liberating black army with "cheers, prayers, and songs. . . . Men and women crowded to shake hands with men and officers." And the soldiers sang "John Brown," "Babylon Is Falling," and the "Battle-Cry of Freedom" followed by intervals of the regimental band playing "national airs, long unheard" in the South. Similarly, black troopers of the 5th Massachusetts Cavalry, followed by the all-black 25th Army Corps, were the first soldiers to enter Richmond after Confederate soldiers evacuated.[139]

Whether near or far away from the battlefields, African American life in various regions of the country was dramatically affected by the war. Black wives and mothers of soldiers receiving unequal pay had to live on less than the families of white Union soldiers. Some were committed to the poorhouse until the policy changed. The federal government also took wages from black government laborers to support refugees who were unable to work.

When the federal government instituted the first national draft system in March 1863, white mobs in New York City attacked the draft office and the homes of the wealthy, and then they targeted black men, women, and children. Without a doubt, the conscription policy was blatantly unfair. Those who could afford to purchase a $300 exemption, or hire a substitute to go in their place, escaped the draft, while the working class and poor, disproportionately immigrants, were forced to serve. Yet rioters blamed, attacked, and killed African Americans for the government policy and, generally, for the war itself. The rioters left thousands of black New Yorkers dead, injured, homeless, and destitute.[140] The rioters destroyed African American physician Dr. James McCune Smith's pharmacy and burned the Colored Orphan Asylum (which housed 233 children) to the ground after stealing the orphanage's furniture, linens, and dishes. The New York City draft riots in July 1863 were the worst, but there were anti-black riots in other cities that same summer, resulting in death, torture, and mayhem.

In several Northern and Western states, African Americans and their white allies demanded that local officials take responsibility for protecting African Americans from mobs, and they also continued to address discrimination and unequal policies. Some demands for change were met. For example, in 1863, black Californians campaigned against the prohibition of black court testimony and gained the legal right to protect themselves and their property. In Syracuse, New York, the National Convention of Colored Men demanded equality and suffrage and formed the National Equal Rights League. While most Northern black men still lacked the right to vote, the federal government reversed some inequities. Anticipating the Fourteenth Amendment, the State

Department issued passports to African Americans, asserting their national identity and citizenship. Beginning in 1862, Massachusetts senator Charles Sumner successfully led the fight to end the prohibition against black men delivering U.S. mail. The bill finally became law in March 1865, over the negative votes of Democrats and conservative Republicans. Following on the heels of a decision in California, the U.S. Congress gave African Americans the right to serve as witnesses in court in the District of Columbia, broadening the policy to all federal courts in 1864. Additionally, activists in Illinois successfully eliminated the state's laws barring black immigration and testimony in February 1865 after decades of protests.[141]

Meanwhile, many Northerners and District of Columbia residents were busy aiding refugees who were fleeing from the South to Union camps, Washington, D.C., and Northern states. African American women were particularly prominent on the ground. For example, Elizabeth Keckley, a free black seamstress to Mary Todd Lincoln and other wives of federal officials, founded, along with some members of her church, the Contraband Relief Association. They provided clothing and other necessities for the refugees crowding into the District of Columbia. While many refugees found jobs, a significant number were too young, old, ill, or pregnant to work. Keckley's organization gained the public support of prominent abolitionists, including Henry Highland Garnet, Frederick Douglass, and Sojourner Truth. Even Mary Todd Lincoln and the president contributed to the cause.[142]

During the war, Northern activists shifted their focus from vigilance committees and the Underground Railroad to meeting the needs of refugees. In April 1862, in Philadelphia, with the support of the Pennsylvania Abolition Society, former Underground Railroad conductor William Still, for example, transformed his fugitive-smuggling activities into an employment and aid office for refugees. Still's office helped hundreds of former slaves find lost relatives, obtain housing, and find work.[143]

In addition, several Northern black men and women joined the band of white teachers and missionaries traveling to Union-controlled areas of the South to teach freedpeople. Northern organizations, mostly white, including the American Missionary Association (AMA), a Protestant abolitionist group established in 1846, sponsored many of these efforts. Freed people of all ages overwhelmed Northerners with their eagerness to obtain a rudimentary education. Just as importantly, Southern blacks, especially women like Mary Peake, were already engaged in establishing schools and other organizations to address this demand. Some simply expanded schools that had served free blacks before the war. And freedpeople (those freed by wartime Union policies)

themselves began using what little resources they had to build schools, even as the war raged around them.

However, the majority of enslaved people remained under the control of the Confederacy until the end of war. Though many tried, they were unable to escape to Union-controlled territories. For them, slavery, already horrific, became worse. After the Confederate defeats at Vicksburg and Gettysburg in the summer of 1863, slaveholders in the Confederacy began forcing their most valuable slaves into interior areas as far away from Union soldiers as possible. And slaveholders in areas near Union-held territory tightened slave codes even more, especially those restricting travel and meeting in small groups, in order to prevent escapes. Passes to see family members were nearly impossible to obtain for those left behind, and the slightest sign of rebellion could mean death. Slaveholders were actually engaged in two wars—a war against the Union to preserve slavery and, increasingly, a war with their own slaves, who were determined to gain their freedom at all cost. Some states imposed fines on white men who failed to perform slave-patrol duty.[144]

Some enslaved people who remained on plantations simply stopped working. They engaged in collective strikes or ignored their slaveholders' wives' supervision. Reports in Southern newspapers of "insolence and insubordination" were common. In Louisiana, some slaves demanded and received wages for their labor, and a Texan slaveholder complained that his slave cursed him when he tried to punish him. Always fearful of slave insurrections, Southern whites were terrified of them during the war. Subversive tactics by slaves, always a fact of life in the slave era, took on greater dimensions and brought greater rewards in the conflict. Some enslaved people ran away from plantations and hid in swamps and forests, often raiding nearby plantations for food and supplies. A Florida Confederate officer reported exchanging gunfire with runaway slaves. "We began to fire at them, and they returned the fire very cool and deliberately. . . ."[145] Slaves who remained on plantations aided Union soldiers; some helped soldiers escape, and others became Union spies.[146]

Many Southern free blacks fled to the North, or to Haiti or Canada if they could. Others were pressed into the service of the Confederacy along with slaves, building fortifications, digging trenches, and doing other work that allowed white men to fight against the federal government. Several of the mulatto elite slaveholders, and a few other free blacks, swore allegiance to the new Confederate government. The loyalty elite free blacks felt to the South reflected their precarious position. They were now closer to being perceived as a threat than they were before the war and in greater jeopardy of losing all that they had worked for generations to build.

Toward the end of war, the meaning of freedom for four million freedpeople was not settled. Generals in the field were making decisions that could easily be overturned by the government when order was restored. Most freedpeople had demonstrated their interest in securing their families and developing independent communities of subsistence farmers, and some officials had encouraged them. In Louisiana, the Sea Islands, and elsewhere, freed men and women were told to work plots of land. In doing so, they contended not only with slave owners who claimed loyalty to the Union in order to keep their slaves and plantations, but also with the influx of Northern investors interested in exploiting the high profits of black labor. When the Union gained control of northeastern Louisiana in 1863, for example, Northern businessmen, who leased land from the government, offered wages, food, and clothing to fugitives gathered near military posts and living in contraband camps. The problem was that these Northerners often failed to live up to their agreements. A government official sent to inspect the condition of former slaves in the northeastern area of Louisiana found that "the negro has been treated by those employing him, as a mere brute" and that in "no case" did he find strict compliance to the contracts the businessmen had agreed upon.[147]

In the South Carolina Sea Islands, slaveholders abandoned their plantations when the Union army arrived. The slaves who remained created communities of small, independent farms, and they hoped to receive or buy the land from the government that they had worked on for generations. These Sea Island black farmers found that one Northern investor, Massachusetts abolitionist Edward Philbrick, stood out among the others in preventing their dreams of land ownership from being realized. Philbrick, who first traveled to the South as a humanitarian to aid the slaves working on abandoned land in the Sea Islands, became a plantation superintendent. He soon urged that Northerners invest in the highly profitable Sea Island long staple cotton. After resigning from his position as plantation superintendent, Philbrick and other Northern investors bought up eleven plantations until they owned more than 8,000 acres with over 900 workers, making Philbrick and his fellow investors the largest planter in Union-occupied territory.

In January 1865, General William T. Sherman issued Special Field Orders, No. 15, responding to freedpeople's constant demands for land by designating the abandoned land of former slave owners for distribution to those who had worked it for generations. In this, Sherman and Secretary of War Stanton, who approved the measure, met freedpeople's primary economic interests and resolved the problem of what to do with thousands of refugees in and around Union camps. To newly freed people, land ownership would be their means of living independently. Land equaled freedom—it defined independence.

Sherman offered each head of household up to forty acres from the 400,000 acres of land the government confiscated along the Florida, Georgia, and South Carolina coastline. Later, some freedpeople received the loan of an army mule to work the land as well. By late June 1865, about forty thousand freedmen had moved onto new farms. However, as we will see in Chapter Three, freedpeoples' success in becoming land owners through Sherman's land policy would be short-lived.[148]

Since early 1864, Republicans in Congress had been certain that the Union would win the war, but at that time there were no means in place to ensure the complete end of slavery. Eventually most congressional Republicans came to agree with President Lincoln, and a few other key legislators, that emancipation through military means, abolition by states, and even congressional legislation could all be legally challenged by a new Congress, the courts, or by southern states. The solution to permanently ending slavery was an amendment to the Constitution. Some key Republicans argued that the founders believed that slavery was declining but were thwarted in their intentions to end slavery by the slaveholders—and their supporters—who dominated the federal government for most of the nation's history. The Thirteenth Amendment would reflect the founders' original intention to secure the blessings of liberty for all. When both House and Senate Republicans introduced bills to permanently abolish slavery through a constitutional amendment, Democrats and Republicans engaged in "sustained and vituperative debate."[149] Historian James Oakes asserts that both sides "understood that slavery was still very much alive and that the outcome of this debate would determine once and for all whether slavery would survive the war or be destroyed by it. The stakes could not have been higher."[150]

The summer and fall of 1864, a presidential-election year, proved precarious for the future of former slaves and the future of the nation. Although many men, women, and children were freed by various means during the Civil War, there were no safeguards that ensured they or their progeny would not be returned to slavery or that the nation would not remain divided over slavery. Unlike the 1860 Republican platform, the 1864 platform endorsed the unconditional and immediate abolition of slavery everywhere in the United States. Democrats, on the other hand, continued to insist that slavery was not the cause of the war and demanded peace without addressing slavery.

The overwhelming Republican victory in November meant that the Thirteenth Amendment had a real chance of passing the House and Senate. In December 1864, congressmen in the House and Senate reintroduced the amendment. Lincoln, Secretary of State William Seward, and many Republican congressmen lobbied fellow Republicans to promote the

amendment and put pressure on Democrats to pass it. On January 31, 1865, it passed with unanimous Republican support and more Democratic support than before. "When the final tally was announced, it took a moment for everyone to realize what had happened. Then the House erupted, Republicans threw their hats in the air; spectators wept and danced."[151] The last of the twenty-seven states necessary finally ratified the bill in December 1865.[152] Additionally, in March of that year, Congress established the Bureau of Refugees, Freedmen, and Abandoned Lands (Freedmen's Bureau) and chartered the Freedman's Savings Bank to help freedpeople transition from slavery to freedom.

When the war ended, more than 186,000 black men had served in the Union army and about 30,000 in the Union navy, with seventeen soldiers and four sailors receiving the Congressional Medal of Honor. Seventy percent of all Northern black males of military age had joined the Union forces, three times the rate for whites.[153] There were 166 black regiments in the Union army by spring 1865. About 37,000 black soldiers died in service to the United States and many more were injured.

Finally, proving right African Americans' conviction that the war would disrupt the slave system, the desperate Confederate Congress, after lengthy debates about the practicality of enlisting slaves as soldiers, belatedly authorized President Davis in March 1865 to call upon slave owners to volunteer their slaves, "offering freedom to those only who elect it."[154] The authorization came less than a month before General Robert E. Lee surrendered at the Appomattox, Virginia, courthouse on April 9, 1865.

"My Children I Have Not Forgot You and Be Assured That I Will Have You If It Cost Me My Life."

PRIVATE LETTERS DESCRIBING MOSTLY PERSONAL AFFAIRS, and generally written to one person, show even more how complex and diverse the African American experience was on the home front, in refugee camps, and for soldiers caught up directly in battles. The public and private letters written by African Americans during the Civil War reflected their belief that the war would end slavery. In each experience, whether enslaved, free born, or newly freed, an individual's kinship remained central. In some instances, fugitive husbands found support from the federal government for rescuing their families from slavery. In other situations, soldier husbands corresponded with their wives for the first time, reporting on the battles and duties in the war.

Correspondence among members of the Douglass family during the Civil War is voluminous. Recruiting black soldiers for the Union, Frederick Douglass was proud that his youngest son Charles Remond was the first of his sons to enlist in March 1863. Douglass's eldest son, Lewis, quickly followed Charles into the 54th Massachusetts Volunteer Infantry Regiment. Army officials almost immediately recognized the two brothers' distinct talents, making Lewis a sergeant major because of his leadership skills and Charles

an army clerk for his precise penmanship. However, because of an illness, Charles did not ship out with the 54th in late spring but stayed at Camp Meigs, the army camp for black soldiers in Readville, Massachusetts. He was appointed a sergeant when he joined the 5th Massachusetts Cavalry later in the war. Lewis, besides writing to his parents, maintained his correspondence with Amelia.

The enslaved Plummer family's commitment to kin was the rule, not the exception. They were unique, though, in their ability to communicate in writing. Fortunately, they were able to continue communicating with one another even when Emily and the children with her were moved farther away from Adam and two of the other children. But the war changed the Plummers' circumstances dramatically. In the fall of 1860, to the anguish of Emily and Adam, Sarah Miranda's slaveholder sold her for $1,000 to a slave trader, because he feared that the incoming Republican government had an abolitionist agenda that would mean the loss of thousands of dollars. The slave trader put Sarah Miranda in an Alexandria, Virginia, slave pen while he waited for an owner or another trader to purchase her. Fearing that she would be "sold south," never to be seen again, Emily, Adam, other family members and friends frantically tried to find a Maryland slaveholder to buy Sarah Miranda, but to no avail. After keeping her in the slave pen for two months, the trader sold Sarah Miranda to another trader, who then sold her to a New Orleans slaveholder a thousand miles away.

Suffering from the loss of Sarah Miranda, and determined not to lose more children, Emily made several attempts to escape from slavery with the children. In October 1863, she finally succeeded—but not according to her plan. Two friends were to escort her and the children to other friends in Baltimore, where she would stay until Adam arrived to get them. That night the friends didn't appear, so Emily set out with the children on her own. Unsure of where she was, Emily asked what seemed to be a trustworthy couple, with a baby, for directions. Apparently, the couple reported her and the children to Maryland authorities, who immediately put her and the children in jail as runaways. According to Nellie Arnold Plummer, her mother believed they were better off in jail than enslaved on the plantation: "except for the thought of being returned to her cruel master for worse treatment. All she wanted was to get word to father to come."[155] By then Henry, the second eldest Plummer child, had escaped to Washington, D.C. He stayed hidden until he joined the United States Navy. Two months later, Adam's slaveholder permitted him to collect his family and bring them to his Riversdale slave cabin. Although Sarah Miranda and Henry were not with them, Emily and Adam Plummer, and five of their children lived together as a family for the first time.[156]

Now more than ever, slaves and freedpeople were able to communicate with loved ones. Several Northern teachers who went South to teach freed-people in Union-controlled areas served as amanuenses for those who fled enslavement (mostly women and children). White New England Quaker abolitionist sisters Lucy and Sarah Chase were part of the early contingent of Northern educators when the U.S. government took control of Norfolk, Virginia, and the surrounding areas. Landing on Craney Island, Virginia, in January 1863, the Chase sisters were responsible for teaching the 2,000 newly freedmen, women, and children on the island. Sponsored by the Boston Educational Commission, one of the many organizations formed to address the needs of former slaves in Union-occupied areas, they also worked as labor superintendents, directing the work of the freedpeople. In May of that year, the army moved the sisters and the freedpeople to the mainland. Besides distributing clothing, opening schools, and engaging in the government's labor interests, the Chase sisters wrote letters dictated to them by wives, children, and lovers, providing glimpses of the values and interests of refugees in the Virginia "Contraband Camp." Lucy Chase also wrote constantly to her "Dear folks at home," telling of the sisters' adventures and their interactions with former slaves. In one letter to her family, Lucy Chase rejoices "with the happy negro in his greed for letters. One word of instruction from a teacher brightens the face of the learner with shining content."[157]

Like the Chase sisters, Northern white schoolteacher Elizabeth Botume traveled South to teach the newly freed people. Arriving in Beaufort, South Carolina, toward the end of war, Botume found former slaves, especially wives of Union soldiers, eager to correspond with their husbands. Although freed women came to the teachers' residence every day to have letters written for them, Botume and the other teachers tried to limit this task to two after-noons a week. The allotted time was never adequate. They found themselves writing into the evening by candlelight to meet the great demand. Botume and her fellow teachers often wrote the letters as they were dictated to them, and they read letters to mothers and wives from their sons or husbands. The Northerners were often amazed at how former slaves found family members, an activity that was routine, even during the war. According to Botume, the "slave boy, now a free man, turned with his whole heart and soul [in search of] ... his wife and child and his mother."[158] The letters also reveal how freedmen, women, and children consistently faced the harshness and brutality of former masters. The horrific effects of slavery affected husband and wives in their most intimate relationships. Enslaved people who were forced to marry, for example, often enacted quick "divorces," and some couples remained silent about children who were obviously the consequence of rape by white men.

Oberlin student Emma Brown, whom we met in the previous chapter, did not have to leave her home in the District of Columbia to be immediately impacted by the war. Her life significantly changed when thousands of refugees fled to the nation's capital in the early months of the war. Recovering from stress and insomnia at home in Georgetown, Brown began teaching first in her home and later at Ebenezer Church on Capitol Hill. Washington, D.C., became the first Southern city to include schools for black children in its public school system. The school at Ebenezer Church experienced record enrollment in a short span of time, and Brown and her assistant, Frances W. Perkins, a white woman supported by the New England Freedmen's Aid Society, worked hard and in limited space.[159]

Unlike the lives of teachers of refugees, the lives of some Northerners were not markedly affected by the events of the war. Even though the war touched everyone in one way or another, many Northerners worked, attended school, and thought of the future without mention of major events of the day. Rosetta Douglass, the daughter of Frederick and Anna Murray Douglass, rarely references the war in her letters. Some of her correspondence reveals the inner dynamics of the Douglass household and the family's attempt to maintain their privacy even as Frederick Douglass became more famous. Rosetta's letters also suggest that she found living with some family and family friends stifling, especially those with overbearing middle-class standards.

Members of the free black Rapier family of Alabama, whom we met in the last chapter, were scattered throughout the United States, Canada, and the Caribbean in the 1850s but remained in contact through letters, especially between John Sr. and John Jr. The most prolific correspondent in the family, aside from his father, John Rapier Jr. lived in the Caribbean for about a year and half, from the beginning of the war, assisting a Jamaican physician. This position redirected young Rapier's life; he returned to the States in 1862 and went to school and worked in Ohio to save money for medical school in Michigan. Rapier Jr. entered the Department of Medicine and Surgery at the University of Michigan in the fall of 1863; the three-year program would be reduced to two years for him because of his studies in Jamaica. Within a few weeks of beginning medical school in Michigan, Rapier Jr. wrote family members that the whole campus was "thrown into convulsions because 'an American of African descent' dared present himself for admission to the Medical class." He wasn't referring to himself, but rather to a young man from Detroit. Because Rapier Jr. listed Kingston, Jamaica, as his residence when he applied, the medical college admitted him as a foreign student. After learning that a local man of color had been admitted to the University of Michigan Medical School, the students were in an uproar at the thought of studying with an African American. Evidently,

they were not opposed to studying with a foreign person of color. The administration and faculty then reversed their decision, and the Detroit man was told to leave. Members of the Detroit black community attacked Rapier Jr. for claiming he was white. By February, Rapier Jr. decided to leave Michigan and enroll in the Medical Department at Iowa State University, where he finished in June 1864.[160] Before graduating, however, he applied to become a medical officer in the Union army. John Rapier Jr. became an admired physician, making hospital rounds in the small, one-story frame building of the Freedmen's Hospital located in northwest Washington, D.C. He was often seen, according to the *Christian Recorder*, visiting the "homes of the lowly, who needed his professional services." In January 1865, Rapier Jr. wrote to Andrew Johnson, soon to be vice president of the United States, asking if it wasn't right that black soldiers should be led by black officers. Rapier Jr. remained at the Freedmen's Hospital, working with African American physician Dr. Alexander T. Augusta, until the end of the war.[161]

In contrast to the majority of Southern blacks, free and enslaved, a few of the so-called mulatto elite swore loyalty to the Confederacy and offered their labor to protect the new government. Yet their freedom, like that of all Southern free blacks, remained in jeopardy. The war might have had a particularly devastating effect on the Ellison family, free black slaveholders in South Carolina. After William Ellison Sr.'s death in December 1861, Henry, the eldest son and now patriarch, took responsibility for providing and protecting the family and, most of all, its freedom, as his father had done so skillfully for more than four decades. Because of the Union blockade on cotton production, planting cotton and making gins could no longer serve as the foundation of the family's wealth. But, like his father, Henry capitalized on providing immediate necessities, enabling the family to maintain its financial security even during the war. The gin shop focused less on repairing gins and more on blacksmithing, a skill his father had insisted the boys learn when quite young.

During the war, the Ellisons apparently hired out their skilled enslaved men to the Confederacy. When the Confederacy required planters to grow food for the military, the Ellison men, Henry, William, and Reuben, began growing food on their plantation. Whereas before the war, the Ellisons and their slaves planted food crops to make the family self-sufficient, now they provided food not just for themselves but also for their neighbors, and most of all for the Confederate army, an effort that was for the Ellisons both patriotic and profitable. According to their biographers, the Ellisons "earned a small fortune from the government" and a "reputation as loyal Confederates."[162] Correspondence between Ellison family members and friends mostly remained focused on their everyday lives.

Finally, romantic letters between enslaved couples, newly freed people, and those born free reveal how love among African Americans reflected the resilience of the human spirit in the face of some of the most brutal ways humans can abuse one another. Early in the war, John M. Washington, the twenty-four-year-old Virginia slave who crossed the Rappahannock River with his cousins in April 1862 to be "a slave no more," became the cook for division commander, General Rufus King, at $18 per month. By May, Washington was guiding the Union army's entrance into Fredericksburg. Before escaping to freedom, John had met Annie E. Gordon, a free person of color, at a Fredericksburg African Baptist church fair. Gordon was four years younger than Washington and, like him, literate. Literacy proved a boon to the young couple during their courtship, when in December 1860, John was hired out to a tavern owner in Richmond, fifty miles south of Fredericksburg. Throughout 1861, while Confederate troops were mobilizing all around them, John Washington and Annie Gordon exchanged letters expressing their love.

Like John and Annie, Lewis Douglass and Amelia Loguen met before the war. In other respects they were unlike the Virginia couple. As children of famous abolitionist fathers who valued education, Lewis and Amelia benefitted from a formal education, and their letters reflected the customs of nineteenth-century Victorian middle-class courtship, in which thoughts that could not be expressed physically could be expressed on paper. Their correspondence gives us insight, like the letters between Annie and John, into courtship during war and underscores the complexity and diversity of African American life.

Free Northern black women and men (as well as a large contingent of white abolitionists) joined Southern black teachers in addressing the basic needs and educational interests of refugees. In 1862, Harriet Jacobs, a former fugitive from North Carolina who referred to herself as "Linda" in her slave narrative, *Incidents in the Life of Linda Brent*, went to the District of Columbia and Alexandria to report on conditions for abolitionists. She found around 400 homeless impoverished men, women, and children. A year later the number had swelled to 10,000, and at the end of the war to 40,000. In her letter to William Lloyd Garrison, editor and publisher of the *Liberator*, Jacobs explains the bleak conditions for most refugees in the nation's capital.

[August 1862, Washington D.C.]

Dear Mr. Garrison:

I thank you for a request of a line on the condition of the contraband, and what I have seen while among them.... Having purchased a ticket through to Washington at the Philadelphia station, I reached the capital without molestation. Next morning, I went to Duff Green's Row, [on East Capitol St.] Government headquarters for the contrabands here. I found men, women and children all huddled together without any distinction or regard to age or sex. Some of them were in the most pitiable condition. Many were sick with measles, diphtheria, scarlet and typhoid fever. Some had a few filthy rags to lie on, others had nothing but the bare floor for a couch. There seemed to be no established rules among them; they were coming in at all hours, often through the night, in large numbers, and the Superintendent had enough to occupy his time in taking the names of those who came in, and those who were sent out. His office was thronged through the day by persons who came to hire the poor creatures.... Single women hire at four dollars a month; a woman with one child two and a half or three dollars a month. Men's wages are ten dollars per month.... It is almost impossible to keep the building in a healthy condition. Each day brings its fresh additions of the hungry, naked and sick....

Hoping to help a little in the good work [being done by two northern white women] I wrote to a lady in New York, a true and tried friend of the slave . . . to ask for such articles as would make comfortable the sick and dying in the hospital. On the Saturday following the cots were put up. A few hours after an immense box was received from the *New York* [a ship]. Before the sun went down . . . every man, woman and child [had] clean garments, lying in a clean bed. What a contrast! They seemed different beings. . . .

Still, there were other places in which I felt, if possible, more interest, where the poor creatures seemed . . . far removed from the immediate sympathy of those who would help them. These were the contrabands in Alexandria. This place is strongly secesh [secessionist]; the inhabitants are kept quiet on at the point of Northern bayonets. In this place, the contrabands are distributed more over the city. In visiting those places, I had the assistance of two kind friends, women . . . [who] felt the wrongs and degradation of their race. These ladies were always ready to aid me, as far as lay in their power. . . . In this place, the men live in an old foundry, which does not afford protection from the weather. The sick lay on boards on the ground floor; some through the kindness of the soldiers have an old blanket. I did not hear a complaint among them. They said it was much better than it had been. All expressed a willingness to work, and were anxious to know what was to be done with them after the work was done. . . . All said they had plenty to eat, but no clothing, and no money to buy any.

Another place, the old school-house in Alexandria is the Government headquarters for the women. This I thought the most wretched of all places. Anyone who can find an apology for slavery should visit this place and learn its curse. Here you see them from infancy up to a hundred years old. What but the love of freedom could bring these old people hither? . . . In this house are scores of women and children with nothing to do, and nothing to do with. Their husbands are at work for the Government. Here they have food and shelter, but they

cannot get work. The slaves who come to Washington from Maryland are sent here to protect them from the Fugitive Slave Law. . . .

Let me tell you of another place—Arlington Heights. . . . Gen. Lee's beautiful residence, which has been so faithfully guarded by our Northern army. . . . At the quarters, there are many contrabands. The men are employed and most of the women. Here they have plenty of exercise in the open air and seem very happy. Many of the regiments are stationed here. It is a delightful place for both the soldiers and the contraband. . . .

Let me beg the reader's attention to these orphans. They are the innocent and helpless of God's poor. If you cannot take one, you can do much by contributing your mite to the institution that will open its doors to receive them.

Linda [164]

Fugitives were critical to the war effort; by fleeing enslavement, they weakened the Confederacy. Union policy soon placed them in refugee camps. When the fugitives were fairly safe, teachers and Northern missionaries established schools and churches in or near the camps. Black Virginian Mary S. Peake, who had secretly taught slaves and free blacks before the war, began working under the auspices of the American Missionary Association during the war. Lewis Lockwood, an AMA missionary, was particularly impressed with Peake's spirituality. Her letter to AMA officials reveals the dedication Southern black teachers had to educating black children before, during, and after the war. Peake's student enrollment increased as thousands of slaves fled to Fortress Monroe, a Union army stronghold. Peake's school had about fifty children enrolled, and she was ready to teach adults in the afternoon. Soon after receiving aid for the school, Peake writes to the association.

Fortress Monroe, Virginia
November 1861

Dear Brethren and Friends:

With many thanks I acknowledge the donation received from you. After our church was burned, we had no place of worship, and we were in a most deplorable condition in respect to our spiritual welfare. . . . Although we have lost many of our earthly comforts, we are better off than many of the poor soldiers, who are suffering from wounds and exposure to weather. Some of them take part in the Sunday school and assist us to teach the children, who improve very fast.

I have been teaching about fifty small children. Some are beginning to read very well, and are very anxious to learn, also quite a number of adults. In regard to the church and school, we feel thankful; our condition is quite prosperous. We have had many interesting marriages performed, since brother Lockwood has been with us.

Most respectfully,

M. S. Peake[163]

Mary S. Peake, ca. 1860s

The AMA received several letters from Northern black women wishing to teach Southern refugees. An example is Sara G. Stanley's letter of application to Reverend George Whipple, a founder and corresponding secretary of the AMA.

Cleveland, Ohio, January 19, 1864

Dear Sir:

I am a colored woman . . . and have been for several years a teacher in the public schools of Ohio. Since the providence of God has opened in the South, so vast a field for earnest and self-abnegating missionary labor, I have felt a strong conviction of duty, an irresistible desire to engage in teaching the freed people; to aid, to the extent of what ability God has given me, in bringing the poor outcast from the pale of humanity, into the family of man.

Possessing no wealth and having nothing to give but my life to the work, I therefore make this application to you. Can I become a teacher under the auspices of the American Missionary Association? I should be very glad and happy if it might be so.

No thought of suffering, and privation, nor even death, should deter me from making every effort possible, for the moral and intellectual elevation of these ignorant and degraded people. I know that the efforts of a single individual seem small and insignificant but to me this is of the most vital importance.

Very respectfully Yours
Sara G. Stanley[165]

As many Northerners and Southern free blacks were attempting to meet the needs of refugees, the enslaved black population sought ways to escape and, if they were literate, contact family members. With the war into only its second month, enslaved Sarah Miranda Plummer somehow managed to get a letter to her parents. Unaware of their attempts to rescue her, she criticizes her father for not seeing her when she was imprisoned in the Alexandria, Virginia, slave pen and hopes the family will not "forget that I am still alive."

New Orleans La May 24th 1861

Dear Mother.

I take my pen and hand to write you a few lines, I am well to day and hope my letter will find you the same; I have been a long time from gorgetown, I suppose you have had so many letters to read that you would not care about hearing from me.

I write with much grief to say that I was in Alexandria two months, and could not hear from any of you; Jackson ogle went to Washington every three weeks to see his wife, he saw my grandmother and of course she knew where I was, I hope you will not think hard of my scolding for that's not half I laid up for you.

I do not blame you because you could not come to see me, I think it very hard that father did not come to see me as he was nearer than you were, though I may hear from you, yet I may never expect to see you again; you will please write to Grandma give my love to her, and tell her I am sorry I didnot come to see her when I went to show my aunt where she lived.... I have been very low spirited since I left you all, but I will try to do the best I can I hope that you will not forget that I am still alive; I send my love to you and to all my inquiring friends, Remember me to my brother, And tell him I hope he has not forgotten to write to me as he promised to do I write you much grief and my heart is full of sorrow, and I can do no better and I hope you will not Grieve after me, but in the good Providence of God I hope we willmeet [sic] to part no more; though you will be sorry to hear I am so far yet you will be glad to hear that I met with my aunt Sarah

and she was very glad to see me yet [s]he did not know me until I made myself known unto her. She has been stopping at StCharles[sic] hotel I do not know whether she has left there or not. she said when I wrote to give her love to sister and all the children I hope you will have a pleasant time over my letter. . . . I suppose you will answer my letter as soon as you can because I want to hear from you as bad as you do from me.

I remain as ever your affect daughter
S.M. Plummer[166]

Constantly suffering from the loss of Sarah Miranda, Emily and Adam Plummer tried to exert some measure of control over their lives and the lives of their other children. Still living on separate plantations but now even farther away from each other, the couple corresponded regularly.

Riversdale, Prince Geo. Col, Md.,
August 11, 1861

For Emily Plummer at Woodlawn,
Ellicotts City, Howard County, Md.
My dear Wife:
I take this opportunity of writing you a few lines today, to inform you that I am not so well today myself, but I hope by the blessings of God, these few lines may find you and all the children well. All are well at Riverdale, Your mother is well and sends her love to all.

I expect or wish to come up to see you on the 24th of August, a. m. You please look for me in the morning.

Your son, Elias Plummer, is well. I have nothing more to say, goodbye till then.

Your affectionate Husband
Adam Plummer[167]

On August 19, unaware of Adam's impending visit because his letter arrived one day later, on August 20, Emily was waiting for him to write. In her letter, she shows that she and Adam tried to find a way to contact their eldest daughter, Sarah Miranda, in New Orleans, but the war made it impossible. Even trusted friends could not find a way to deliver concealed letters to slaves. Still mostly illiterate, Emily now relied on a white seamstress friend to read and write for her instead of her slaveholder. Importantly, Emily's sentiments are consistent throughout the period of the couple's separation, whether written by her slaveholder or the white friend, indicating that the slaveholder wrote Emily's words as she expressed them. Of course, enslaved people could not express all their true feelings to slaveholders but Emily's primary wish that she and her family be reunited is evident in all her letters to her husband.

Woodlawn, Ellicotts City,
Howard County, Md
Monday, August 19, 1861

My ever dear Husband:

I have been hoping each day to hear from you, as you may imagine it gives me intense pleasure to hear of your welfare and happiness.

Your inquiring as to the proper address for Miranda's letters should have been sent, but you cannot send any letters South. I have had one written to her, and for two months watched in vain for an opportunity to send the letter. Her address is to the care of Hanson Kelly, New Orleans, La.

We are all well. The babies grow and improve rapidly. They can almost walk. And Papa, Saunders is not with me, he is hired to Miss Eliza Dorsey, as house servant, is doing very well, and is much better satisfied. He and all the children are so anxious to see you, they send all their love.

But what shall I say of myself, my dear husband? I think each day I cannot longer wait for a visit from you. My heart aches at the thought of this long and painful separation. I do pray to God for patience to

hear my trials. He only knows how hard I struggle with myself for my little children's sake. I dream of you and think you are once more with me, but wake to find myself alone and so wretchedly unhappy.

Could you come up early some Sunday morning to breakfast? I have flattered myself you thought of doing some such thing. O what joy it would bring to the almost broken heart of your poor wife and family! Do try this plan, my dear husband, and let us hear from you soon, that you will come, but under any circumstances write very frequently. It is our next great pleasure to seeing your kind face, and hearing your voice of affection.

William and Clarice send their best love, each and all want to see you.

God bless and speedily reunite us, ever prays

Your truly affectionate wife,
Emily Plummer[168]

In October 1863, Emily Plummer and her children were some of the thousands of enslaved people who fled slavery during the war. As noted previously, after she escaped and made her way to Maryland, Adam, Emily, and five of their children were together for the first time. Another Maryland fugitive, John Boston, escaped to Union lines early in the war. In this letter, he informs his wife, Elizabeth, of his safe arrival at the camp of a New York regiment in Virginia. Boston expresses his joy in freedom and, like other blacks, believes that black freedom was God's design.

Upton Hill [Va.] January 12 1862

My Dear Wife it is with grate joy I take this time to let you know Whare

I am i am now in Safety in the 14th Regiment of Brooklyn this Day i can Adress you thank god as a free man I had a little truble in giting away But as the lord led the Children of Isrel to the land of Canon So he led me to a land Whare freedom Will rain in spite Of earth and hell Dear you must make your Self content i am free from al the Slavers Lash. ... I am With a very nice man and have All that hart Can Wish But My Dear I Cant express my grate desire that i have to See you i trust the time Will Come When We Shall meet again And if We dont met on earth We Will Meet in heven Whare Jesas ranes. ... Dear Wife i must Close rest yourself Contented i am free i Want you to rite To me Soon as you Can Without Delay Direct your letter to the 14th Reigment New york State malitia Uptons Hill Virginea In Care of Mr Cranford Comary Write my Dear Soon As you C Your Affectionate Husban Kiss Daniel For me

John Boston
Give my love to Father and Mother[169]

It is not known if Elizabeth Boston received her letter or if she was free or enslaved; as with so many stories of enslaved people, we do not know what happened to the couple. Because John Boston ran away from a loyal slave owner in a border state, the Maryland government, which somehow obtained the letter, demanded that the federal government explain how Boston's owner could recover his slave.

Meunomennie L. Maimi was an African American Union soldier in the 20th Connecticut Volunteer Infantry Regiment. He was one of the few black men in a white regiment who was able to join the army before the Emancipation Proclamation, perhaps because of his light skin color. Apparently, when he wrote his wife that he was ill and described the racism evident among white Union soldiers, she urged him to recuperate at home. In his response, Maimi chastises her for not considering the great significance of the war and what would happen if the Confederates won.

Buckingham Legion, Co. I, 20th

Reg[iment]t., C.V.

Camp near Stafford C[ourt]

H[ouse], [Virginia]

March, 1863

My Dear Wife:

When I wrote you the last letter I was quite sick, and did not know as I should ever be able to write to you again; but I am better now and write to relieve your mind, in case you might worry too much about me. When I wrote my last letter, I did not expect to be able to write another; but some good news which I received and the kind usage of a few friends who came to my hut and did what was needed for me, have saved you your husband, and I am enable to write again. There is one thing which your selfish love for your husband has made you forget, and that is, that he is naturally a soldier, and in time of war, and particularly in times like the present, a good soldier has something else to do besides enjoying himself at home with his family. I shall come, if permitted to go home, but as soon as my health will admit, will return to duty.

Do you know or think what the end of this war is to decide? It is to decide whether we are to have freedom to all or slavery to all. If the Southern Confederacy succeeds, then you may bid farewell to all liberty. If our government succeeds, then your and our race will

be free. The government has torn down the only barrier that existed against us as a people. When slavery passes away, the prejudices that belonged to it must follow. The government calls for the colored man's help and, if he is not a fool, he will give it. . . .

Now, wife, although I love you and would grant anything in reason to one who has been so kind and so faithful and true to her husband, yet there is something which the true man should hold dear and for which he should be willing to die, besides the wife of his bosom or the children of his loins: first, his God; then his country or his government, when it is a just one; and if he cannot do that he is no man, but a useless piece of machinery. If I did not know why you spoke those words, I would be very angry indeed. I know that it was your wifely anger at the mean treatment which your dearly beloved husband has suffered at the hands of some of his fellow soldiers that made you speak so quick and without forethought, bidding me desert my flag and leave my country to fall into the hands of its worst enemies. You did not speak such words as those on the day when I stood before you with the uniform of a volunteer, the uniform of a free man on. You told me at the door with a smile on your face, but a tear in your eye, that if I thought it was my duty to go to what was then a white man's war, to "go, and may God bless you!" I was prouder of you that day than the day the minister bid me salute my wife.

You have never doubted my true and faithful love for you; it is still the same, or else I would come running home like a little cur that some large dog had badly frightened, and leave you to become a slave to those wretches who hate us. For if these Southern demons conquer, then you, with your Indian and Negro blood mixed in your veins, must bow down to them and become their slave or perhaps some white man's mistress, not an honored wife, loved and respected by her husband, but a mere plaything, to be cast aside as soon as he discovers a fresh victim to administer to his beastly lusts. . . . This he has been doing for years, and the only cure that can or will relieve this disease is the present war, which he in his foolish and wicked plan began.

I do not blame you altogether for what you said about returning home, as it was cowardly in me to complain to you of the fools' bad usage. I forgive you, as it was prompted by your too-selfish love for your husband. But I want you to remember hereafter that you are a soldier's wife, a warrior's bride—one who has not a single drop of cowardly blood in his veins, and who will not desert his flag, or country, or his brother in bonds, not even for his dearly beloved wife, the friend of his bosom. Ponder this well; take the right sense of it and be proud that you have such a man for a husband. What is money but trash? And is trash to be compared to a country's and my own liberty? If the government gets so poor, before the war ends, that it cannot pay but $40 per month and no bounties, I will take that and fight on. That will buy bread for you and my poor old grandmother. If I return at all, let me come back to your arms a free man, of a free country and a free flag, and my brothers free, or else let me rest in death on the battlefield, with my face to the slave-holders, a continual reproach and curse unto him, as long as the world shall stand or a slaveholder breath. This from your soldier-husband,

M. L. Maimi[170]

Maimi soon joined one of the first black units, the 54th Massachusetts Volunteer Infantry Regiment. The sons of Frederick Douglass and Peter Vogelsang Sr., prominent black abolitionists and recruiters for the army, were some of the first to enlist in the regiment, which was organized by Massachusetts Governor John A. Andrew after President Lincoln announced the Emancipation Proclamation. Two of Frederick Douglass's sons, Lewis and Charles, were in the 54th, and in July 1863, Lewis participated in the famous assault on Battery Wagner, a well-armed fortress in the Charleston harbor. In his letter to his parents, Lewis describes the battle, unaware that his commander, Robert Gould Shaw, had been killed.

Union soldier and family, ca. 1863–1865

Morris Island S[outh]C[arolina]

July 20th [1863]

My Dear Father and Mother:

Wednesday July 8th, our regiment left St. Helena Island for Folly Island, arriving there the next day, and were then ordered to land on James Island, which we did. On the upper end of James Island is a large rebel battery with 18 guns. After landing we threw out pickets to within two miles of the rebel fortification. We were permitted to do this in peace until last Thursday, 16th inst., when at four o'clock in the morning the rebels made an attack on our pickets, who were about 200 strong. We were attacked by a force of about 900. Our men fought like tigers; one sergeant killed five men by shooting and bayoneting. The rebels were held in check by our few men long enough to allow the 10th Conn. to escape being surrounded and captured, for which we received the highest praise from all parties who knew of it. This performance on our part earned for us the reputation of a fighting regiment.

Our loss in killed, wounded and missing was forty-five. That night we took, according to our officers, one of the hardest marches on record, through woods and marsh. The rebels we defeated and drove back in the morning. They, however, were reinforced by 14,000 men, we having only a half a dozen regiments. So it was necessary for us to escape.

I cannot write in full, expecting every moment to be called into another fight. Suffice it to say we are now on Morris Island. Saturday night we made the most desperate charge of the war on Fort Wagner, losing in killed, wounded and missing in the assault, three hundred of our men. The splendid 54th is cut to pieces. All our officers, with the exception of eight, were either killed or wounded. Col. Shaw is a prisoner and wounded. Major Hallowell is wounded in three places, Adj't James in two places. . . . Nat Hurley is missing, and a host of others.

I had my sword sheath blown away while on the parapet of the Fort. The grape and canister, shell and minnies swept us down like chaff, still our men went on and on, and if we had been properly supported, we would have held the Fort, but the white troops could not

be made to come up. The consequence was we had to fall back, dodging shells and other missiles.

If I have another opportunity, I will write more fully. Goodbye to all. If I die tonight I will not die a coward. Goodbye.

Lewis[171]

As Lewis Douglass's letter to his parents shows, black soldiers fought with pride in several battles and, because many were learning to read and write, they were able to keep in touch with family and friends at home. Private Rufus Wright, a soldier of the 1st USCI regiment, exchanged letters with his new bride, Elizabeth, while he was stationed at Fort Monroe, Virginia. In April 1864 he informed Elizabeth that he was well and wished to see her.

Camp 1st U.S.V.T. Near Hampton [Va.] apl the 2 1864 My Dear Wife I thake this opportunity to inform you that I am well and Hoping when thoes few Lines Reaches you thay my find you Enjoying Good Health as it now fines me at Prisent Give my Love to all my friend I Recived you Last letter and was very Glad to Hear fome you you must Excuse you fore not Riting Before this times the times I Recive you Letter I was order on a march and I had not times to Rite to you I met witch a Bad mich-fochens I Ben Sad of I Lost my money I think I will come Down to See you this weeck I thought you Hear that I was hear and you wood come to see me Git a Pass and come to see me and if you cant git Pass Let me know it Give my Love to mother and Molley Give my Love to all inquiring fried

No more to Say Still Remain you Husband untall Death

Rufus Wright

Derect you Letter to foresess Monre VA

MARRIAGE CERTIFICATE.

This is to Certify,

That Mr. _Rufus Wright_
of _Richmond Va_ and
Miss _Elisabeth Turner_
of _X Barsknaith va_ were lawfully joined in
HOLY WEDLOCK, on the _Third_ day
of _December_ in the year of our Lord one
thousand eight hundred and _Sixty three._

    May the God of all grace enable you faithfully to fulfil the
solemn covenant made in His presence, and after having lived
together in a state of holy joy and pious friendship, may you meet
in Heaven in perfect happiness never to be terminated.

H M Turner   Pastor of the

Evang. Lutheran Church in _Chaplain U, S. Army_

Sold by T. NEWTON KURTZ, 151 Pratt-st., Baltimore, Md.

In his letter to Elizabeth in May, Wright proudly describes one of his unit's successful battles.

wilson Creek Va May 25th 1864

dear wife I take the pleasant opportunity of writeing to you a fiew lines to inform you of the Late Battle we have had we was a fight on Tuesday five hours we whipp the rebls out we Killed $200 [sic] & captured many Prisener out of our Regiment we lost 13 Thirteen Sergent Sephensen killed & priate out of Company H & about 8 or 10 wounded we was in line Wednesday for a battele But the rebels did not Appear we expect an Attack every hour give my love to all & to my sisters give my love to Miss Emerline tell John Skinner is well & sends much love to her. Joseph H Grinnel is well & he is as brave a lion all the Boys sends there love them give my love to Miss Missenger You must excuse my short Letter we are most getting ready to go on Picket No more from your Husband

Rufus Wright[172]

The following month, Private Wright was wounded in action at Petersburg. He died in the U.S. General Hospital at Fort Monroe of an abdominal wound on June 21, 1864. Seeing death all around them, soldiers continued to sacrifice their lives for the great "cause" even as they knew their risks were even greater than those of the white soldiers. The Confederacy's refusal to take black prisoners of war should have caused many to desert but instead, according to Sergeant Charles Douglass, it made black soldiers more determined.

Elizabeth Turner and Rufus Wright's marriage certificate, 1863

amp Hamilton City Point Virginia May 31 1864

Dear Father

I received your letter with Lewis yesterday afternoon I was very much pleased to hear from home and to know if any were sick I hope that you will be about soon. It is pretty warm here at present and has been so for several days. Sunday we all had green peas for our dinner this morning I had chicken for breakfast our Company went out on picket yesterday afternoon and Capt. [Erik] Wulff made a raid on an old farm house outside our picket lines and shot seven chickens one he sent to me I staid in from picket [a small group of soldiers assigned a specific duty] just as I am writing this there is heavy firing just above our picket line I expect to be called into line of battle every moment we have been fighting ever since our Regt. came here I mean our forces. . . . I suppose you hear of it through the papers . . . our boys are very anxious for a fight I think their wishes will be complied with shortly as for myself I am not over anxious but willing to meet the devils at any moment and take no prisoners remember Fort Pillow will be the battle cry of the fifth Mass Cavalry although I have been the first to take a prisoner last week when on picket I espied a man in grey clothes dodge behind a tree (Capt Wulff had just left me) in a moment I had my piece to bear on him I was only about a dozen yards off once the old wild cat had got so near me without being perceived I ordered him to step from behind the tree so I could knock a hole through him he stepped out I could see no gun I then ordered him to go in ahead of me which he did very reluctantly as soon as he had passed in front of me I cocked my piece which went click: click he stopped stone still and wanted to know if I meant to murder him I spoke in a harsh tone for him to go on and if he stopped before I ordered him that I would shoot him he went on I took him to Capt. Wulff who was sitting under a tree Capt. ordered me to search him which I did well making him strip off every rag for he was covered with them I found a revolver dirk knife $50 in reb money $15. in gold and some silver coin and green backs he proved to be the man that owns the land where we were picketed. I have the revolver that I took from him . . . I also brought in . . . contrabands from a farm house. I have had the praise of bringing the first prisoner. . . .

Your Affectionate Son
C R Douglass 1st Sergt Cold[173]

146

Enslaved women and children were particularly vulnerable, especially families of soldiers still in the Confederate South or in border state areas sympathetic to the rebel cause. Ann Valentine dictates a letter from Missouri to her soldier husband asking for money and describing her slaveholder's abuse. At the same time, she tries to assure her husband that, in spite of her distress, things will get better. Some officers in black regiments consistently reported slave owners' abuse of soldiers' wives and children to their superiors, usually asking what they should do about it. And when the soldiers' families escaped to be with their husband or father, officers noted "we cannot raise enough for them to eat."

Paris Mo Jany 19, 1864

My Dear Husband I r'ecd your letter dated Jan'y 9th also one dated Jany 1st but have got no one till now to write for me. You do not know how bad I am treated. They are treating me worse and worse every day. Our child cries for you. Send me some money as soon as you can for me and my child are almost naked. My cloth is yet in the loom and there is not telling when it will be out. Do not send any of your letters to Hogsett especially those having money in them as Hogsett will keep the money. George Combs went to Hannibal soon after you did so I did not get that money from him. Do the best you can and do not fret too much for me for it wont be long before I will be free and then all we make will be ours. Your affectionate wife

Ann

P.S. Sind our little girl a string of beads in your next letter to remember you by. Ann

The Valentines' friend, James Carney, who wrote the letter for Ann, included a note telling Andrew Valentine not to write too often and not to acknowledge that he had received letters from Ann. "Hogsett has forbid her coming to my house so we cannot read them to her privately. If you send any money I will give that to her myself. Yrs &c Jas A Carney."[174] As we have seen, soldiers' wives and lovers often relied on teachers in refugee camps or other Union-controlled areas to write for them. In Virginia, teacher Lucy Chase explains that she "laid aside my pen a moment ago" to write a letter from a young woman to her *"beau,"* probably a soldier, reminding him of their commitment to one another.

Feb 7 1863

My dear Dick: I hope you will not forget me, and I will not forget you. I am a lady of my word, and I hope you will prove to me that you are a gentleman of yours. I am doing very well on Craney Island. Don think that I dont think as well of you as you do of me. So I write to you, hoping that you will keep the same word you told me in Hampton, that you would not forget me, and that you would come and see me where ever I might be. I shall be a lady of my word, if you are not a gentleman of yours.[175]

Union soldier and companion, ca. 1863–1865

Lucy and Sara Chase not only wrote letters dictated to them by former slaves, but they also helped enslaved people send letters to family members written by slaves themselves. One such letter was written by Emma Bolt. She described a slave owner's depiction of "yankees," showing the type of scare tactics slave traders used to prevent enslaved people from escaping. We also see how eager former slave women were to practice their new writing skills and how important phonetics were to those learning to spell.

Norfolk, Va 1864

Norfolk is a Dole place three years ago I was Dasant [hesitant] to say that I was free but thank God i can say so now the man I lived with is named W W hall he says that Woebelong to him in hell and he says that he wishes that yankees was at the Devel when I came a way I Diden no my a b c he had sould my brothers and sisters and would have sould me and mother and father if he coud for he had us paced upsen in richmond to sell he sead that the Yankees had horns and thaer eyes was be hind them and thay had but one and . . . they us[e] to beat me this man was a negro byer he says before meny years he will be Doin the same bisniss he ses that the rebles will be her in may thank God that yankees come mond [Monday]he was goin to send us to richmond the next monday that Yankees come satday night he carad my brother away he sad that youal black that you all had for legs like a hors and had one eye before and one behind and a horn on each side

Emma Bolt [surname not clear][176]

When former slaves under Union protection tried to legitimize their marriages, the process was fraught with heartache and pain. The letter below shows that during the war, they made decisions based on their own values and needs. It seems Hannah Standing had been forced into a relationship with Willis Criss, who did not live on the same plantation as she did. Slaveholders generally preferred enslaved people to form intimate relationships with individuals living on other plantations, because they felt it gave them a better means of control: They could punish slaves more easily, without interference from spouses. However, Hannah and Jerimiah Standing had formed a relationship while working on the same plantation and considered themselves husband and wife, even though Criss insisted Hannah was his wife. In her letter to her family in New England, Lucy Chase included Hannah's letter requesting the help of Dr. Orlando Brown, surgeon and superintendent of Negro affairs in Virginia.

June 13, 1863

Upon one of the farms this letter was handed me for Dr. Brown.

Mr Willis Criss has been hear and wanted me to have him, and I don't want to have anething to do with him and I don't [want] him to come here whare I am. Mr Jerimiah Standing has been hear and has ben hear ever since last Cristmust on the place and I want to take him as my Husband and he has ben my husband ever since he has ben hear. I want to keep him as my husband. Mr Criss has ben hear and has threatened to kill my husband. I want you to keep him a way from hear and he does not belong to the farm at tall.

Hannah Standing [177]

In another instance of how the slave system's refusal to legitimize marriages created seemingly impossible problems as slavery was ending, teacher Elizabeth Botume tells of being approached by Sarah Barnwell, an elderly woman who needed a letter read in February 1865 "just after the surrender of Charleston." In her book, *First Days Amongst the Contrabands*, Botume describes her encounter with Sarah and her daughter-in-law:

"Well, Sarah, who do you think wrote this?"

"I spects it's William, ma'am. Him's wid de soldiers in Virginny."

"But have you no other sons?"

"You 'member, ma'am, I bin telling you . . . de rebels catch my biggest boy an' hang him for a spy. An' Martin, the next boy been sell off by de secesh, an de Lord know where him is ef him living."

"This letter is from Martin, Sarah."

After Sarah recovered from the shock that her son was alive, Botume learned that Jane Ferguson, Martin's wife had taken another husband, assuming that Martin was dead. Botume became perplexed: How could the situation be resolved? Martin's mother and his wife, however, had no such confusion. Jane was Martin's wife and that was the end of it.

"Why Sarah! Jane has another husband!" I exclaimed. She looked earnestly at me.

"Never mind, ma'am. Jane b'longs to Martin an' shell go back to him. Martin been a sickly boy and de secesh treat him too bad, an' we never 'spect him to lib t'rough all."

Just then Jane came in.

"Bless de Lord, gal!" said Sarah. "Martin is alive an' coming back to we."

"What will you do now, Jane?" I asked. "You have got another husband." She drew herself up, and said deliberately,

"Martin Barnwell is my husband, maam. I am got no husband but he. Wen de secesh sell him off we nebber 'spect to see each offer more. He said, 'Jane take good care of our boy . . . You see, ma'am, w'en I come here I had no one to help me. . . .

So Ferguson come . . . an' axed me to be his wife. I told him I never 'spects Martin could come back, but if he did he would be my husband above all others. . . . Martin is my husband, ma am, an' the father of my child; and Ferguson is a man. He will not complain. And we had an understanding, too, about it. And now, please, ma'am to write a letter for me to Ferguson—he was with the Thirty Fourth Regiment. I want to treat the poor boy well."

Botume explains that she "wrote the letter word for word as . . . dictated. It was clear and tender. But decided." Despite Jane's understanding, Ferguson was unwilling to give her up. In his response to Jane's "letter of divorce," he begged her to reconsider.

"Martin has not seen you for a long time. He cannot think of you as I do. O Jane! Do not go to Charleston. Come to Jacksonville. I will get a house and we will live here. Never mind what the people say. Come to me, Jane."

After listening to Botume read Ferguson's letter, probably written by the chaplain of the regiment, Jane instructed Botume to write one last letter to Ferguson.

"Tell him, I say I'm sorry he finds it so hard to do his duty. But as he does, I shall do mine, an' I shall always pray de Lord to bless him."[178]

Botume wrote a letter for Savannah, South Carolina, freed woman Peggy Owens, "exactly in her own words." Owens had been driven out of Savannah by a cruel master and fled with her husband, Caddy, to General William T. Sherman's army, then slashing and burning much of South Carolina on its way to North Carolina and then Virginia. The couple was sent from Sherman's army to a remote house in the Beaufort, South Carolina district, where they became ill and their baby died. In her letter, she informs her pastor and church community about her husband's more recent death.

Winter 1865

Father Cuffy Anderson,

I beg you to have praise in the church for me. Ask all the friends to pray for me, for I have lost my husband—am a lone woman. There is no one left for me now but God. I give my best love to all my fellow-servants. The morning before my husband, Caddy Owens, died, he called me to him and said, 'Peggy, I was in a house last night not made with hands, -a big white house. I am going to leave you gal, but I ain't going to fret 'bout you, for we been fight together a long time, and you'll brush on till you come to me. . . . I'm going now, gal, but don't fret. When I git up there I'll prepare a place for you.' I cried, 'O boy, don't leave me all alone! But he just laid back and folded his hands, and looked up to heaven and smiled. Oh, Father Cuffy! he didn't die but he sleeps.

Peggy Owens[179]

Fannie, a woman who remained in slavery in Texas, probably dictated the letter below to her husband, Norfleet, who was serving as the personal servant to the son of his slave owner. The letter was possibly written by the slave owner's seventeen-year-old daughter, meaning that Fannie would have been careful about expressing all of her sentiments. But, like so many enslaved men and women, she is able to express her love and commitment, a discreet counter to one justification for enslaving people of African descent. According to racial ideology, Africans lacked human emotions and thus, as Thomas Jefferson and others claimed, could be separated from kin.

Spring Hill, [Texas] Dec. 28th 1862.

My Dear Husband,

I would be mighty glad to see you and I wish you would write back here and let me know how you are getting on. I am doing tolerable well and have enjoyed very good health since you left. I haven't forgot you nor I never will forget you as long as the world stands, even if you forget me. My love is just as great as it was the first night I married you, and I hope it will be so with you. My heart and love is pinned to your breast, and I hope yours is to mine. If I never see you again, I hope to meet you in Heaven. There is no time night or day but what I am studying about you. I haven't had a letter from you in some time. I am very anxious to hear from you. I heard once that you were sick but I heard afterwards that you had got well. I hope your health will be good hereafter. Master gave us three days Christmas. I wish you could have been here to enjoy it with me for I did not enjoy myself much because you were not here. . . . Mother, Father, Grandmama, Brothers & Sisters say Howdy and they hope you will do well. Be sure to answer this soon for I am always glad to hear from you. I hope it will not be long before you can come home.

Your Loving Wife
Fannie[180]

A significant number of women in refugee camps were able to write directly to their soldier husbands. Writing from Fernandina Beach, Florida, an area occupied by the Union forces since March 1862, Emma Steward tells her husband, Solomon Steward, of the death of their daughter and her own near starvation. Though the recruits were promised allotments and rations of food for their families, government provisions were often in arrears or insufficient.

Fernandina, Florida, February 8, 1864

My Dear Husband:

This Hour I Sit Me Down To write you In a Little world of sweet sounds. The Choir In the Chapel near Here are Chanting at The Organ and Thair Morning Hymn are sounding and The Dear Little birds are joining Thair voices In Tones sweet and pure as angels whispers. But My Dear a sweeter song Than That I now Hear and That Is the song of a administering angel Has Come and borne My Dear Little babe To Join with Them. My babe only Live one day. It was a Little Girl. Her name Is alice Gurtrude steward. I am now sick in bed and have Got nothing To Live on. The Rashion That They Give for six days I Can Make It Last but 2 days. They don't send Me any wood. I dont Get any Light at all. You Must see To That as soon as possible for I am In want of some Thing To Eat.

All the family send thair love to you. No more at pressant

Emma Steward [181]

By late 1864, black soldiers began collecting their children with even greater certainty of the outcome of the war. In a letter to his daughters, former Missouri slave Spotswood Rice explained that he would come to get them in the company of about 1,600 black and white troops. Rice then wrote to Kittey Diggs, the woman who owned his daughters, informing her that her ownership of his children would soon be at an end.

[Benton Barracks Hospital, St. Louis, Mo. September 3, 1864]
My Children I take pen in hand to rite you A few lines to let you know that I have not forgot you and that I want to see you as bad as ever now my Dear Children I want you to be contented with whatever may be your lots be assured that I will have you if it cost me my life on the 28th of the mounth. 8 hundred White and 8 hundred blacke solders expects to start up the rivore to Glasgow and above there thats to be jeneraled by a jeneral that will give me both of you when they Come I expect to be with, them and expect to get you both in return. Dont be uneasy my children I expect to have you. . . . Your Miss Kaitty said that I tried to steal you But I'll let her know that god never intended for man to steal his own flesh and blood. . . . And I want her to remember if she meets me with ten thousand soldiers she [will] meet her enemy I once [thought] that I had some respect for them but now my respects is worn out and have no sympathy for Slaveholders. And as for her cristianantty I expect the Devil has Such in hell You tell her from me that She is the frist Christian that I ever hard say that aman could Steal his own child especially out of human bondage . . . now my children I am a going to close my letter to you Give my love to all enquiring friends tell them all that we are well and want to see them very much. . . . I you father have a plenty for you when I see you Spott & Noah sends their love to both of you Oh! My Dear children how I do want to see you

[Spotswood Rice][182]

To his daughters' slave owner, Rice writes:

"I received a leteter from Cariline telling me that you say I tried to steal to plunder my child away from you now I want you to understand that mary is my Child and she is a God given rite of my own and you may hold on to hear as long as you can but I want you to remembor this one thing that the longor you keep my Child from me the longor you will have to burn in hell and the qwicer youll get their for we are now making up a bout one thoughsand blacke troops to Come up tharough and wont to come through Glasgow and when we come wo be to Copperhood rabbels and to the Slaveholding rebels for we dont expect to leave them there root neor branch but we thinke how ever that we that have Children in the hands of you devels we will trie your [virtues?] the day we enter Glasgow I want you to understand kittey diggs that where ever you and I meets we are enmays to each orthere I offered once to pay you forty dollars for my own Child but I am glad now that you did not accept it Just hold on now as long as you can and the worse it will be for you . . . now you call my children your pro[per]ty not so with me my Children is my own and I expect to get them and when I get ready to come after mary I will have bout a powrer and autherity to bring hear away and to exacute vengencens on them that holds my Child you will then know how to talke to me I will assure that and you will know how to talk rite too . . . I have no fears about getting mary out of your hands this whole Government gives chear to me and you cannot help your self

Spotswood Rice[183]

Letter from Union soldier Spotswood Rice to Kittey Diggs, the woman who owns his children, 1864

Maryland fugitive Grandison Briscoe escaped with his pregnant wife, infant child, and mother to Washington, D.C., a few days before the enactment of the District of Columbia Compensated Emancipation Act of April 16, 1862. Within days, a slave catcher recaptured Briscoe's family and returned them to slavery in Maryland. Almost two years later, Briscoe, now a private in the Union army, describes his family's fate in an affidavit to federal officials.

[Washington, D.C.] 6th day of February 1864 Grandison Briskoe being duly sworn says he is about 25 years of age was born in Maryland & has been married to his wife since 1861 Came to reside with his wife in this City in April—4th day of April 1862 & has resided in said City Since that period of time except a part of the time he has been in the Service of the United States all the time & now in Said Service in Virginia— That his wife & his mother were taken away from Washington in April (on the 7th day) 1862 & as fugitive Slaves & taken to Piscatawa to Broad Creek to their master's [farm?] whose name is John Hunter & My mothers masters name was & is Robert Hunter—They were both taken to the barn & severely whipped Their clothes were raised & tied over their heads to keep their screams from disturbing the neighborhood & then were tied up & whipped very severely whipped and then taken to Upper Marlborough to jail My wife had a Child about nine month's old which was taken from her & died soon after. Some six of eight months after my wife was imprisoned she had a Child but the inhuman master & mistress though the[y] knew she was soon to be Confined or give birth to a Child made no arrangements provided no Clothing nor anything for the Child or mother I have sent them Clothing & other articles frequently until the first or near the first of January 1864 Since which the new jailor has refused to allow them to receive any thing from me

They have been in prison for the Crime of Coming to Washington to reside, ever since about the fourth of April 1862 now a year & ten months. They are confined in Jail at Upper Marlborough Prince George's County Maryland

Grandison Briscoe[184]

Mothers and wives of soldiers actively engaged in protesting the Union government's policy of paying black soldiers less than white soldiers. Rosanna Henson's letter to President Lincoln is one of many letters written by wives of soldiers explaining how the government's unequal pay for black soldiers caused suffering to their families.

Mt Holly [N.J.] July 11 1864

Sir, my husband, who is in Co. K. 22nd Reg't U.S. Cold Troops. (and now in the Macon Hospital at Portsmouth with a wound in his arm) has not received any pay since last May and then only thirteen dollars. I write to you because I have been told you would see to it. I have four children to support and I find this a great struggle. A hard life this!

I being a cold [colored] woman do not get any State pay. Yet my husband is fighting for the country. Very Resp'y your

Rosanna Henson[185]

Buffalo July 31 1863

Excellent Sir

My good friend Says I must write to you and she will send it   My Son went in the 54th regiment, I am a colored woman and my Son was Strong and able as any to fight for his country and the colored people have as as much to fight for as any, My father was a Slave and escaped from Louisiana before I was born more forty years agonee I have but poor education but I never went to School, but I know just as well as any what is right between man and man. Now I know it is right that a colored should go and fight for his Country, and so ought to a white Man, I know that a Colored Man ought to run no greater risques than a White, his pay is no greater. his obligation to fight is the Same. So why should not our enemies be Comp=elled to treat him the Same, Made to do it.

My Son fought at Fort Wagoner but thank God he was not taken prisoner, as many were

Wives and mothers also protested the Confederate army's refusal to take black Union soldiers as prisoners of war. Black soldiers were either enslaved or shot on the battlefield. Unaware that the president would issue a statement of retaliation for this practice the very next day, Hannah Johnson, whose son was part of the 54th Massachusetts Volunteer Infantry Regiment, tells President Lincoln to make sure that black soldiers are treated the same as white soldiers not only with their pay but also as prisoners of war. She also instructs Lincoln on the immorality of slaveholding.

Buffalo [N.Y.] July 31 1863

Excellent Sir My good friend says I must write to you and she will send it My son went in the 54th regiment. I am a colored woman and my son was strong and able as any to fight for his country and the colored people have as much to fight for as any. My father was a Slave and escaped from Louisiana before I was born morn forty years agone I have but poor edication but I never went to schol, but I know just as well as any what is right between man and man. Now I know it is right that a colored man should go and fight for his country, and so ought a white man. I know that a colored man ought to run no greater risques than a white, his pay is no greater his obligation to fight is the same. So why should not our enemies be compelled to treat him the same, Made to do it.

My son fought at Fort Wagoner but thank God he was not taken prisoner, as many were I thought of this thing before I let my boy go but then they said Mr. Lincoln will never let them sell our colored soldiers for slaves, if they do he will get them back quck he will rettallyate and stop it. Now Mr Lincoln don't you think you oght to stop this thing and make them do the same by the colored men they have lived in idleness all their lives on stolen labor and made savages of the colored people, but they now are so furious because they are proving themselves to be men, such as have come away and got some edication. It must not be so. You must put the rebels to work in State prisons to making shoes and things, if they sell our colored soldiers, till they let them all go. And give their wounded the same treatment. It would seem cruel, but their no other way, and a just man must do hard things sometimes, that shew him to be a great man. They tell me . . . you will take back the Proclamation, don't do it. When you are dead in Heaven, in a thousand years that

action of yours will make the Angels sing your praises I know it. Ought one man to own another, law for or not, who made the law, surely the poor slave did not. So it is wicked, and a horrible Outrage, there is no sense in it, because a man has lived by robbing all his life and his father before him, should he complain because the stolen things found on him are taken. Robbing the colored people of their labor is but a small part of the robbery their souls are almost taken, they are made bruits of often. You know all about this

Will you see that the colored men fighting now, are fairly treated. You ought to do this, and do it at once, Not let the thing run along meet it quickly and manfully, and stop this, mean cowardly cruelty. We poor oppressed ones, appeal to you and ask fair play.

Hannah Johnson[186]

For black civilians, things got worse on the home front. Not surprisingly, soldiers' families experienced constant stress. Wives, parents, and children worried about the soldiers' safety and about their own financial survival. In her letter to President Lincoln below, Jane Welcome asks that her son be released from the army so that he could care for her.

Carlisles [Pa.] nov 21 1864

Mr abarham lincon I wont to knw sir if you please wether I can have my son relest from the arme he is all the subport I have now his father is Dead and his brother that wase all the help that I had he has bean wonded twise he has not had nothing to send me yet now I am old and my head is blossoming for the grave and if you dou I hope the lord will bless you and me if you please answer as soon as you can if you please tha say that you will simpethise I the poor thear wase awhite jentel man told me to write to you Mrs jane Welcom if you please answer it to

he be long to the eight rigmat co a u st collard troops mart welcome is his name he is a sarjent

[Jane Welcome][187]

President Lincoln forwarded Mrs. Welcome's letter to the Bureau of Colored Troops, which informed her that "the interests of the service will not permit that your request be granted." Familial concerns were compounded by political concerns for African Americans. Like the families of military personnel everywhere, black soldiers' wives and other family members lived in constant anxiety, not knowing from day to day if their loved ones were dead or alive. Three months before the war ended, Sarah Brown wrote from Philadelphia to Secretary of War Edwin M. Stanton to learn if her husband and his cousins were dead. She and his cousins' wives had not heard from their spouses for more than a month.

Philad February 8th 1865

Honl Sir I am in great trouble of mind about my husband it is reported that he is dead he has been gone over a year and I have not hear from him his name is Samuel or Sandy Brown Co. C. 25th regiment U.S. Colored Troops Penn he went with his brother and five cousins to list they are all in same Co. and regiment none of them have been heard from only reports that they were dead which causes their wifes great grief. You will be doing charity by letting us know there whereabouts if alive so that we may write to them. Their names are Samuel or Sandy Brown Co. C. 25th regt Daniel Brown. Asa Miller. Daniel Horsey. George Horsey. Samuel Horsey George H. Washington. . . . We have not received a cent from them since they left we are all bad off it would do us a great favor if you would give the information as soon as your time will permit I am your obedient servant

Sarah Brown[188]

In great contrast to the experience of most people of African descent, the Ellisons of Stateburg, South Carolina, and their extended family in Charleston, continued to correspond about both serious and mundane matters during the war. On December 5, 1861, William Ellison Sr. died. Though he and other family members had considered leaving the state, only the children of William Jr. left South Carolina just before the war. The Ellisons, Johnsons, Westons, and others would have raised suspicion even if they had been successful in disposing of their extensive property holdings in a short span of time. In the letter below, free black (mulatto) tailor James D. Johnson, whose son was married to Ellison Sr.'s daughter, Eliza Ann, expresses condolences to the Ellison family on the death of their father and patriarch.

Charles[ton] Decr 9th, 61

Dear Friend

... with feelings of the Deepest condolence [in y]our recent affliction in the loss of my Esteemed friend your father. I take up my pen to write you these few lines hoping they may find you enjoying the Blessing of health and all of family also. I was in hopes of seeing your Dear Father before he breathes his last in this world, but alas! little did I think that I would have been deprived of the Brother William and all of the family and that I deeply simpathise with them in their affliction. My Wife is deeply Distressed on account of the death of your Father and with the exciting times down her on account of the war, that I am almost afraid she will become distracted & therefore am very sorry but I am compelled to send you some things for [from?] her by the R.R. to day. I hope you will receive them for me in good order as I send them. Northing more at present & remain your Esteemed friend

J.D. Johnson[189]

Though hardly representative of most free blacks, even among the elite, the Ellison brothers grew food for their family, friends, and community and thrived financially because of their contract to supply food for the Confederate army. Below, Ellison family member Louisa Weston writes to her brother-in-law, Henry Ellison, in Stateburg, thanking him for the corn he sent to her and apologizing for not being able to send salt, a precious commodity in those years. She also shares news about family and friends in Charleston. News of the death of Jacob Weston, a free mulatto elite who, like William Ellison Sr., had been a slave and became a slaveholder, would have particularly saddened the Ellison family.

Charleston March 23 [18]64

My Dear Brother

This will acknowledge the receipt of the corn sent for which accept my thanks and would herein express my regret that I was unsuccessful in getting the salt off to you. Mr Johnson apprised me about sunset of his intentions to go to Stateburg, and I had just gone to see Martha at the time. I returned home a little after dark, and started immediately to his house, requesting him to call in the morning for the salt. He said it would be out of his power to stop, as he was going up King St road. I returned home and strove my best to get a dray but it was too late. I could not succeed. . . . I however trust God willing to get up there in about 3 or 4 weeks time and if that time will suit, I will bring it up myself.

I hope you are well and that your Brother has recovered. Your kind Sister and our Dear Tilda, I hope are quite well. Mr Weston was quite indisposed when I left the country. The girls are both well together with myself. I am sorry to inform you of the Death of our Friend Mr Jacob Weston, who Died last night of Paralysis [probably a stroke]. . . . Excuse this scrall and believe me as ever

your sister

Louisa P Weston[190]

Unlike Louisa Weston's life, Emma Brown's life would change significantly soon after the Confederacy attacked Fort Sumter. However, in her letter, dated three days before the war began, Brown appears unaware of the major events swirling around her. Brown, who had entered Oberlin College in spring 1860 at sixteen years of age, continues her correspondence with her friend Emily Howland. She shares her current reading interests and excitement about having access to a significant library collection. Like other students, especially black students, who had to contend with the burden of racism, even at Oberlin, Brown suffered from stress, which manifested itself in the form of headaches and insomnia.

Oberlin, Ohio, April 9, 1861

Dear friend:

Your last letter accompanied by the sleeves came some weeks ago, for both I thank you, also for the package you sent by Miss Searing. I wanted to write some time ago, but have not been very well. This must be my apology. Mother thinks I can stay in Oberlin until next fall. I am glad of this. I shall return your kind loan pretty soon. I did hope to return it with this letter but was disappointed.

I have been reading Carlisle's "Sator Resartus." Have you read it? What a strange thing it is. I have all the books I want from the library. The members of the Ladies Society get them for me. There are two of these Societies; in August they have an exhibition, at which time several ladies read essays. I was invited to join and read next summer, but refused. I guess I have enough of reading essays at exhibitions.

I am compelled to stop. I am ashamed of this letter, but I despair of being able to write a better one. I am too nervous to write.

Yours sincerely
Emma[191]

Emma V. Brown,
ca. 1874–1876

Three years later, now a teacher in Washington, D.C., Emma writes again to Emily. She refers to school trustee Dr. Daniel Breed, who was instrumental in getting her a position at the school for Black students on Capitol Hill, and to significant events of the war. Two of her references were on the minds of many African Americans at the time: Confederate General Jubal Early's attempt to attack Washington, D.C., and Confederate Lieutenant General Nathan Bedford Forrest's attack on Fort Pillow in April, which resulted in the savage murder of black troops after they had surrendered, now known as the Fort Pillow Massacre. Still under stress, this time likely due to the difficulties of teaching 130 pupils in one room, Brown reveals the dilemma of educated nineteenth century women with few career choices.

Georgetown, [D.C.] July 18, 1864

Dear friend:

I have not seen you since I have been teaching in Washington. Dr. Breed offered me the Corporation school and I felt that I should like to help establish the first district i.e. colored school. We have had an average attendance of one hundred and thirty pupils. There is only one room for this multitude. Miss Perkins prefers to have the primary department. She teaches from the charts you gave. Her scholars recite in concert and I must have my classes at the same time. We have a regular Bedlam.

This is hard work—it has been too hard for me and Dr. Breed closed the school a week earlier than he intended because I was too sick to teach longer. I gave completely out.

Would you believe that I hate teaching now? I grow sick at the very thought of going back to teaching. I can scarcely realize that I who loved teaching so dearly should feel so. Dr. B. is kind and considerate, Miss P. I am devoted to, she is a faithful friend and an excellent teacher, the children have been good, yet the mere thought of going back to that school makes me sick.

I must work—there is no alternative, yet it is not right to teach with this feeling. What shall I do? How can I overcome this loathing, this hatred of teaching?

I have boarded in Washington but am at home now. The enemy made a daring attempt recently. Many of our citizens were alarmed. I did not believe they could get in. Is it not a shame that W. is so poorly defended? The rebels are far more solicitous about Richmond. The rebels are so daring, so courageous that were it not for the remembrance of Fort Pillow I fear I should be a sympathizer.

Yours ever,
E.V. Brown [192]

Like many teachers, Emma Brown had little personal time of her own. She seems to have spent nearly every moment working with the freedpeople. Brown also served as secretary to the Auxiliary Freedmen's Relief Association in Washington, D.C.[193] Whether African American teachers lived in the North or the South, their personal lives were complicated in many ways by their own particular teaching situation. Rosetta Douglass, a graduate of Oberlin College's "Young Ladies Preparatory" department and the daughter of Anna Murray Douglass and Frederick Douglass, found it hard to live under the constraints of Philadelphia's Black middle-class community standards when she was rooming with caterer Thomas J. Dorsey and his family, who demanded she demonstrate the utmost propriety. Douglass describes her loneliness and her despair that her hostess did not trust her ability to judge the character of new acquaintances, independently stop for tea with Mrs. Dorsey's sister-in-law, explore the city unaccompanied, or find herself a teaching position.[194]

My Dear Father:

To night your letter has reached me. You cannot imagine how grateful I was to receive it for I need something to cheer me for I am gloomy. I thank you so very much for reminding me I have a home and parents to come to. I did not know I could be so unhappy and friends so false or at least unkind but six weeks have shown me. To night for the first time in my life have I ever heard anything detrimental to my character and I ought not be so surprised if I would consider the source and know I am amidst slanderers. Since I have been here I have felt more or less ostracized.

Mrs Dorsey told me to night that I was a *street runner* and used some pretty harsh language she said that my father had told her that she was to keep me from the boys, and said it to me before a room full of folks and it sounded quite badly that you should send me here but that I must be kept from the boys as if that was my particular failing and she was to watch me. Now the reason for her passion, twice since I have been [here] I went out walking by myself so as to feel at home in the city and feel a little independent and also because Mr Dorsey who is quite genial told me he would like to see me go out and walk that I staid in the house too much.... So yesterday afternoon I dressed myself and told Mrs Dorsey I was going out for a walk. I went out and called on a Miss Gordon a young lady who had previously made me a call after stopping she ask to accompany in a walk and show me part of the city. I accepted and we went and she came around by Mrs Dorsey's and left me at the door before tea time.... Mr Dorsey appeared to be much pleased Mrs Dorsey was out. About noon today I went out to mail a letter of course I did not think it necessary to tell Mrs Dorsey I was going out though I might have done so if I had thought. I mailed my letter and found my way to Mrs William Dorsey's who was glad to see me as I had been there but once since my arrival she had wondered why I had not been and prevailed upon me to stay to dinner. I did so and got back before tea and now Mrs Dorsey called me a *street runner?* I asked what she meant by that term and she said I knew devilish well or something to that amount for words of that kind escape her lips often.... I never had any one speak to me in that manner before.... I should not have minded it so much if she had not spoken before strangers in that manner.... I am surprised and grieved with those around me Mr Dorsey I like very much. Mrs Dorsey is tyrannical.... You and Mother are satisfied

of my capacity to take care of myself now I see no reason why others should doubt it and I had no idea of being a hermit. . . . There are plenty of young ladies who are ready and willing to take me about but Mrs Dorsey will not allow it and would treat them in such a way they dare not approach . . . if I go I go at the risk of another outburst of temper and . . . that is something Mother and yourself never did if you were satisfied that those with whom I went were respectable. . . .

Miss Ada Minton's coming tomorrow to ask me to go walking with her. I do not know how Mrs Dorsey will receive her but I am fearful of an explosion. But two gentlemen have called and they have called twice, Mr Minton the young man and Mr Catto a teacher in the school both times they came and asked for me the family did not like it and they are respectable, too. I anticipated so much pleasure in an innocent way and nothing but unhappiness has followed. . . . For as to my running the streets that is all nonsense for every time I have been out has been with her [Mrs. Dorsey] excepting the couple of times I have already mentioned. All the time I am here I feel in bondage for I must not even go out which is necessary to get out at least to try and negotiate for a school. Mrs Dorsey does not wish me to go out unless I tell her when I am going and where I am going I am willing to tell her *when* but I wish people to think me capable of going just *where* is right. That is more than Mother and yourself have required of me to always tell *where* I am going. After this I never expect to visit any Colored family who make such great pretentions. . . . O cannot tell all that experience I have had in my six weeks sojoun here. I try never to complain unless there is some cause I have ample cause here. . . .

I would like to come home but feel ashamed because I did so very much wish to get a school and pay my board and I then could feel independent but a school here I cannot get. . . .

Please give my love to my mother and the boys. Much love to yourself

> Yours affectionately
> Rosetta Douglass

Father please write soon. Are there to be any meetings in New York in May if so are you going? I might wait until then, if best.

> Your affectionate daughter
> RD[195]

Rosetta Douglass left the Dorsey home, enrolled in the Salem Normal School in Salem, New Jersey, and finally secured a teaching position after receiving her license to teach. This time she roomed with family—her mother's brother and his wife, Perry, and Elizabeth Murray, who had left Maryland immediately after the war began. Her living arrangement, however, improved little. First, the family was barely able to support themselves, and second, "Aunt Lizzy," like Mrs. Dorsey, proved overly concerned with community perceptions and resented Rosetta's sense of independence. Perhaps because of Frederick Douglass's fame, Rosetta faced constant gossip about her and her family. The rumors were often vicious, with no basis in fact, and sometimes confused the Douglass family and with that of William Wells Brown, another fugitive slave. Rosetta tried to ignore the rumors but feared they would prevent her from getting a teaching position. She soon moved out of her aunt and uncle's home, but before she did, her aunt and uncle threatened her physically. At this time, Aunt Lizzy and Uncle Perry were upset because Rosetta had challenged two Quaker women for denigrating children at a black school where she had taught before accepting the new position in Salem. Rosetta's letters indicate that her parents allowed their children to express their ideas and feelings at a time when children were urged to be silent. We also see that Rosetta was as resourceful as her mother—she took in sewing to supplement her teacher's income. Demonstrating her close ties to and constant communication with her parents, Douglass's letter expresses her frustrations to her mother and father.[196]

Salem September 24th, 1862

My Dear Father and Mother:

I anxiously awaited an answer to my last letter and last evening was greeted with one. It found me in a new home. Father, your conjectures were right when you supposed my home with Uncle was growing unpleasant. My reason for not saying much of them lately was because I . . . did not wish to utter any more complaints for two reasons, 1st because I told you much of my disappointment in Philadelphia that I thought if I began to utter more from here you would begin to think me a great-faultfinder and 2nd I was anxious to obtain this situation since I was from home to make a beginning when if I should come home and I should want to get another place I would

have money to start out with without calling on you for I thought if I was not successful after having asked you to give me a little start you would not feel like risking again so that I was determined to make one desperate effort even if I did undergo a few hardships though when I begin to communicate these trials they will appear trifling to those you have undergone. I am now with a family of the name of Gibbs. . . . During my stay in Uncle's family they never exacted board from me nor from the time I went there until I left. When I had money the most of it went in the family. If I had not done so I should many times have gone supperless to bed as Uncle is busy paying for his house and his family were obliged to just live on as little as possible. When I went there I found they had just one towel and every body used it I could not get use to that. I bought three towels. I found that while I was going to bed the rest remained in the dark and as I usually take my time when I am in my room I was often hurried so that I bought myself candles which the family used also and so I went on getting little things when I had money only saving enough for myself to buy my paper and ink and postage stamps and thread. This I considered with what sewing I could do would go towards my board see the money that I made in my little school last summer amounted to nearly ten dollars. All went in the family except what I spent for my paper and stamps so that I feel I have been more a help than a hindrance to them and the $11 you sent and they tell I have done more for them than Uncles own daughters, that is the reason I did not say anything about the board money.

But towards the end my reasons for becoming disconsolate are these. Uncle's wife was repeatedly asking me questions about my former habits she had heard I was not altogether what I should be. I was driven from my home on account of my growing intimacy with men and again on account of my quarrelsome disposition towards my mother that there was some minister had come from Rochester who was acquainted knew of you having been obliged to send me away and some Lucy Oliver from New Bedford had said I was in New Bedford living as our Martha Fletchers but had gone on living from there and

my father had come and removed me. He had taken much pains with my education having taken me to England for that purpose. This part of the story I knew who was meant Mr Brown's daughter I supposed the girl meant. I was questioned had I been in New Bedford did I know the Fletchers. I told them yes New Bedford was my birth place but I left when but little more than a baby. I knew Mrs Fletcher that was a lady of respectability living there but I was too small to have any recollection of her that was enough I had been in New Bedford knew of Mrs Fletcher. The fact is not believed that I left a mere child and the story goes. I wanted the school and I became a little frightened about these stories but did not heed them much as those circulating them I cared little for until some of the Quakers getting hold of some letter came and questioned me, where was thee from. Was thy father married to Perry's sister before he left slavery and many more inquisitive questions.

One day a lady and daughter called and talked about many things questioning mostly about my school in Claysville as those in that district were very low indeed the daughter said I wonder at thee going there to teach them. I told her I did not feel the least ashamed of the task admitting that they were of course much neglected and were quite low and degraded. She curled her lip she said I would not care to go to school with such children and would not be engaged in teaching them. She could not do it she was sure. I was quite indignant then and I tried to show as well as I could that much of degradation was owing to the whites. Much was said on both sides. A week or so afterwards Uncle who having heard the conversation repeated by someone else came home and told me he had not liked it. . . . I asked why but he could say no more. Did not think it was proper to say such things to persons who were our friends. . . . I told him I should certainly say what I thought when people speak so carelessly of Slavery. Well he says you cannot speak here. I saw he was cross and said many things concerning these stories about me, I need not mention here but I certainly did not wish to hear them and as soon

as I could conveniently proceeded to go to my room, when his wife jumped up and dodged me first one way and then another to prevent my going up stairs. . . . I seated myself and then waited patiently and seized another opportunity and started up when she followed accusing me of closing the door in her face and shook her fist in my face saying what she should do if I did it again. . . . I laughed and said you seem determined to have a little row with me Aunt Lizzy for I left you to escape and you have followed me here. I thought I had made a pretty mistake in the character of the household and if it were not that I was soon to be employed I would not have staid. I remained until now which is three weeks since the above happened. She did not wish me to go off then although I spoke of doing so. She said Uncle had promised himself if I left he should report it that I was saucy and was quite unruly as he went among those who had shown a friendly interest for me. She thought I had better leave quietly. . . . During this time three weeks she often persisted in my staying. She . . . was more exacting and overbearing than ever. . . . I [was] determined to find a place to board. I have done so, Monday she shook me as if I were a child and threatened to pitch me out doors and my washing after me. I was washing preparing to leave. . . . [the rest of the letter is apparently lost][197]

In her October 9, 1862, letter to her father, Rosetta Douglass shows that she had finally achieved the independence she craved. She describes how she had taken on more teaching responsibilities, and other work, to support herself and save her teacher's salary. She walked a mile and a half from her boarding place to her school, taught night school as well as day school, and made "a few cents at spare times by knitting edging and doing embroidery. . . . With my night school and knitting and embroidery, I can make sufficient pin money and save my salary which is my object."[198]

The exigencies of life remained constant during the war. Harriet B. Henson writes to successful businessman and prominent black abolitionist Jacob White Sr. concerning the burial of her niece. One of White's businesses owned and operated the Lebanon Cemetery, established in 1849 for the Philadelphia black community. After gaining their freedom in the late eighteenth and early nineteenth centuries, African Americans in the North almost immediately established their own cemeteries to avoid the indignity of having their family members segregated in plots for paupers and criminals. Henson, who had evidently purchased more than one plot, wants her niece to be buried close to her mother's grave.

August 19 1862

Mr. Jacob White

Office of Lebaner Cemetery Lombard St Philadelphia

Respected Sir

My little neice died quite suddenly and it is my wish to have her buried in my lot in Lebaner Cemetery, will you please by my special request [have] the grave to be digged there without my sending the deed as it is at present in Bordentown with the papers and it is not convenient to send it, will you have the other Babe put into the same grave first and the one that is to be buried tomorrow to be put on the top of the same grave. I mean the Babe of James Campbell that you was speaking to me about and with as little expense as possible, please not to let interupt my Dear Mothers grave by no means as there is plenty of room and I will call at your office and see you about the matter as soon as possible.

Very respectfully yours

Harriet B. Henson[199]

In the letter below, Dr. John Rapier Jr. writes to his father's youngest brother, James Thomas, a barber in St. Louis, about his strenuous work schedule while simultaneously revealing his great pride in becoming an officer. Noting that the number of patients who died in his care was acceptable, based on the medical standards of the time, he hopes for a promotion to major in the spring. Rapier reported that white soldiers respected him as an officer, unlike their view of the other black physcans, just as they respected General Oliver Otis Howard, the highly regarded white Union army officer who became head of the Freedmen's Bureau in 1865. White soldiers, according to Rapier, did not treat him like a Pompey or Cuffe, derisive names slaveholders often gave to slave men. The District of Columbia area, though, had limited accommodations for African American "gentlemen." Besides commenting on the astounding work done by the teachers for the newly freedpeople, and a potential love interest, Rapier writes excitedly about the opportunity to meet and dine with Frederick Douglass and mentions a possible teaching appointment in D.C. for his cousin Sarah Thomas, Uncle Henry's daughter, who was teaching in Canada.

Freedman's Hospital Washington D.C.
Aug[ust], 19, [18]64

James P. Thomas Esq
St. Louis Missouri
Dear Uncle
Your letter of the 13th is before me. I had come to conclusion to "damn" you if I might use the expression—I am always glad to hear from you and our St Louis friends but I am a little afraid I will be considered as a very poor correspondent after awhile on account of the few letters I write— Indeed Uncle James I never worked so hard, and had so little rest, and felt so tired at night as I do now.

  Of my success and failures, for I have both, it does not become me to speak, for your satisfaction and of those others who kindly feel an interest in me, and my welfare, I may venture to say that my mortality

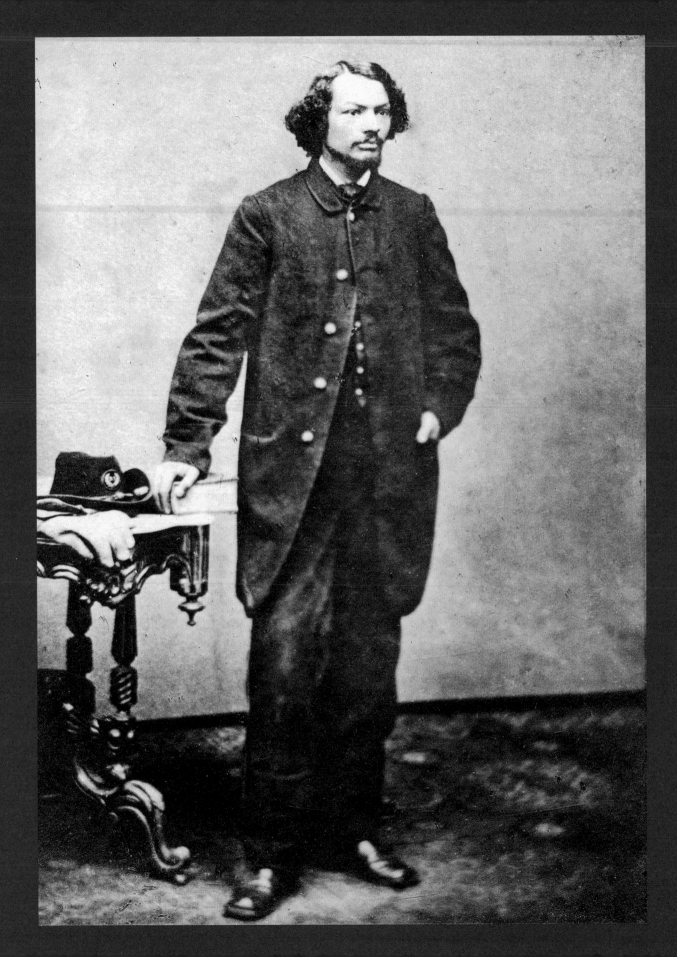

list so far stands approved by the Mid-Director of the Department to whom I make daily, weekly monthly and quarterly Reports—

There are many Ladies here from the East. blessed old Massachusetts always in the lead in good works engaged in teaching and general supervision of the interest of the Freedmen in this City—They are as a class the most indefatigable and earnest laborers I have ever seen engaged in any cause—Wind, Rain and Storm never stop them—Night and day these Angels of Mercy may be found engaged in the miserable filthy hovels of these poor people doing the most servile and menial duties

Foremost and bravest of these is a Miss Harritte Carter of Mass—Do not imagine Miss Carter to be an old and homely one who has [sighed?] for some one to love for many years in vain, and has taken up this occupation, perhaps as a penance for youthful indiscretion in saying "no" when somebody thought she ought to have said "yes"—By no means—Miss Carter is 24 with rosy cheeks, pretty eyes and [illegible] of the softest brown hair you ever felt, and as full of learning as an Episcopal Minister or a Catholic Priest and would make even Henry Green laugh at her humour and wit. She is never seen with a sober face—And in making my daily rounds I always encounter her, and have a half hour pleasant chat before I resume the duties of the day. I have but little time to visit and therefore have but few acquaintance, and these poorly cultivated—I am socially speaking a stick and take but little pleasure as you know in making new friends. I much rather presume upon those I know—

In our Hospital some changes have taken place—Surg Korner (white) supercedes Surg Powell (Col) The change was for the good of the service and I believe complexion had nothing to do with it—Surg. Korner is a skillfull and well educated Surg, and polite-agreeable gentleman— Dr. Powell is retained as Asst. I have thought of resigning in Oct for the purpose of attending Lectures in the University of Harvard in Boston and hoping for a Surgeon's Post in the spring—Perhaps I may perhaps I may not give up this idea—I am undecided—

On the 14th the most eventful event of my life occurred—I drew $100 less war tax 2.50 for Medical Services rendered the US

Union Army surgeon Dr. John Rapier, 1864

181

Government—My draft was in favour of "Acting Asst-Surgeon Rank 1st Lieut U.S.A. I read the address several times—I liked it—Tho' I confess it read strange to me—In the spring I want my drafts payable to Maj[or] John H. Rapier Surg U.S.A.

I do not like the U.S. Service—However half loaf is better than no loaf—It is better to have a blue coat than no military coat—I would rather have the Mexican Green or English Purple—But I must tell you Colored men in the U.S. uniform are much respected here and in visiting the various Department if the dress is that of an officer, you receive the Military Salute from the guard as promptly as if your blood was a [Oliver Otis] Howard . . . instead of Pompey or Cuffee's I had decided not to wear the uniform but I have altered my mind—And I shall appear hereafter in full dress gold, lace, pointed hat straps and all—

Mr Fred Douglass spoke here last night to an immense audience—and today the Pres—Sent for him to visit him in the Capitol—Did you ever hear such nonsense. The president of the U.S. Sending for a "Nigger" to confer with him on the State of Country—I have been invited to take supper with Mr Douglass to night—I am proud of it—He visited the Hospital today—He is a fine looking gentleman. He made a fine impression on the public. . . .

I have an opening here for Lady Teacher—pay depends on her qualifications it may be $50 or $30 per month—If I had the money I would send for Sarah—I believe she could get $50

If you go to New York come by Washington if you can—I am sorry I have not money in my pocket to offer you a big time—But wait until September 30th and I will do the clean thing by you—In all Washington there is not . . . a number one place for a Col'd Gentleman to stop—But I will fix you up—if you give "due and timely" notice—Write to me—Direct my letters John H Rapier M.D. Actg Asst Surg-U.S.A. Tell Mrs Baily I have written to her—Remember me to Mr Clamorgan and the Johnsons Mrs Pritchard & Mr Pritchard Write Soon I am as usual Yours

John Jr.[200]

The few extant intimate letters written by mid-nineteenth-century African Americans provide important insights into love and courtship under diverse circumstances. Elizabeth Botume and other teachers quickly found that some freedpeople expected their amanuensis to write letters with limited guidance from the sender. One Saturday afternoon, Botume, who like other Northern teachers tended to portray freedpeople as a kind of exotica, was met by a "party of young girls," each waiting with paper in hand to have letters written for them and requesting that Botume's colleague "Miss Fanny" write the letters as she "knew best what to say." One young woman instructed Fanny to write a not-too-romantic letter to her fiancé. Fanny was to state that "I 'member him sometimes. You mus' talk stiff but kind' a easy too." When Fanny read the letter back the young women shouted with delight, one exclaiming: "I tell you, writing-larning's a powerful thing."[201] Rather than have Fanny write her love letter for her, another young woman, according to Botume, "walked boldly to the table and said, 'Now I'm going to talk my letter. . . . I know jes' w'at to say.' " The young woman's letter follows.

To Mr. John Gardiner, orderly sergeant. . . . I can't forgit him, an' I 'specs him ain't forgit me. I stan' jes' where he lef me, an' I shall stan' there 'till he gits back; an' ef he never comes back, I shall stan' there still as long as I live.

One woman, Susannah, apparently determined to dissuade a suitor who had written to her, wanted her letter written last, so she sent the other young women away. Botume explains that the young woman gestured very low and raised her arms high while dictating her letter to make her point.

Sir, fur I don't call him my friend. Tell him he needn't exscuse fer writing, for I is more'n sprise to get his letters, sence he ain't no cause for writing of. I ain't know w'at he t'inks of me. Does he t'ink I is an apple way down on de groun', under his foot, that he can stoop down, [making a low gesture] an' pick up wid his hans' ? . . . I isn't that. I is an [apple] high up on de top branch ob de tree. I ain't fur drop in his mouth, an' he can't reach me wid his ban's [stretching her arms high above her head]. Ef he jump an' jump, till he jump his head off, he can't reach up to me. Susannah[202]

Contrary to Susannah's letter, most romantic letters express affection, love, desire, and longing. In a letter dated October 27, 1861, hired-out slave John Washington writes from Richmond to tell free-born Annie Gordon, still living in Fredericksburg, that he wants her to be his wife.

Richmond Oct 27th 1861

I seat myself to write you a few lines as I have a few . . . moment to think of you I was up to our Jim Gilki this evening to a fine dinner with Arthurs and some others we had a nice dinner and agreeable time of it. The report about Sarah is well known down her Now. of course I cant. Contredict it. So I let it go. I did hope for a letter from you Saturday but as it did not come, I can hardly expect one too-morrow for I never get you sweet letters before Tuesday or Wednesday. The air is quite bad her and it feels much like winter it makes me feel like a different man as time wines on and Christmas hastens. I wonder What you are doing Now. and I Wonder if You have any Company to cheer the lonesome hours. oh if I was home with you to-night how happy I should be I would endeavor to cheer thee. I think some times I will have a thousand little love storys to tell you when I come home. Wont we be happy together once more. for I think we might be married soon next year. I am really anxious to marry Now. more than ever. things that has been in the way heretofore can now be over come. I think my mind better settled and really want some one to call wife.

Annie Gordon Washington, 1880

John M. Washington, 1880

Three days later, John writes to Annie again reassuring her that his visits with friends mentioned in the previous letter did not mean that he was socializing with other women.

Wednesday night Oct 30th, Your sweet letter came to hand to-day and made my heart leap for joy for it always makes me happy to hear from you and I have been hoping for the last letter ever since Monday but I got it now. Do you really tries to scold me & what for I don't know. . . . I have not even been up to see Arthurs 3 times since I was up home. . . . I went to see the girls 5 or 6 times while they was here only for old acquaintance sake and bought 3 tickets to go and carry them to a party. But they did not go. . . . I did not speake to a Lady the whole night. For I did not know but one and that slightly. I played non. I admired non. That was my first party this year and will be my last. . . . Oh my own sweet Annie. I *know* you love me and I am so proud of it and it sends a thrill of joy to my heart when I think of my heart tells me, when you are unhappy and then I become anxious to hear why but your sweet letters tells me all

I think your fears groundless about my coming back to Richmond. I'd do most any thing first. . . . I must stop now for it is nearly 12 o clock and I have to stay on watch quite late now. . . . Good Night my Dearist

I am as ever
Your John[203]

The couple was married January 3, 1862, in Fredericksburg, only a few months before John's escape.

Six months after Confederate troops fired on Fort Sumter, Amelia Loguen indicates that she is interested in more than a casual relationship with Lewis Douglass when she expresses concern about his health. She writes to Lewis about an event in which both their famous fathers were involved: the rescue of fugitive slave William "Jerry" Henry in October 1851. Henry had been captured and was about to be returned to slavery under the Fugitive Slave Act of 1850. Amelia's father, Jermain Loguen, and other abolitionists rescued Henry and he was scurried off to Canada. Amelia also references a Reverend Wright, who helped Lewis's father escape from slavery.

Syracuse, [New York]
Oct. 3rd, 1861

My Dear Lewis:

I was very glad to Receive yours of Sept 29. I had expected a letter but had given up all hopes of ever hearing from you again, but when I learned of your sickness all was explained and I found myself mentally saying "poor Lew I am so sorry that he has been sick." How lonely you must have been during those long seven nights that you could not sleep, and had I known it- I should have been tempted to come and dispel in a slight measure their gloomy monotony; that is if it –were in my power so to do. Now you are so much better do take care of your-self, and I hope you may be very soon strong and healthy as ever.

I should like to propose something but-being confident-of, and at the same time disliking so much that gallant- "No, I could not-make it convenient- I refrain.

We last-week had a pleasant-visit from a Mr. Wright-of Washington Co. Pa. the same uncle Charlie that assisted your father on a certain occasion from Baltimore; you have doubtless heard him spoken of. A fine old man but- so funny, he would sit all day like an old lady and knit, -and when Sunday came he was ready to preach and sing. The Sunday night-that he was here I was very anxious to hear

him, but-as I was half way sick with the asthma, no one would give their consent-to my going out. All came home at-about half past eleven and gave me such a glowing description of the sermon that I resolved that if teasing would do any good I would be there the next-night-, and sure enough when the time came father said I might-go, and I was well paid for we had a regular methodist-shout."

I received your kind letter on the memorable 1st of October, and it was almost-provoking to think that it-should be so pleasant-, but had we "poor colored people" held a convention I do believe it-would have rained "pitch-forks and [hoe?]-handles" all day. On the quiet-evening of that beautiful day Memory and I took a pleasant stroll in the well-known past; ten long years have past but since Jerry was rescued. I was only eight then and yet I remember that day as distinctly as though it were but a short time ago. I can never forget the strange feelings that past over me, when I heard all the bells in the city tolling before we had heard what was the matter. I know many changes have taken place since that day, four dear ones who were then in the enjoyment of life and health are now silently sleeping their last long sleep. Some that we did not know then are now dear friends. I will remember the celebration held three years ago, how I did want to have a little chat with some one but alas! had not the courage. I had forgotten the first letter. "I do not say I wish I were or wish I were not: -you can't guess what that means and I will not tell you.

We are all quite well and I take it for granted that we all join in sending kind regards. My special regards to Charlie [Lewis's brother] and love to your mother. I want to hear from you but do not write if it tires you, but wait til you are stronger.

Yours truly and affectionately
Amelia[204]

In response to one of Amelia Loguen's earlier letters, Lewis Douglass wrote a lengthy description of how Amelia's greetings had changed from "Dear Brother" to "Dear Lewis" to "my own Dear Lewis." In the letter below, he exclaims, "I want to marry you simply because I love you."

Rochester, Sunday, Dec. 8, 1861

My Own Dear Amelia,

I have just finished reading all the letters I have filed, received from you, these are a great many letters from you that I must confess I took no account of, more than to read them and whatever became of them after that, I cannot tell. The first letter that I received from you is on file with the ones I have received more recently.

Those letters are remarkable, the meaning of many of them can be construed differently, we will take for example the first, it is as I have once before called it a "spunky letter,' it pretends that you the writer does not care a fig whether I remember you more than a week or not after you returned home from your visit to our house, and ends with "I am Your Friend." However sagacious you are in many things if you intended to show to me an independent spirit in that letter, you took exactly the wrong course, although in my answer to that letter I tried to make it appear that I understood the letter in its offensive sense. That letter gave me good grounds to hope that the dear little heart you professed to be afraid of losing might by me be found. The double dealing of that letter was to me and is a source of great pleasure. You will confess that the spunk of that letter was all sham and that there was no real spunk intended, that the spunk was a kind of blind for your real feelings which delicacy prevented you from expressing, so I understand your first letter. And as with the first so it has been with many others, the brother arrangement which was invented by you, was intended as another blind or disguise of your real feelings and to me another oasis in the desert of uncertainty of winning your love.

Through the medium of the mighty pen a love has grown up between us that baffles all description, and my prayer is that then may nothing arise that may in any way shake the firmness or overturn the foundation of our love which we have each made to know one another. It may be easy for you to find a man to love other than myself, but for me to find a lady more suited to my mind and love than my own dear Amelia, never!

How well I could enjoy my self were you here or I with you in Syracuse, but such is not the case and it may be well it is not so. Though a sweet kiss and fond embrace from you is something even to travel as far as Syracuse for. There is no language that can express the real joy of love experienced by me when on the Sunday evening after the family had all retired we sat together saying never a word for the reason that words could express nothing of the real sentiments of the hearts that were beating as one. Yes those were happy moments, can there be happier? Will not the familiarity of marriage blunt in a measure the real happiness of such moments, I trust not, yet we can see how others live who are married. There are some men however who marry because it is fashionable to be married not stopping to find whether he is in that blessed state love, and soon sickens of his companion in life and seeks pleasure in corner groceries and grog shops.

I want to marry you simply because I love you, and as my love for you has stood the test of nearly two years, and those years spent in absence from you and a portion of time not even having the pleasure of a letter from you. I base the hope on such a foundation that my love and your love may remain undying. Such should be the love of husband and wife.... Now my own dear Amelia... I shall leave off what may have been to you a decided bore to read. Remember me to everybody in the family and you who was first timid friend, then dear friend, dear sister, and last but by no means least my *own dear* Amelia . . . receive for yourself, the fullest and highest affection of a heart of Love overflowing for thee.

Ever thine in true Affection

Lewis[205]

Sergeant Major Lewis Douglass, 1863

Helen Amelia Loguen, ca. 1860s

Courtship at any time requires that couples reckon with certain exigencies of life—occupational and educational goals, for example. The demands and politics of the Civil War exacerbated such tensions, making it even more difficult for couples to focus mainly on each other. Studying to become a teacher, nineteen-year-old Amelia expresses "dread" about the yearly school examinations to Lewis. She refers to a Cincinnati crowd heckling and pelting white abolitionist Wendell Phillips when he connected the cause of war to slavery in a lecture at the city's Opera House in late March.

Syracuse April 10th/62

My Dear Lewis:

Pardon my negligence in allowing so many weeks to pass away without writing and accept this tardy letter. Your note of Apr. 8, has acted as a reminder, and I with pleasure write. Since I last wrote to you I have lost by death a dear aunt whose name was Marry Wills and her home was with my grandfather in Rusti Chautauque Co. N. Y. The Dr. called her disease Billious Fever, She died on the 10th of March. Father and Mother attended her funeral, leaving me to keep house and care for aunt Tinnie and little Tinnie who were both sick. I flatter myself that I did remarkably well considering.

Spring has brought with it as usual, the ever dreaded, yearly school examinations, *dreaded* because they are *so very tedious*. Monday I thought of nothing but Chloride of Sodium, Nitrate of Silver detection of arsenic, uses of Zin etc etc; Tuesday, Parlez-vous francais? Comment-vous appelez-vouz? And Je me porte tres bien, yesterday oh! terrible thought Plane Trigonometry: do you wonder then that last night I dreamed of being in France? After of trying to show that Chemistry is one of the most useful and interesting studies imaginable and lastly I was alone in some queer place trying to accertain the height of a "fort on a distant hill inaccessible on account of an intervening swamp." O! how refreshing on awaking this morning to know that all *such* is for a time past and that vacation is close at hand.

Quite a contrast in the reception of Wendall Phillips in Washington and the manner in which he was treated in Cincinnati, how filled up this world is with mean unprincipled men, will they ever be reformed? Prof. Porter is in town and his little lady is at some water cure East. Please let me know when your sister Rosa returns and I will write to her.

Give my love to your mother and believe me

Yours truly

H. Amelia Loguen[206]

A year later, Lewis Douglass enlisted with his younger brother Charles in the 54th Massachusetts Volunteer Infantry Regiment at Camp Meigs in Readville, Massachusetts. Within a week, Lewis was appointed sergeant major, the highest rank an African American could hold at the time. In addition to describing camp life, he continued to express his love for Amelia in letters written throughout his time in the war.

Camp Meigs, April 8 1863

Readville Mass

My Own Dear Amelia: I am once again the happy recipient of a good letter from you of whom I think so much. You wish me to tell you of camp life. I will after first stating that with the exception of a slight cold, I am enjoying good health. The first thing I did was to be examined by the surgeon to see if I was in any manner deformed, after which I was told to go to an officer whose business it is to take a description of my looks and then swear me in to the service. I'm promising to obey all orders from the President of the United States down. After taking the oath I proceeded to the Quartermasters department, there to receive my clothing, which consists of everything that "our sex" uses excepting a vest. My badge of office is three stripes placed on my coat in the shape of half diamond, and three circular stripes rounding off from the diamond somewhat like this [Lewis includes a drawing] on

each sleeve, and a wide stripe down the leg. After I was dressed I reported to the Adjutant who instructed me in my duties. We have every morning for breakfast over third of a six cent loaf of bread nearly a quart of coffee a large piece of fish or corn beef or ham as the case maybe. For dinner we have beef and potatoes and the same quantity of bread, sometimes bean soup at night constantly rice and molasses. The men sleep in barracks in bunks two in each. I not having my quarters prepared yet the weather being so stormy that there is building going on, I have to stop in the barracks along with the privates. The rules are that I shall have a room of my own with writing materials & which I hope soon to occupy. The soldiers amuse themselves by fighting each other, speaking up to the officers, for which they are immediately punished by chaining large balls of iron to them, or making them hold heavy weights for hours for striking a superior officer. Death is the punishment, yet in the face of this penalty one of the men knocked a Lieutenant sprawling the other night-and the Lieutenant's good nature would not allow him to report the rascal, for if he had he would have certainly been shot.

Thursday last I went into Boston and staid all night at some friends of mine. I attended a levee [reception] in the evening of colored people which was just nothing. I did not stay in the hall long having soon found out that there were "all sorts" present. I thought it would not be well for me to be known there. This morning we had an addition to our regiment of seventy-three men making our number five hundred and forty-eight. My dear girl I would like to have you occasionally send me a Syracuse paper or send to those young men who have come from Syracuse they will take it so kindly. And I shall tell them that you sent it. Direct all papers and letters to me as usual. The young men from Boston and New Bedford receive many little niceties from their friends which keep them in cheerful spirits.

I shall always love you, never give me up for dead until you are certain of it. My fear is that I may be reported dead when I am not, it is often the case in battle. Remember me kindly to your mother and father and sisters and Miss Lewis. Oh for our sweet kiss. Do not cry,

Every Lovingly
Lewis[207]

Consistently urging Amelia not to worry about whether he will survive the war, Lewis repeatedly explains that if he is killed, the sacrifice of his life is for a higher cause. The letter dated May 20, 1863, is an example: "My dear girl while I am away, do not fret yourself to death. Oh! I beg of you, do not. Remember that if I fall that it is in the cause of humanity, that I am striking a blow for the welfare of the most abused and despised race on the face of the earth, that in the solution of this strife rests the question."

After arriving with his regiment on the South Carolina coast in early June, Douglass describes the 54th Massachusetts Volunteer Infantry Regiment's role in the July 18 battle at Fort Wagner, during the war department's heavy assault on Charleston. Shortly after writing this letter, as a sergeant major Douglass would lead his men into battle and suffer a permanent injury.

Morris Island. S. C. July 20

My Dear Amelia: I have been in two fights, and am unhurt. I am about to go in another I believe to-night. Our men fought well on both occasions. The last was desperate we charged that terrible battery on Morris Island know as Fort Wagoner, and were repulsed with a loss of 3 killed and wounded. I escaped unhurt from amidst that perfect hail of shot and shell. It was terrible. I need not particularize the papers will give a better [description] than I have time to give. My thoughts are with you often, you are as dear as ever, be good enough to remember it as I no doubt you will. As I said before we are on the eve of another fight and I am very busy and have just snatched a moment to write you. I must necessarily be brief. Should I fall in the next fight killed or wounded I hope to fall with my face to the foe.

If I survive I shall write you a long letter. DeForrest of your city is wounded, George Washington is missing, Jacob Carter is wounded. The above are in hospital.

This regiment has established its reputation as a fighting regiment not a man flinched, though it was a trying time. Men fell all around me. A shell would explode and clear a space of twenty feet, our men would close up again, but it was no use we had to retreat, which was a very hazardous undertaking. How I got out of that fight alive I cannot tell, but I am here. My Dear girl I hope again to see you. I must bid you farewell should I be killed. Remember if I die I die in a good cause. I wish we had a hundred thousand colored troops we would put an end to this war. Good Bye to all Your own loving, Write soon   Lewis[208]

Douglass was so severely wounded at Fort Wagner that he was shipped to Manhattan for recovery in the fall. His African American physician and family friend, Dr. James McCune Smith, explained that Lewis was "too feeble" to be moved home to Rochester and that it would take months before he could "do even the lightest military duty." Lewis might live, according to McCune Smith, but he could never father children.[209]

The thought of only being a creature of the present and the past, troubled me, and I longed to have a future—a future with hope in it. To be shut up entirely to the past and present is abhorrent to the human mind; it is to the soul—whose life and happiness is unceasing progress.

FREDERICK DOUGLASS 1855[210]

PART THREE:

In the Aftermath of War

WITH THE MILITARY DEFEAT OF THE "WORLD'S MOST POWERFUL SLAVEHOLDING CLASS," the consequences of the Civil War emancipated and freed more slaves than abolition did in all other New World societies. The United States ended the legal right to own persons, eliminating human property valued at billions of dollars without compensating former slave owners and demanding that former slaves be paid for their labor. Within a few short years, the United States took the unprecedented action of making former slaves citizens of the nation, placing citizenship under federal jurisdiction and enfranchising all black men, former slaves and free.[211] Yet, the revolutionary nature of the Civil War and its consequences were thwarted by the very forces that had contributed to slavery. Actor and Confederate sympathizer John Wilkes Booth's assassination of President Lincoln on the evening of April 14, 1865, signaled the persistent resistance of those who, in both the North and South, intended to profit from black labor and maintain white supremacy at all costs.

The assassination of the president hit the nation like a ton of bricks. Having just experienced the upheaval of a four-year-long war, supporters of the Union cause, black and white, were in shock. A famous actor had killed the president of the United States. As the news spread that Easter weekend, Northern cities that had only two days before ecstatically celebrated Robert E. Lee's surrender at Appomattox now shrouded their buildings in black drapery and sounded more somber bells in mourning. When the president died from the gunshot early the next morning, city officials and clergymen held impromptu memorial services to help mourners grieve and comprehend the meaning of Abraham Lincoln's death.

Just back from the East Coast, where he had celebrated the Union victory, Frederick Douglass silently entered the packed, standing-room-only memorial service in Rochester City Hall. He was not included in the program, so he took a seat in the rear. But when the news surfaced that the famous abolitionist was in the audience, the crowd demanded to hear from the great orator. Shaken, like so many other Americans, Douglass explained that the occasion was not for speech-making but for "silence and meditation; for grief and tears." To loud applause, he insisted that Lincoln's death was not in vain. The "noblest man [to] trod God's earth, is struck down by the hand of the assassin, yet I know that the nation is saved and liberty established forever." Rather than focus on the assassin, Douglass blamed slavery for the president's death. Anticipating a conciliatory mood among many Republicans toward Confederates, he argued for vigilance in ensuring the future of a strong republic founded in freedom and equality for all Americans. "Let us not forget that justice to the negro is safety to the Nation." No man should be judged by his complexion, but "every man by his loyalty, and wherever there is a patriot in the North or South, white or black, helping on the good cause, hail him as a citizen, a kinsman, a clansman, a brother beloved. Let us not remember our enemies and disenfranchise our friends."[212]

Douglass articulated the feelings and goals of African Americans residing all over the country. Lincoln's death was a time for mourning and, simultaneously, for promoting the idea that the dead president had been committed to black citizenship and equality. There was no other way to define freedom. To be free meant to live as equals in a society that argued that liberty and equality were its foundational principles. Newly freed people specifically demanded the right to have a family, the right to own property, the right to be compensated for their labor, the right to participate politically as citizens, and the right to create communities that included schools, churches, and other organizations to nurture a vibrant and purposeful existence.

During wartime, the federal government had provided temporary food rations and living quarters to fugitive slaves and white refugees who came to Union lines. With the employment of tens of thousands of ex-slaves by army officials and the enlistment of more than 186,000 black soldiers (134,000 from the slave states), the government became more involved in providing relief for the soldiers' and military laborers' families, mainly at refugee camps, home farms, and government farms. Union officers assigned the able-bodied to work for private employers, generally planters or farmers who agreed to pay, house, feed, and clothe freedpeople and their non-working family members. Thus, those who remained in the refugee camps were young mothers, small children, and the elderly who could not work.

This was the situation at the end of war. Thousands of freedpeople were living either in refugee camps or on government farms, mostly in the Upper

South.[213] When the Union army no longer needed them, they survived as day laborers or by foraging or begging. Black Southerners mobilized to meet the needs of the destitute. In June 1865, residents in Memphis took care of more than two hundred indigent former slaves. In Augusta, Georgia, freedpeople raised money to establish a hospital and employ a physician. In Chattanooga, Tennessee, blacks formed a benevolent association and taxed themselves to aid the poor, the ill, and the orphaned, while blacks in Columbia, South Carolina, during and after the war, supported invalids through their "Church, Pension Society of Freedmen."[214]

In December 1865, the Thirteenth Amendment freed four million people from enslavement, and left them mostly without food, clothing, or any means to support themselves. Before his death, President Lincoln signed the Congressional bill establishing the Bureau of Refugees, Freedmen, and Abandoned Lands to assist people with their transition to freedom. Known as the Freedman's Bureau, agents of the organization would be involved in issuing food and clothing rations, supervising labor contracts between former slaveholders and former slaves, managing confiscated lands, and contributing to establishing schools, and legitimizing marriages. The records of the Freedmen's Bureau are filled with evidence of persistent conflicts throughout the South between freedpeople and those who refused to countenance the idea of black freedom. Even simple acts of independence could mean death.

Testimonials in the Freedmen's Bureau's records reveal how hard gaining their freedom was for many former slaves. In June 1865, in Texas, Charles Brown's former slaveholder, D. B. Whitesides, decided to kill his former slaves rather than recognize their freedom. When Brown responded "They tell me so master" when Whitesides asked him if he was free, Whitesides exclaimed that Brown's freedom would be of no benefit. He told Brown to run to the nearby woods as he counted to ten, but Brown took only a few steps before he was shot. Asking Brown if he was shot "good," Whitesides then declared, "it will learn you G--d niggers to put on airs because your free." When freedman Frank Frazier tried to help three women with three children escape from their former Georgian slaveholder in June 1865, dogs were set upon them. "The bridge across the lake was burned The dogs were pressing us hard. the bank was about fifteen feet high. I went down to the water as quick as I could. I climb down on the posts of the trestle work to the water, One woman threw down her child to me I caught it. This was her babe. She then threw down to me her little daughter about five years old I could not catch it and the current swept it away and it was drowned." Neither was Frazier able to catch a seven year old. "It was swept away and drowned." When helped by another escaping freedman, the mothers and the remaining child successfully got across the river.[215]

The Freedmen's Bureau, along with Northern aid societies, tackled the gargantuan task of addressing relief not only for blacks but also for nonslave-holding destitute whites. Having once been self-sufficient, many were reduced to tenancy and indebtedness. Southern white officials wanted relief only for whites, but the Freedmen's Bureau attended to everyone.[216] For example, in June 1865, military authorities in Richmond, Virginia, fed 940 freedpeople and nearly 8,500 white people. These numbers, as historian Steven Hahn and other editors at the Freedom Project note, were "far out of proportion to the city's roughly equal mix of black and white residents. In regions where yeoman farmers predominated, white recipients of relief often outnumbered their ex-slave counterparts many times over—as much as fifty to one in east Tennessee."[217]

Freedpeoples' utmost desire was to reunite with their families, a process that had begun with the coming of war. Having been once legally kinless, African Americans continued to define themselves, as they had always done in spite of slavery, as part of a family and a community. Husbands, wives, fathers, mothers, daughters, and sons traveled from camp to camp, town to city searching for family members. The searches, sometimes successful, lasted into the early twentieth century through advertisements placed in black newspapers and journals. Freedom meant the right to be in a family, the right to marry, and the right to name yourself. Often unknown to slaveholders, enslaved people had surnames. Those who did not have a surname immediately established one, rejecting the disparaging names given to them by slaveholders. The arbitrary power of slaveholders was revealed in how they named their human property. Rather than allow individuals to name themselves, or parents to name their children, some slaveholders gave enslaved men, especially, fanciful names or names from classical antiquity, such as Nero, Caesar, Scipio, or, most common, Pompey. These names were jokes—they were meant to humiliate. Anthropologist Susan Benson argues that these names were not names a slaveholder would give his or her child but to a pet—a dog—as a way to underscore the powerlessness of the individual named, to separate the individual from "real" human beings, to assert that the bearer of the name is "in another class altogether."[218] Once free, Pompey might name himself John or William, a name he viewed as indicating freedom or a name his kinfolk called him. Reflecting the adaptations to slavery, when so many families were separated, free families often included extended family members who were living in the community—their families didn't necessarily resemble the nuclear-family household of the white majority. As a consequence of enslavement and war, many former slaves were widowed and many children were orphaned. Freedom to be in a family also meant that mothers would prioritize children over working in a field. Large numbers of freed women temporarily withdrew from the workforce in the early days of emancipation.[219]

In addition to searching for their family, newly freedmen and women also immediately sought compensated work if they were not already employed. Aware that slave labor enriched individuals, the region, and the nation, they expected wages to be more than a mere symbol of black freedom. With savings from their wages, they would build homes, send their children to school, and establish churches and other institutions reflecting their interests. Freed people aspired to be independent from their former owners in all aspects of their lives.[220]

Above all, newly freedpeople expected to own or rent land. To them, land ownership defined economic independence. There were signs that land would be available either for purchase or for rent, or available as outright compensation for generations of toil. Just before the end of the war two prominent federal officials signaled the possibility of black land ownership. In January 1865, General William T. Sherman issued Special Field Order No. 15, granting thousands of acres along the Atlantic coast to freedpeople in lots of no more than forty acres per family. And in March 1867, Representative Thaddeus Stevens of Pennsylvania proposed redistributing land to former slaves and poor whites to pay for the war debt and transform Southern society into a region of small farms:

> Nothing is so likely to make a man a good citizen as to make him a freeholder. Nothing will so multiply the production of the South as to divide it into small farms. Nothing will make men so industrious and moral as to let them feel that they are above want and are the owners of the soil which they till. . . . No people will ever be republican in spirit and practice where a few own immense manors and the masses are landless. Small and independent landholders are the support and guardians of republican liberty.[221]

As largely agricultural people in an agricultural region, most former slaves imagined freedom as owning their own small plots of land and working mainly as self-sufficient farmers. Even before the war ended, indeed as consequence of the war, about 10,000 slaves were working in the South Carolina Sea Islands when their owners fled the arrival of the U.S. Navy in November 1861. With the absence of owners, slaves took possession of the land, sacked the owners' houses, destroyed cotton gins, and planted corn and potatoes—not the "slave crop" cotton but food for their own subsistence.[222] Already accustomed to working in a task system that gave them independence to cultivate their own crops, hunt, and fish after completing specific tasks, these farmers became "de facto freedpeople by their owners' exodus."[223] At the end of the war, hope for land ownership was high.

Freedpeople continued their pursuit of land late into the post–Civil War period, or Reconstruction. Many mobilized collectively in "scores of communities" to purchase land. Former black nationalist Major Martin Delany, who had become a Freedmen's Bureau agent, advised freedpeople in South Carolina to "get up a community and get all the lands you can—if you cannot

get any singly."[224] In Lenoir County, North Carolina, a group of freedmen agreed to raise $10,000 by January 1868 to purchase homes for "ourselves." By September 1865, eighty-nine laborers on a Louisiana plantation had accumulated $1,200 and were applying to lease the estate that they had been farming. In Wilkes County, Georgia, an association of freedpeople raised $7,000 to buy a plantation in a nearby county. Black soldiers were especially active in obtaining land. In Louisiana, a regiment accumulated $50,000 to purchase "four or five of the largest plantations on the Mississippi," and soldiers in Kentucky explained to a Freedmen's Bureau agent that they were "laying up money for the purpose of purchasing a home."[225]

Freedpeople also imagined freedom as the ability to get an education and establish their own churches and other social institutions. Like so much else that began during the war, the development of black schools and churches continued after the war ended. As education history scholar James D. Anderson explains, "the former slaves' fundamental belief in the value of literate culture was expressed most clearly in their effort to secure schooling for themselves and their children. . . . The value of self-help and self-determination underlay the ex-slaves' educational movement."[226] Although Northerners were critical to educating freedpeople, during the war newly freed men and women often initiated getting an education for themselves and their children. They bought the land, built the schools, and hired the teachers. Secret and private schools had existed for free Southern black children in several states since the early nineteenth century. A black female teacher who had secretly educated black children since the early 1830s openly taught them in Savannah, Georgia, after the war. The invisible schools became visible, testifying to the resourcefulness of teachers and the determination of parents to have their children educated.

When New England school teachers Lucy and Sarah Chase arrived in Savannah in 1863, they found that African Americans had formed an educational association and supported teachers and several schools in the area. Reflecting their self-reliance and what Anderson refers to as their "deep-seated desire to control and sustain schools for themselves and their children," Southern blacks soon started a universal-education movement that provided Southern public-school education for all Southerners, a phenomenon almost nonexistent in the South before emancipation. Part of the aforementioned sense of control involved hiring black teachers and keeping the schools under the aegis of Southern blacks. By 1868, more than half the teachers in Southern black schools were black, and most were women. Teacher success was evident in the significant decline in black illiteracy. According to the 1870 census, 81 percent of the black population was illiterate, but by 1900 the census reported that that number had decreased to 48 percent. Twenty years later, the number of illiterate African Americans had

decreased by 24 percent. Within fifty years, nearly half the black population in the United States was literate.[227]

Freedpeople often migrated to towns and cities where education might be available for their children, and plantation workers were sometimes able to make the establishment of a school a condition of signing a labor contract. The existence of a schoolhouse symbolized independence, especially when it was built and run by former slaves. In Louisiana, for example, a contract specified that the planter pay a 5 percent tax for supporting black education. During Reconstruction, Northern benevolent societies, the Freedmen's Bureau, and state governments provided most of the funding for educating black people. The Freedmen's Bureau coordinated Northern educational societies for freedpeople rather than establish schools of its own. In addition to the many evening and private schools operated by missionary societies and African Americans, close to 3,000 schools, serving more than 150,000 students, reported to the bureau. Though most of the teachers were Northern middle-class white women, black Southern women and men played a critical role in educating blacks in the South. They raised funds through various societies to purchase land, built schoolhouses, and paid teachers' salaries, especially in the early years of freedom. Black artisans donated their labor to build schools, and black families offered room and board to teachers to supplement their salaries. For instance, freedpeople built the first public schoolhouse in Beaufort, North Carolina. Yet outside aid was necessary to tackle the enormous task of educating millions of people.[228]

Soon after the war, Southern black colleges were also established by African Americans and those who supported their educational interests. The three black colleges already in existence were located in the North. Pennsylvania had two, Cheyney College, established in 1837, and Lincoln University, established in 1854. And in 1856, the African Methodist Episcopal denomination in collaboration with the Methodist Episcopal Church established Wilberforce College in Ohio, only five years before the war. Yet by 1877, there were more than a dozen Southern black colleges and at least two medical and law schools.

When a school was erected, a church quickly followed or was housed within the same building. In fact, with the end of war former slaves immediately left Southern white churches and established their own, joining one of the two existing black denominations—the African Methodist Episcopal Church and the African Methodist Episcopal Zion Church—or joining the new Colored Methodist Episcopal (established in 1869). Freedom meant controlling not only their intimate family lives but their spiritual lives as well. Largely invisible to Southern white society, the black church immediately became central to the social, economic, and political lives of black communities.

While schools and churches were the primary social institutions freed-people established after the war, they also created hospitals, orphanages, mutual-aid societies, lodges, and unions. With the help of the medical division of the Freedmen's Bureau, former army hospitals became hospitals that served African Americans.[229]

Finally, former slaves joined with the Northern free black population in demanding the right to vote to protect their freedom, especially as they continued to experience horrific violence. Political participation became an utmost necessity for the reconstruction of the nation.[230]

African Americans' refusal to accept anything but genuine freedom matched the determination of Southern whites to retain absolute power over all blacks throughout the South. Most intended to control Southern labor, land, and other resources. Violence, the main means of controlling enslaved people and free blacks before the war, continued unabated. Even before the war ended, most Southern whites signaled their rejection of the very idea of black freedom, and in this they were aided by newly installed President Andrew Johnson. Though more likely a political and military strategy to end the war in late 1863, President Lincoln had offered "full pardon and the restoration of all rights" except the ownership of slaves to former rebels (excluding the highest ranking civil and military Confederates) who took a loyalty oath and pledged to accept the abolition of slavery. When 10 percent of Southerners who had voted in the 1860 election took the oath, they could establish a new state government. Johnson continued this lenient plan, rapidly giving amnesty to former Confederates who swore a loyalty oath to the United States.

Johnson indicated in the spring and summer of 1865 that he would leave laws and policies, except for the abolition of slavery, up to the former Confederate states. To the great disappointment of freedpeople, Johnson overruled Freedmen's Bureau commissioner Oliver Otis Howard and ordered the return of confiscated and abandoned land to pardoned Southerners in August. And, signaling his belief that the Confederate states should determine the reconstitution of their governments, Johnson overruled a Union Major General's prohibition of the Mississippi governor's establishment of a state militia. Major General Henry Slocum rightly suspected that the militia would be composed of Confederate veterans who could not be trusted to deal fairly with freedpeople and Southerners who were loyal to the Union. In addition, Johnson acquiesced to Southern white demands to remove black troops whose presence was "a painful humiliation" to white Southerners and an interference to plantation discipline. By 1867, most black soldiers had been mustered out of the service. In the fall of 1865, Johnson removed a Freedmen's Bureau assistant commissioner when Louisiana whites complained about him. Throughout the spring and fall of

that year, pardoned former rebels re-created their state governments with laws and policies that were not dissimilar from their old governments. By December, President Johnson, a strong advocate of white supremacy, declared the Union restored.[231] Reconstruction was over.

And yet, it wasn't. To most Northerners, Southern whites went too far. Northern white feelings about the loss of more than 700,000 lives were very raw, and Southern laws were too similar to laws during the slave era. The problem was that most Southern whites could not imagine their economic and social lives functioning without exploitative black labor and inferior black status. They could only imagine "slavery by another name."[232] South Carolina planter William H. Trescot explained in December 1865 to the state's governor, "you will find that this question of the control of labor underlies every other question of state interest."[233] Historian Eric Foner shows how South Carolina and other Southern states took the place of former slaveholders in controlling black labor in 1865 and 1866. State legislatures, with the urging of planters like Trescot, created the legal means to continue subordinating a people convinced that economic independence equaled freedom and that the system of white control over black labor was the same as slavery[234]. When Confederate troops returned home in the summer of 1865, local whites throughout the region quickly passed laws that undermined black freedom. These laws affected African Americans' right to move freely, to rent or own land, and to practice skilled trades. Southern whites' interest in continuing to exploit black labor underlay the entire re-enslavement project. When local laws proved unsatisfactory, state legislatures stepped in to become the arbiters of black labor.

Called Black Codes, these laws centered on continuing the goal of slavery: creating a malleable, docile, and a stable black workforce. They also aimed to keep all blacks, whether workers, teachers, or businesspeople, subordinate to all whites. Mississippi and South Carolina's laws were the most draconian, but Black Codes in all Southern states demonstrated white Southerners' primary interest in maintaining white power for their own interests and financial gain. Black Mississippians were treated as criminals if they lacked written evidence of employment for the coming year or if they left their jobs before the contract expired—to do so would mean forfeiting any wages already earned. Additionally, Mississippi's code provided for arresting and imprisoning African Americans who were idle or disorderly, or who misspent what they earned. Breaking these "vagrancy" laws was punishable by fines or involuntary plantation labor. Additionally, white employers were subjected to fines or possible imprisonment if they tried to hire a laborer already under contract. Mississippi blacks could also be imprisoned for using "insulting" gestures or language, "malicious mischief," or "preaching the gospel without a license." As in slavery, any black person was subject to arrest by any white person. To ensure that African Americans had

limited economic opportunities, Mississippi forbade black people to rent land in urban areas. Wanting to be sure that they had not overlooked a law, the Mississippi legislature declared that all penal codes defined as crimes for slaves and free blacks before 1865 were in "full force" unless specifically changed legally.

Under the South Carolina Black Codes, African Americans were restricted to working only as farmers or servants unless they paid an annual tax ranging from $10 to $100. This law hit the Charleston free black community especially hard, but satisfied the white urban workers who had been set on eliminating competition for jobs from skilled black urban workers since the antebellum era. As in Mississippi, South Carolina legislators focused on their demand for black labor by requiring black farmworkers to sign annual labor contracts, work from sunup to sundown, not leave the plantation without permission, and not entertain guests. South Carolina's vagrancy law applied to all unemployed blacks—"persons who lead idle or disorderly lives," as interpreted by the state.[235]

Early on, hearing the rumblings that Northerners perceived Black Codes as another form of slavery, some Southern states began modifying their codes to some degree, yet they still aligned with Mississippi's and South Carolina's focus on black labor. As Foner notes, the former Confederate states virtually all "enacted sweeping vagrancy and labor contract laws" that included "antienticement" measures to prevent employers from competing for black labor. Some states had distinct and specific provisions. Virginia, for example, included within its vagrancy laws a measure to prevent African American workers from attempting to force employers to increase wages. Florida's code made disobedience, impudence, and disrespect to employers a criminal offense; black workers who broke labor contracts could be whipped, placed in a pillory, and sold for up to one year's labor without compensation of any kind. In contrast, white workers in Florida who violated contracts were threatened with civil suits. Louisiana and Texas went after black women who sought to make their home their top priority rather than a planter's profits. Contracts in these states required that all members of the family who were able to work must work. The language of the laws in Southern states engaged in a kind of linguistic gymnastics, in which a construction of black dependency, rather than white dependency on black labor, justified neo-slavery.

In the immediate aftermath of war, Southern states also criminalized all African Americans for hunting, fishing, or allowing their livestock to graze freely—if they were lucky enough to own a mule or a pig. Criminalization and imprisonment became the means by which Southern whites controlled black men, women, and children in order to extract their labor and contain black aspirations. In many states, blacks were forbidden to own guns, or faced taxes if they owned guns or a dog. Rather than individual slaveholders, it was now the state (through its police force, state militia, and courts) that punished and controlled all black

people. While employers, according to law, could not whip black men, women, and children any longer, the courts could mandate whipping and the state could sentence black people to "long prison terms, force them to labor without compensation on public works, or bind them out to white employers who would pay their fines." In this revised labor system, leasing out convicts was a primary means for planters and other employers to gain easy access to black labor. Again, the critical difference between slavery and this new form of negotiating and profiting from black labor was that the state replaced the slave trader and auction houses. Beginning on a small scale during the war, these convict-lease laws pervaded the entire South in the first years of emancipation.

The white-dominated police force, state militia, and judicial system enforced these laws, providing almost no space for blacks to challenge them. Although most Southern states allowed blacks to testify in court, to appease Northern critics and rid the South of Freedmen's Bureau courts, the same states did not allow blacks to serve on juries, thus ensuring that the outcome for black plaintiffs would favor white interests. Paralleling the work of the courts, the state militia (usually composed of former Confederate soldiers, often in uniform) patrolled black areas and terrorized blacks through intimidation. They ransacked homes, seized guns and other belongings, and violently accosted those who refused to sign labor contracts.[236]

Perhaps the most galling to freedpeople were the apprenticeships laws in Southern states, which provided planters and other former slaveholders with the unpaid labor of black minors. First instituted when Maryland abolished slavery in 1864, the laws allowed judges to bind black orphans and children whose parents were deemed unable to support them to former owners or other employers without the consent of their parents.[237] Apprenticeship laws spread rapidly throughout the South in the immediate aftermath of emancipation. Mississippi approved a new state law in November 1865 governing the apprenticeship of black children. The law charged civil officials with reporting to county probate courts "all freedmen, free negroes and mulattoes, under the age of eighteen . . . who are orphans, or whose parent or parents have not the means, or who refuse to provide for and support said minors" and required probate courts "to apprentice said minors to some competent and suitable person." Boys were to be bound until they were twenty-one and girls until they were eighteen. The master or mistress was required to furnish the apprentice with food, clothing, and medical care, "treat said minor humanely," and "teach or cause to be taught him or her to read and write, if under fifteen years old." The law prohibited "cruel or inhuman punishment" but authorized the use of "such moderate corporeal chastisement as a father or guardian is allowed to inflict on his or her child or ward."[238] Apprentices who left without permission could be legally forced to return, and anyone who enticed an apprentice, including parents or other relatives, from the master's or mistress's service was subject to prosecution.[239]

These laws, like other laws at the end of war, completely undermined freedpeople's goal of reconstituting their families.

Responding to Southern whites' rejection of black freedom, African American men gathered at conventions all over the South. Delegates delivered speeches and passed resolutions about the multiple inequities they faced as newly freed people. Union soldiers often dominated the debates at these conventions.[240] Their concerns about the draconian apprenticeship laws and Black Codes topped their agenda. And the franchise was one of their primary demands. Having a voice in the political leadership of their state would not only enable Southern blacks to protect themselves, their family, and their property but also affirm black freedom.

When Congressional Republicans met in December 1865, they immediately addressed the violence being perpetrated against African Americans by Southern whites. It was then that Congress began developing legislation that came closer to defining black freedom as African Americans understood it. Overriding President Johnson's veto, Congress expanded federal authority over the former rebel states, reauthorized the Bureau of Refugees, Freedmen, and Abandoned Land Act, and passed the Civil Rights Act of 1866, which for the first time defined U.S. citizenship. The act mandated that all persons born in the United States (except Native Americans) were citizens of the nation, without regard to race. Just as important, the Civil Rights Act overturned the Black Codes and gave blacks the right to make contracts, bring lawsuits, and enjoy "full and equal benefit of all laws and proceedings for the security of person and property." No state law or custom could deprive any citizen of these "fundamental rights belonging to every man as a free man."[241] The Republican majority Congress, already in battle with the Democrats and the president, then proposed the Fourteenth Amendment in 1866 and sent it to the states for ratification. This amendment stated that "all persons born or naturalized in the United States" are "citizens of the United States." It also prohibited a state from making or enforcing any law that "shall abridge the privileges and immunities of citizens of the United States" or deprive "any person of life, liberty, or property without due process of law; nor deny to any person within its jurisdiction the equal protection of the laws."[242] As a consequence of these laws, historian Eric Foner explains, for the first time the Constitution "enshrined . . . the ideas of birthright citizenship and equal rights for all Americans."[243]

During the midterm election of 1866, Northern white voters demonstrated approval of this radical Republican agenda by returning their representatives to Congress. In March, Congress passed the Reconstruction Acts of 1867, which dissolved state governments in the former Confederate states, except for Tennessee, and divided the South into five military districts under martial law and military government. Congress then required that these states call constitutional

conventions, with delegates elected by manhood suffrage (only men could vote) and approval of the new constitution by the majority of voters, in order to reenter the Union. This meant that black men could be delegates to the state constitutional conventions. The act also required that the former Confederate states ratify the Fourteenth Amendment and write a state constitution that guaranteed black men suffrage. Congress passed three other acts in 1867 and early 1868, giving military commanders the power to ensure the process of congressional reconstruction in their district. The struggle between the Republican Congress and Johnson nearly ended with the president's impeachment in 1868; the House voted for impeachment, but the Senate did not convict. Johnson was saved by one vote.

The Fourteenth Amendment was ratified in 1868, affirming the Civil Rights Act's definition of citizenship and guarantee of equal protection of the laws to all citizens. And Congress agreed with African Americans' belief that the franchise was essential for their freedom when it passed the Fifteenth Amendment in 1869. This amendment declared, "The right of citizens of the United States to vote shall not be denied or abridged by the United States or by any State on account of race, color, or previous condition of servitude."

Because the new laws made many former Confederates ineligible to vote in the elections for delegates to the state constitutional conventions, and because many whites refused to participate in elections in which black men could vote, some state delegations had a black majority. The constitutions drafted in these states were far more democratic than the South had ever imagined. They provided for "universal male suffrage, public schools, progressive taxes, improved court and judicial systems, commissions to promote industrial development, state aid for railroad development, and social welfare institutions including hospitals and asylums for orphans and the mentally ill."[244]

During Congressional Reconstruction—1867 to 1876—more than 2,000 African American men served as officeholders at various levels of government in the South. They were postmasters, registrars, city council members, county commissioners, members on boards of education, tax collectors, land office clerks, sheriffs, police officers, and justices of the peace.[245] Although propaganda spread by Northern and Southern racists insisted that black office holders were ignorant former slaves, the evidence shows that those who had been enslaved were literate and well qualified to create a society in which they were part of the political community. They contributed to the development of a public school system in the South, pioneered civil-rights legislation, and created plans to rebuild the demolished Southern economy. Black office holders represented a range of occupations, including artisans, laborers, businessmen, carpenters, barbers, ministers, teachers, editors, publishers, storekeepers, and merchants. Some black politicians were more than prepared to serve in office.

Alabama congressman James Rapier and other African American congressmen, 1870s

Francis L. Cardozo, the son of a free black woman and a Jewish man, attended the Charleston school for free blacks and, later, the University of Glasgow and seminaries in Edinburgh and London. As the South Carolina secretary of state, he was the first of several African Americans to serve in a statewide office during this period. A few, like Cardozo, filled high positions in states where there was a large or even a majority black population. More than six hundred African Americans served in state legislatures, fourteen were elected to the House of Representatives, and two, Hiram Revels and Blanche K. Bruce, served in the United States Senate. This was an era of possibility, a moment when the United States was moving toward a true democracy.[246]

Northern and Southern whites alike were shocked at the rapidity with which freedpeople became politicized. Even before the end of the war, black men were members of Union Leagues and other organizations demanding the vote and an end to all discriminatory laws. In the spring and summer of 1865, freedpeople, sometimes armed, gathered in cabins, churches, and secluded places to discuss labor contracts, self-defense, education, politics, and other matters requiring immediate attention. They also organized a constant series of mass meetings, parades, and petitions demanding civil equality and the franchise. When President Johnson's Reconstruction program provided only for white participation, freedpeople held their own state conventions in seven Southern states. With Congressional Reconstruction, black men participated in official Southern state constitutional conventions from 1867 to 1869.[247] And with the passage of the Civil Rights Act of 1866 and the Fourteenth and Fifteenth Amendments, Southern blacks had representation in local, state, and federal governments. Voting, however, was a communal process. Former slave men and women gathered before elections and determined how they would vote; women participated right along with men at these gatherings. Most black politicians were moderate in their efforts to represent the interests of Southern blacks while also attempting to mollify white Southerners, most of whom repudiated even the thought of the black franchise. For example, few black politicians advocated land redistribution and some supported amnesty for former Confederates.[248]

At the same time, black men in state and federal political offices generally spoke strongly for civil rights, particularly for equal access to public transportation. Black Americans throughout the North and South had been consistently subjected to the indignities of segregated railway cars since the early nineteenth century. It was especially galling after the end of slavery and the passage of the Fourteenth and Fifteenth Amendments. Segregated and unequal access to railway cars signaled to Africans Americans their continued inferior status, in spite of abolition and Congressional Reconstruction.

Reconstruction, however, barely began before it ended. While the timing of Reconstruction was distinct in each state (states with large white majorities barely experienced Reconstruction), white supremacy eventually prevailed through horrific violent means from the late 1860s to the mid-1870s. The Southern white majority formed organizations, including terrorist organizations like the Ku Klux Klan, to "redeem" the South to white rule. Using the language of "states' rights" and stressing the necessity of white domination, they gained momentum and, eventually, success in all the Southern states.

The Civil Rights Act of 1875, which outlawed racial discrimination in juries, transportation, or public accommodations, did pass (without the equal and integrated public education proposal that was in the original bill), but the act had no real means of enforcement. The two strongest white congressional proponents of black freedom and equality, Thaddeus Stevens and Charles Sumner, had died. After 1877, the Republican Party's new "let alone policy" put Southern blacks at the mercy of Southern white politicians, the Ku Klux Klan, White League Clubs, and other paramilitary organizations, when "Redeemers" eventually kept black men from elected offices and black voters from voting in the Deep South. The last black Southern congressman from that era left office in 1901.

When they regained control, Southern Democrats trimmed taxes and cut state government functions under the guise of fiscal conservatism. They particularly scaled back and ended programs that assisted freedpeople, and they insisted that African Americans were incapable of understanding and participating in the political process. They charged incompetence, corruption, and dereliction of duty. None of it was true, but the propaganda campaign depicting black politicians as ignorant Sambos continued into the mid-twentieth century, driving persistent disenfranchisement in the South. At the same time, Southern white terrorists targeted black political leaders and successful businessmen and women, killing, raping, or maiming anyone who challenged white supremacy in word or deed. Throughout Reconstruction and after, black women were regularly subjected to beatings, rape, and other forms of violence by Southern white men merely for expressing that they were free, or acting as if they were free. If they placed their children before their employers' work demands, they were "playing the lady." White women not only supported this kind of violence but engaged in it themselves.

Meanwhile, white Northerners believed their role in Reconstruction was over. New congressmen were willing to let the white South handle its "Negro problem." After an economic downturn in 1873, the Northern electorate was more interested in addressing the economy than in ensuring the freedom of all Americans. Indeed, many Northern whites were as reluctant to allow universal suffrage for black

men in the North as Southern whites were. Antagonism to African Americans as part of the body politic remained in most of the nation. Reconstruction ended, according to Eric Foner, "not because propertyless blacks succumbed to economic coercion, but because a politically tenacious black community, abandoned by the nation, fell victim to violence and fraud."[249]

Thus, in the aftermath of slavery, most Southern black labor looked very much like slavery. White dependency on black labor and white interest in maintaining white supremacy decided the fate of black freedom. Deprived of land and forced to work for former slaveholders and others, most freedpeople became tenant farmers or sharecroppers, renting and working the land on terms that favored the white owners. A sharecropper worked the land for a "share" of the crop, usually one-third or one-half. The landowner, or merchant (often the same person), generally supplied the cabin in which the sharecropper's family lived, as well as the seed, work animals, and tools the sharecropper needed to work the land. If he had his own mule and plow, he might warrant a larger share of the crop. The crop raised belonged to the landowner, and he sold it in the market. There was no exchange of cash. Instead, the sharecropper received credit for buying food and clothing from the planter or merchant. When accounts were settled at the end of the year, the sharecropper received a bill indicating his indebtedness to the planter or merchant. Many sharecroppers were forced into debt by a lien system on their crop that required they borrow seed and supplies against anticipated harvests. This reduced black households to a kind of debt peonage. Additionally, though freedpeople were not supposedly threatened by the prospect of being sold—they were no longer property—most southern states reinstituted the convict-lease system they had established right at the end of the war. The convict-lease system was another form of slavery. During and especially post-Reconstruction, state courts could sentence freedpeople to long prison terms and force them to work without wages on public works projects or be bound out to planters and other employers who paid their fines. The system devastated individuals, families, and communities.[250]

Still, freedom held meaning during Reconstruction and after for most African Americans in the South and North. They were determined to live and work in family and community. Their letters reveal the degree to which they continued to fight for their understanding of freedom, a freedom indelibly linked to family and community.

CHAPTER THREE:

"Send Me Some of the Children's Hair."

IN MANY PRIVATE LETTERS, AFRICAN AMERICANS SEEMED TO AVOID DISCUSSING the issues described above, though they were often life-threatening. Philadelphian seamstress Emilie Davis generally referred only to the most immediate and mundane events involving herself, close family members, and friends in her diary written during and immediately after the Civil War. The private letters written during this period were usually about specific issues having little to do with the national project of reuniting the Union. Indeed, as we have seen, former slaves defined Reconstruction as reconstructing their families, during and after the Civil War. Searching for family members was their highest priority, and freedmen, women, and children traveled great distances in search of loved ones. But finding one's child or other relatives was often difficult or even futile. Still, family members persisted. When husbands and wives did find each other, most legitimized their marriage with the hope of ensuring control over their most intimate relationships and, for soldiers' widows, of qualifying for the veteran's pension.

The Plummer family was completely reunited when Henry found his elder sister Sarah Miranda and brought her back from New Orleans in October 1866. The family had saved and borrowed money for the train fare and was able to pay back their loan the following year. In July 1868, Adam Plummer put down $344.75 as the first installment for ten acres of land in Maryland costing a total of $1,000. The family worked and saved, sacrificing "the necessities of life"[251] to make the payment. Then the speculator demanded another payment of $160.25 in December. According to Nellie Plummer, the youngest daughter, the family pooled their money again, working long hours and giving all they could make and borrow from friends. On January 17, 1870, much to the surprise of the land speculator, Adam paid the full amount for the land. The speculator had told the neighbors living next to the land the Plummers were buying, who worried about living next door to a black family, that the Plummers would never be able to raise the money to buy the land. Although he had encouraged Adam to build a house on the land while still making

payments—Adam refused—the speculator had assured neighbors that "In time, I'll take the land back."[252] In September 1870, Adam built a four-room log cabin on the land; in March 1872, the Plummers paid back all their loans. The home expanded and the family grew as the Plummer children got an education, married, and had children. Adam and Emily Plummer's children became physicians, teachers, and ministers. They and their children lived for several decades at Mount Rose, the home Adam built in Maryland, a former slaveholding state.[253]

In contrast to that of the Plummers, some slave marriages were troubled from the beginning. Enslaved women and men weren't always able to choose their mate—the slaveholder made the decision—and, consequently, these couples decided to end their undesirable relationships. In marriages that continued after the war, some husbands chose to exert control over their spouses and children that they did not have as slaves. Anglo-American law was slowly changing from allowing husbands near-absolute rule as heads of households and requiring wives and children to obey without question to making physical abuse illegal. This would take decades, and the law generally gave men authority, including to physically strike wives and children. Interestingly, the Ku Klux Klan and powerful Southern whites often sided with abused black wives as a means to continue their control over black men.[254] In their clearly vulnerable and precarious state, former enslaved parents were also confronted with the dreaded apprenticeship system that swept the South in the post–Civil War era. Mothers, fathers, grandparents, and other relatives attempted to end this form of slavery, in which minors were bound by the state to former slaveholders or anyone interested in wage-free labor. Family members searching for one another often found their children bound to white employers for more than a year.

There is at least one interesting example of a different kind of family search. The Grimke sisters, Angelina and Sarah, abolitionists and feminists, sought out, communicated with, and supported the sons of their slaveholder brother and a woman he had enslaved. As correspondence between Sarah Grimke and her nephew Archibald Grimke shows, the reconstruction of family included relationships between black and white family members. Archibald and his brother Francis Grimke would go on to become important leaders in their respective careers. Archibald, who graduated from Harvard Law School in 1874, was a lawyer and a journalist in Boston and was later appointed consul to Santo Domingo, in the Dominican Republic, by President Grover Cleveland. Francis, who married schoolteacher Charlotte Forten and graduated from Princeton Theological Seminary in 1878, became the minister of the Fifteenth Street Presbyterian Church in Washington, D.C., a position he held for forty years. While the positive interaction between the Grimke brothers and their white aunts suggested the possibility that race would matter less in the nation, race demagogues and their supporters made sure that race defined American political, economic, and social life for the next century and beyond. Racism infected

relationships between parents and children. Archibald's marriage to Sarah E. Stanley, a white woman, ended in tragedy. Her father, an abolitionist, made clear that her new husband would never be welcome in his home. The couple separated soon after their daughter Angelina was born, and a few years after sending her daughter to live with her father, Sarah committed suicide. Race remained a dominant factor in almost all of American life.

Another interracial couple's beginning was not unlike the Reconstruction era's—full of promise but overcome by unchanged attitudes and practices. Carrie (Carolyn Victoria) Highgate was teaching in Jackson, Mississippi, with her mother when she met Albert T. Morgan, a former Union army officer who became active in Mississippi state politics after the war. As a state senator during Congressional Reconstruction, Morgan pushed through a bill to repeal the law against interracial marriages. After the Mississippi Reconstruction government was violently removed, the Morgans lived in Washington, D.C., for a decade, where Albert clerked in the federal government's pension office until he was forced out by Southern Democrats. The couple then fled to a racially mixed community in Lawrence, Kansas, where Albert experienced several business failures. He left for Colorado to mine silver, leaving Carrie and their six children in Kansas. Carrie (who was of mixed African and European ancestry) and her children went on the stage with a musical act, passing as whites. The mother and children performers experienced some success, but tragedy ensued when a son died in an accidental shooting; one daughter committed suicide, and another was placed in an asylum when her mixed racial ancestry was exposed. Carrie lived the remainder of her life with her daughter Angela, a poet who tried to support the remaining family.[255]

The Reconstruction era's great promise of freedom and equality lasted but a moment in the history of the nation. But its positive legacy is evident in the zeal with which freedpeople built and attended schools, and the way teachers worked, often at great expense to their health and endangerment of their lives, to educate the newly freedpeople. Emma Brown continued her correspondence with her friend Emily Howland, in which she illustrated the toll teaching took on young African American women working in the South.

While Southern whites' determination to maintain white supremacy at all costs filled the South with violence and contentious politics, letters written by Northern blacks reveal the price racism exacted on African Americans living in that region as well. Many black men and women were unable to support themselves and their families in a Northern society still rife with racial discrimination in jobs, housing, and education.

Still, African American men and women throughout the nation persisted in their determination to live as free Americans with dignity and purpose, during Reconstruction and after. Letters expressing love and hope for a brighter future are especially evident between young men and women who came of age during the war.

African Americans' definition of freedom involved reunification of their family, financial security, and the right to protect themselves, their family, and their community. Whether in the North or the South, African Americans consistently defined freedom as holding the same rights as white Americans, meaning political, social, and economic rights. In this letter to the regional Freedmen's Bureau, Tennessee freedpeople sum up their definition of freedom.

[Lincoln Country, Tenn.] July 27th 1865

Genl

We the colored People of Lincoln County, State of Tennessee, would respectfully submit the following representation.... We now, simply ask that we may be secured as others, in the just fruits of our toil: protected from unjust, and illegal punishments, and we are sure we will keep our families from want, and do our part as good citizens of the United States to add to the wealth and glory of the Country. We are recognized as men by the Constitution of the land: we only ask to be treated as such, and we will, in the future as in the past, be law abiding men.[256]

Four months after the war, Northern white teacher Joseph R. Johnson reports to the Freedmen's Bureau commissioner on a celebratory meeting of Virginia's freedpeople that included a set of resolutions spelling out their economic and social expectations in freedom.

Halls Hill Va August 4th 1865.

Dear Sir: On Tuesday August 1st 1865, the Colored People of Halls Hill and vicinity . . . celebrated West India Emancipation, and American Emancipation.

During the business part of the celebration, the Rev Jacob Ross, (colored) of Georgetown—was chairman, and the following resolutions were unanimously adopted:

"We feel it to be very important that we obtain HOMES—owning our shelters, *and the ground,* that we may raise fruit trees, concerning which our children can say—*"These are ours"* also: that we may regularly and perseveringly educate our children, having our own school house in a central location, and also maintain public worship, and a Sabbath School, so that we may be an established and growing people, and be respected, and recognized by all loyal people, as welcome and efficient citizens of these United States—which is now *our* Country—made emphatically so by the blood of our brethren recently shed to save *our* Country."

Resolved: That we appoint a Committee of seven to visit the Freedmens Bureau, and enquire—Can the Bureau give us any aid, or advice, in regard to obtaining Homes in this vicinity, or elsewhere?..."

I trust that they will receive such a response as may much encourage them, and those whom they represent. Yours for the Freedmen—

Joseph R. Johnson[257]

Former slave Jourdon Anderson responds to his former master, who asked Anderson to return with his wife and children to carry on the work they did as slaves. His definition of freedom is representative of the black majority. Anderson, who probably gained his freedom by joining the Union army, expresses concern for his family if he returned to the South and explains that he expects wages for future work and back wages for work while in slavery. He also wants assurance that his wife and children will be respected, be protected from rape, and have access to schools.

Dayton, Ohio, August 7, 1865

To My Old Master, Colonel P. H. Anderson,

Big Spring, Tennessee

Sir: I got your letter and was glad to find you had not forgotten Jourdon, and that you wanted me to come back and live with you again, promising to do better for me than anybody else can. I have often felt uneasy about you. I thought the Yankees would have hung you long before this for harboring

Rebs. they found at your house. I suppose they never heard about your going to Col. Martin's to kill the Union soldier that was left by his company in their stable. Although you shot at me twice before I left you, I did not want to hear of your being hurt, and am glad you are still living. . . .

I want to know particularly what the good chance is you propose to give me. I am doing tolerably well here; I get $25 a month, with victuals and clothing; have a comfortable home for Mandy (the folks here call her Mrs. Anderson), and the children, Milly, Jane and Grundy, go to school and are learning well; the teacher says Grundy has a head for a preacher. They go to Sunday-School, and Mandy and me attend church regularly. . . .

As to my freedom, which you say I can have, there is nothing to be gained on that score, as I got my free-papers in 1864 from the Provost-Marshal-General of the Department at Nashville. Mandy says she would be afraid to go back without some proof that you are sincerely disposed to treat us justly and kindly—and we have concluded to test your sincerity by asking you to send us our wages for the time we served you. This will make us forget and forgive old scores, and rely on your justice and friendship in the future. I served you faithfully for thirty-two years and Mandy twenty years. At $25 a month for me, and $2 a week for Mandy, our earnings would amount to $11,680. Add to this the interest for the time our wages has been kept back and deduct what you paid for our clothing and three doctor's visits to me, and pulling a tooth for Mandy, and the balance will show what we are in justice entitled to. Please send the money by Adams Express, in care of V. Winters, esq, Dayton, Ohio. If you fail to pay us for faithful labors in the past we can have little faith in your promises in the future. We trust the good Maker has opened your eyes to the wrongs which you and your fathers have done to me and my fathers, in making us toil for you for generations without recompense. Here I draw my wages every Saturday night, but in Tennessee there was never any pay day for the negroes any more than for the horses and cows. Surely there will be a day of reckoning for those who defraud the laborer of his hire.

In answering this letter please state if there would be any safety for my Milly and Jane, who are now grown up and both good-looking girls. You

know how it was with poor Matilda and Catherine. I would rather stay here and starve and die if it comes to that than have my girls brought to shame by the violence and wickedness of their young masters. You will also please state if there has been any schools opened for the colored children in your neighborhood, the great desire of my life now is to give my children an education, and have them form virtuous habits.

From your old servant, Jourdon Anderson

P.S.—Say howdy to George Carter, and thank him for taking the pistol from you when you were shooting at me.[258]

Immediately after the war, private letters between soldier husbands and their wives often concerned finding the financial means to reunite with one another and to escape from the clutches of former slaveholders who intended to keep wives and other family members at work on the plantations. Catherine and Norman Riley's correspondence from August to September in 1865 shows the difficulty of reuniting with family even when they were separated by little more than forty miles. Norman wants his wife to ask his brother, George, for help.

Nashville Tenn Aug 12th 1865

Dear wife I Received your letter that was written on the 8th to day and was glad to hear that you was well and that the children was well also. I am well as to health and well Satisfide all to Seeing you and as I can't tell when I can come to see you my wishes is for you to come and See me I am in earnis a bout you comeing and that as Soon as possiable it is no use to Say any thing a bout any money for if you come up here which I [hope] you will it will be all wright as to the money matters I want to See you and the Children very bad and my love for you and the Children is as great to day as it ever was. I can get a house at any time I will Say the word So you need not to fear as to that So come wright on just as soon as you get this. I also wish you to get George to give you Some money to bare your exspences here. and if you cant

get off you must write to me a gain and I will try and Send you Some money I want you to tell me the name of the baby that was born Since I left that is if you can't come up here. and I want you to bring my son George with you for I want him. and if it Suits you you can leave your daughter Elisabeth there with George. I am your affectionate Husband untill Death

    Write soon

                                  Norman Riley

Impatient for his wife's response, within two weeks Norman writes to Catherine again, urging her to come.

                         Nashville Tenn Aug 26 1865

Dear and affectionate Wife I Seat myself to write you a few lines to let you know that I am well hoping that these lines may fine you the same. Dear wife I would like you to come down if you Possible can I wrote to you some time a go to come and you did not come and I dont know the reason for I have not got any letter from you to hear how you was nor to know cause of you not comeing. I cant tell when I shall get out of service and I want to See you very bad and if you [want] to See me you will have to come and see me and I would like for you to come for I think that you can make a great deal more here then you can. and you George I think very hard of you for not coming and Seeing me for you know that I cant come and See you and therefore you ought to come and See me and if you dont feel like coming down here I want [you] to come and bring my family and you can go back if choose.

    now if you cant come I want you to write me an answer to this as Soon as you Receive it. I have Nothing more at Preasent but I Remain Your Most affectionate Husband Until Death. . . .

                                  Norman Riley

Write Soon yes I have got a house all Ready for you and if cant come I Shall reant it out a gain in the coure of ten days so good by

Catherine Riley finally responds from Clarksville, explaining the circum-stances. When Norman's brother, George, and a friend, Jessie Boyd, tried to get Catherine's personal belongings from the plantation—perhaps intimate clothing or blankets, and so on—her former slaveholder nearly killed them.

Clarksville Tenn Aug 28. /65

Dear husband It is with pleasure that I Seat myself for the perpose of Writing you afew lines. acknoklage the recept of your letter. which came to hand in Dew time. it finding [me] very Well as I trust this may find you. I am sorry to Inform you. that your brother George is very badly Wonded he went out After my things and Jessie Boyd also. Jessie went with him. he was also shot. But not so bad as Geo. and George wants that you should come down To see him if you posible Can. do so he thinks that if you cannot come now. you Need not to come at all for he is very badly wounded I guess you would like to know the reson why that I did not come when you wrote for and that is because that I hadnot the money and could not get it. and if you will send me the money. or come after me I will come.... dear husband If you are coming after me. I want you to come before it Get too cold. that I cant Travel I don't want you to Rent that house out. for if there is a better chance to make a living there. then what there is here. I want to get up there.

George was badly Shot through the Back. the shot still remains in him and Jessie boyd was shot through the thigh. I seen Uncle Moses Riley. Sunday and he told me to give you his best respect. and tell you that he was well and doing very well. dear husb I havenot got my things from home yet but I shell. as soon I can. having nothing more to Write. I shell close hopeing to hear from you soon I Remain as ever your affec-tionate and Loving Wife

Catherine Riley

African American woman, ca. 1860–1870

Norman Riley continues to urge Catherine to join him.

Nashville Tennessee Sept 22 1865

M[y]Dear Wife I again the pleasure of writing to you To let you know that I am In the enjoyment of Good health. I would like to know the reason why you did not answer my last two letters. I am very anxious to hear from you. and particularly to know if you are coming Here. if you are coming I would like for you to come immediately, as there is A man here about. to buy a house and he has no person to go into it to take care of the things. also let me know if George has got well or not I am very anxious to hear from him I want you to write to me inside of an hour after you receive this and let me know what you are going to do I will now conclude hoping to hear from you son I remain your affectionate & Loving Husband

Norman Riley[259]

Living in Nashville, Norman Riley was unaware of the brutal circumstances that prevented Catherine from writing regularly. Their former slaveholder was refusing to release one of their children and beat Catherine for trying to escape with their son. Evidently, Norman took his wife's letter concerning the shooting of George and Jessie Boyd to his company commander, who then forwarded it to the Freedmen's Bureau assistant commissioner, requesting bureau action against the former slaveholder. From Clarksville, the agent reported the Riley situation to the headquarters of the Kentucky and Tennessee Freedmen's Bureau assistant commissioner.

Clarksville Tenn Dec 19. 1865

Sir I have the honor to call your attention to the following statement and ask your advice thereon

On the 9th ult [ultimate] I gave Catherine Riley, the wife of a soldier, an order to James Riley of Logan Co Ky. for her child which the said Riley

still claimed as his Slave. She got the child & started on her return to this place & when about three miles from said Rileys, he overtook her, & did unlawfully beat her with a club, & left her senseless on the ground after which he returned home with the child. Catherine Riley reported to me the following day. and substantiated the above facts by competent witnesses & at the time was all covered with blood. could scarcely talk & was barely able to stand alone. The above facts have also been told to me by a neighbor of the said James Riley I sent a guard for him but he could not be found, as he had gone from home & taken the said child with him, as he remarked. to a neighbor, to "put the child out of the reach of the d---d Yankees Not long since this same man Riley shot a negro soldier, & ran away from home to prevent his being arrested.

Cases of the above kind are reported to me about every day, but many of them I cannot attend to on account of not having soldiers to enforce my orders at a distance

I respectfully refer this matter to you & as your advice theron Resp ct Your obt Sevt

W. G. Bond[260]

Eventually the family appears to have been reunited, and the former slaveholder James Riley was arrested, tried, convicted on charges of having "maltreated" Catherine Riley and fined $100, including $48.80 damages to the freedwoman.[261]

Black soldiers' lives were pulled back and forth between their commitment to their families and the requirements of the Union army. Husbands were particularly fraught with emotion as they tried to protect their wives and children still living on former slaveholding plantations. In Louisiana, Emily Waters writes to her husband, who is stationed far away, about her former slaveholder's threat to evict her and their children if they don't pay rent. According to a Freedmen's Bureau official, evictions were common and widespread.

Roseland Plantation [La.] July 16th 1865

My Dear Husband I received a letter from you week before last and was glad to hear that you were well and happy.

This is the fifth letter I have written you and I have received only one— Please write as often as you can as I am always anxious to hear from you. I and the children are all well—but I am in a great deal of trouble as Master John Humphries has come home from the Rebel army and taken charge of the place and says he is going to turn us all out on the Levee unless we pay him (8.00) Eight Dollars a month for house rent— Now I have no money of any account and I am not able to get enough to pay so much rent, and I want you to get a furlough as soon as you can and come home and find a place for us to live in. and besides Amelia is very sick and wants you to come home and see her if possible she has been sick with the fever now over two weeks and is getting very low— Your mother and all the rest of your folks are well and all send their regards & want to see you as soon as you can manage to come— My mother sends her compliments & hopes to see you soon

My children are going to school, but I find it very hard to feed them all, and if you can not come I hope you will send me something to help me get along

I get all the work I can and am doing the best I can to get along, but if they turn me out I don't know what I shall do— However I will try & keep the children along until you come or send me some assistance

Thank God we are all well, and I hope we may always be so Give my regards to all the boys. Come home as soon as you can, and cherish me as ever Your Aff wife

Emily Waters[262]

Rejecting the emancipation, former slaveholders took vengeance on any person of color, particularly the wives and children of Union army soldiers. Jane Coward reports to her soldier husband, Pharoah, that she was now living with the Reed family to escape her slaveholder's wrath. Sarah Reed wrote the letter for Jane and, after transcribing Jane Coward's greeting and description of the beating, included

a message to Pharoah's captain—and all government officials—that they must address former slaveholders' brutal behavior toward soldiers' families. There was no real escape without the force of the Union authorities.

Green Cty Ky. July the [6] 1865

Dear Husband i set my self down to write you a few lines to let you know that Mr Reed twoke [took] to me and my three children to live with him to live and R. L. Moor and Mr. Frank Coward come her to day and beat me nearly to death he says that he will kill any man that will take me in to a house to live with him Pharoah this is roat by Sarah M Reed i want you to hand this to your captain Stranger i want to know of all you that is a friend to the cullard people that you have got thar husband in survice i want you to come to greens burg and treat old Coward just like he did Pharoah wife to day and he said that if i said one word that he would searve me the same way he knocked hear down and old dick more hell hear and Coward beat hear nearly to death he took the older girl with him home and he said to jane that before she should live with me he would killer de[ad] and all of the Reeds that was on top of earth in less than one weak i would ceap you wife but R L more says that he will kill every woman that he knows that has got a husband in the army he said that i was no better than a negro rage and i think that i am just as good as he is i never treated nothing as he did Pharoah wife to day I want you to come to greens burg and let me see you and tell you all about it i think we will have to leve hear on the account off the rebels that is hear for is a man ever leaves his wife and children at home by thar selves thay are abusded by some one of them you must do some thing for Mr Frank coward in return to his treatment to day to Pharoah wife i never was so abused in my life by no man my husband is not at home to day i have two children in the uion army and we have two children that was killed in the union army and i think that aught to have some peace at home when my husband leaves me at home do pray do come to our relieaf at home nothing more but this your wife

jane coward

rote by Sarah M Reed[263]

Former slaveholders and other Southern whites' violence, including burning ex-slaves' meager belongings, only exacerbated the multiple complications freed couples experienced when they finally found one another. Philip Grey had been sold and separated from his wife, Willie Ann, and their daughter, Maria, in the 1850s. When Philip searched for his wife and daughter after the Civil War, he learned not only that Willie Ann had remarried but also that she was a war widow with three more children. In her letter to Philip, Willie Ann expresses her continued love for her first husband while urging him to accept her and the other children as family.

Salvisa, Kentucky, April 7, 1866

Dear Husband:

I received your letter the 5 of this month and was very glad to hear from you. You wish me to come to Virginia. I had much rather you would come after me but if you cannot make it convenient you will have to make some arrangement for me and family. I have 3 little fatherless girls. My husband went off under Burbridge's command and was killed at Richmond Virginia. If you can pay passage I will come the first of May. I have nothing much to sell as I have had my things all burnt. You must not think my family to large and get out of heart for if you love me you will love my children and you will have to promise me that you will provide for them as well as if they were your own. I heard that you spoke of coming for Maria but were not coming for me. I know that I have lived with you and loved you then and I love you still. I was very low spirited when I heard you was not coming for me. My heart sank within me in an instant. You will have to write and give me directions how to come.

Maria sends her love to you but seems to be low spirited for fear that you will come for her and not for me. No more at present but remain your true wife. (I hope to be with you soon.)

Willie Ann Grey[264]

As Philip and Willie Ann show, reuniting family after the Civil War could be difficult, if not tortuous. Not only had wives or husbands often remarried but they also may have had two distinct families. Lucy Chase continued to share the letters of former slaves living in refugee camps with her family in Massachusetts. She wrote, "I don't know whether I have told you Laura Spicer's story." Laura Spicer and her husband had been separated for some time after being sold. Believing that Laura was dead, her husband remarried. When he learned that Laura was still alive, he wrote her several letters expressing his undying love for her and the children and simultaneously urging her to remarry because he had another family.

I read your letters over and over again. I keep them always in my pocket. If you are married I don't ever want to see you again . . . I would much rather you would get married to some good man, for every time I gits a letter from you it tears me all to pieces. The reason why I have not written you before, in a long time, is because your letters disturbed me so very much.

You know I love my children. I treats them good as a Father can treat his children; and I do a good deal of it for you. I was very sorry to hear that Lewellyn, my poor little son, have had such bad health. I would come and see you but I know you could not bear it. I want to see you and I don't want to see you. I love you just as well as I did the last day I saw you, and it will not do for you and I to meet. I am married, and my wife have two children, and if you and I meets it would make a very dissatisfied family.

Having resolved not to meet again, her husband asks Laura for locks of the children's hair.

Send me some of the children's hair in a separate paper with their names on the paper. Will you please git married, as long as I am married. My dear, you know the Lord know both of our hearts. You know it never was our wishes to be separated from each other and it never was our fault. Oh, I can see you so plain, at any-time, I had rather anything to had happened to me most that [than] ever have been parted from you and the children. As I am, I do not know which I love best, you or Anna. If I was to die, today or tomorrow, I do not think I would die satisfied till you tell me you will try and marry some good, smart man that will take good care of you and the children; and do it because you love me; and not because I think more of the wife I have got that I do of you. The woman is not born that feels as near to me as you do. . . . Tell them they must remember they have a good father and one that cares for them and one that thinks about them every day—My very heart did ache when reading your very kind and interesting letter. Laura I do not think that I have change any at all since I saw you last.—I thinks of you and my children every day of my life. Laura I do love you the same. My love to you never have failed. Laura, truly, I have got another wife, and I am very sorry, that I am. You feels and seems to me as much like my dear loving wife, as you ever did Laura. You know my treatment to a wife and you know how I am about my children. You know I am one man that do love my children. . . .[265]

Inquiries posted in the *Christian Recorder* and other black journals and news-papers are representative of the methods used by husbands, wives, sons, and daughters in their search for family members, a practice that continued into the early twentieth century.

Information Wanted

Of my mother and father, Matilda and William Reynolds, well known in Essex Co., Va., from which place they were sold some eight or nine years ago, being at that time the "property" of Dr. John Taylor. I hope that the ministers of our respective churches will make public announcement of the same. Any information concerning the missing parties will be most thankfully received. Please address me at Davenport, Iowa.

Lucinda Reynolds

Davenport, Iowa, March 9th, 1866.

Information Wanted

Of my father, Joshua Clarke, my mother, Polly Clarke, my brother, Joshua, and sister Kate. In our family there were four daughters and one son. I am the oldest daughter. I was sold about thirteen years ago, to Alabama. My father, mother, brother and sisters were then living in Richmond, Va. Please address any information to

Alice Mitchell

(Care Rev. Levi Walker)

Glennville, Barbour Co., Ala.

Ministers will please read in their congregations.

Information Wanted

Susan Arnot wishes to learn the whereabouts of her children, three girls and one boy, who were taken from Martinsburg, Berkley Co., Va., four years ago. Their names are - 1, Nelson Alexander Arnot; 2, Elizabeth Mitchell Arnot; 3, Lucy Virginia Arnot; 4, Harriet Matilda Arnot. My children were formerly owned by Geo. Morrison.

> Susan Arnot
> Richmond, Virginia,
> Corner of Tenth and Clay Streets.
> July 12 - 3mo.[266]

Some notices offered rewards.

$200 Reward. During the year 1849, Thomas Sample carried away from this city, as his slaves, our daughter, Polly, and son, Geo. Washington, to the State of Mississippi, and subsequently, to Texas, and when last heard from they were in Lagrange, Texas. We will give $100 each for them to any person who will assist them, or either of them, to get to Nashville or get word to us of their whereabouts, if they are alive. Ben. & Flora East.[267]

As we have seen, former slaves put reuniting with family members at the top of their list of expectations in freedom. While there were many who engaged in long, tortuous, and usually unsuccessful searches for family members, others knew exactly where their family members were but were unable to get them. In his letter to Tennessee Governor William Brownlow, Urbain Ozanne, a white Nashville brewer, is trying to help his employee and wife free their children from their former owner.

Nashville, Tenn., April 10 1865

Sir, I have the honor to make the following representation, and invoke your interference in behalf of justice.

At the inception of the rebellion Samuel Emery (colored) together with his wife, and four children, were slaves, resident in Wilson County Tenn,

During the progress of the war, this man Emery was pressed to labor upon the fortifications erecting for the defence of this city. Soon after, his wife, the bearer of this, who with her children was owned by Mrs Eveline Blair, was likewise brought to this city by the federal Army, and subsequently joined her husband and under the operation of the emancipation proclamation began and continue the honest, industrious pursuit of a livelihood, The husband now being in my employ,

On several occasions, the last of which was but a day or two since, these parents presented themselves before the former Mistress of their Children who *now* retains them in bondage, and supplicated her for them, On each occasion she has indignantly spurned their united supplication uttering the most opprobrious epithets against the federal government and declaring the children should never be granted their freedom thus evincing an utter disregard for the federal government and the earnest solicitations of these oppressed people. I therefore beg that you may take such action, if consistent with your official duty, as shall warrant the rendition of the children to their parents, who are fully competent to properly care for them, or if not within the sphere of your official province that you will ind[icate the] process proper to s[ecure the end] desired. . . . Very Resp[ectfully] Your ob'd[t servant]

Urbain [Ozanne][268]

In August 1865, Daniel Chase, reflecting the anguish of hundreds of parents whose children were caught up in the so-called Southern states' "apprentice-ships," testified before the District of Columbia Freedmen's Bureau that his former slaveholder refused to allow him to remove his children from bondage.

Washington, D.C. Aug. 24. 1865

Danl. Chase of the City of Washington, being duty sworn states:

That he was formerly the slave of Virgil Gant, of Prince Frederick, Calvert Co Md., that when he left said Virgil Gant, in 1863, he left with him his five children, viz. Rachael Ann, aged 8, Hanson, 7-Sias & David (twins) 6- & Caroline, 3 years, who, about the time of the passage of the emancipation act, were bound by the Orphans Court of Calvert Co. to the said Virgil Gant; & further-that the said Gant has hired out to Mr. Danl. Bowen-the boy Hanson, & "Sias," to Mr. Thos. Hutchins-he (Gant) to receive their wages: that he went to Mr. Gants house in Prince Frederick, the 19th" inst. And asked for his children, he wishing to bring them to Washington. He was refused possession of them: he further states that the children were bound without the Knowledge or consent of either himself or his wife-, the mother of the children: that his wife, Mina, the mother of the children went after them in Decembr 1864, as soon as she heard they were free, but was refused possession of them by Mr. Gant.

His mark

(Signed) Danl. X Chase[269]

African American boys in the South, ca. 1860–1870

Nelson Gill, Freedmen's Bureau sub-commissioner at Holly Springs, Mississippi, expresses concern that the apprenticeship system has spread to his area.

Holly springs Miss. Dec. 20, 1865

Sir I think the apprentice act is being used here to the injury of the Freedmen. For instance yesterday a woman complained to me that her daughter had been taken from her and bound to her former owner till She is 18. The woman complaining is young and able bodied. The girl is her only child and is 12 ½ years old. And will hire readily for more than her Support. The girl was bound on the ground that her mother had not the means to support her, the *falsity* of which was proven by the man to whom the girl was bound offering the mother (*in court*) *"good wages'* if She would go and work for him. The mother Says She could not live with (the former owner) because he always abused her and She is very much grieved by the fear that he will misuse her daughter. The worst thing proved against the mother was that She had been known to be for two days with nothing but bread in her house to eat. She Says She will contract for next year to anyone I select and I can hire her and the daughter for at least $100 more than their food and clothes. What can I do in the matter? I have written to the Judge who ordered the binding protesting against it on the ground that the mother was not proven unable to support her child. If this is allowed they will have every negro between the ages of 12 and 18 bound. No matter what their circumstances The *little* children they will leave for the parents to support.

> I could give other instances but will not this time
> I await advice   Very Respectfully
> Nelson G. Gill[270]

Former slaveholders' persistence in keeping children in slavery matched newly freed parents' determination to establish their families. The oath Harriet Saunders took before a Freedmen's Bureau officer reveals how illiterate parents were tricked into the illegal apprenticeship system, while Elizabeth Pollard's statement shows her determination to rescue her grandchild.

Starkville, Mississippi, September 14, 1867

Harriet Saunders, a colored woman states on oath that she is the mother of Lucius & Gracy Ann two minor children, that these children were bound out to Green W. Walker with her consent but that her consent was obtained by fraud & misrepresentation and that she did not know what "bind out" children meant, that he promised to give up the children whenever she became dissatisfied & left, but she has some time since left & he refuses to give them up—that her son Richard Oliver is over fourteen years of age & was bound out to Dr. Josephus Walker. That she is able to take care of & provide for said children & prays for an order setting aside said letters of apprenticeship.

Her mark

(Signed) Harriet X Saunders[271]

[Athens, Georgia, June 22, 1868]

Elizabeth Pollard (Col'd) states that she has been to get her Grandchild Georgiana of Mr. Mobley Forsythe Geo., that Mobley refused to give her & says that she is properly bound to him until she is 18 years old. Elizabeth now wishes that the indenture be cancelled on the ground that Georgiana is treated badly & is beaten by Mr. Mobley & she wishes to get the child to educate her & bring her up properly.[272]

Freedmen's Bureau officials and Southern white supporters or friends of freedpeople consistently wrote letters on behalf of newly freed parents who wished to restore their family. Joseph Hall, a white Union supporter from Maryland, writes to the Freedmen's Bureau on behalf of Rindy M. Allen. He believes a military court is necessary as "the only way justice can be done."

Prince Frederick [Md.]

September 14' 1865

General Howard or those having charge of freedmen. at Washington DC. I have been Called upon by Rindy M Allen the barrer of this. [she wants] me to state to you her condition and situation in regard to her children. whis is as follows.

She has a boy which she had hired last Christmas for which she was drawing wages. besides the boy was Clothed and fed, but it seems some time after the boy was hired out by his mother. that Ira Young her former master complains to the orphans Court and the said Court bound the boy to him [young] the boy stayed with his employer about a month. Young then replevys the boy. and the Justice or something in shape of a human being called a Justice of the peace decided that the boy was the property of young, notwithstanding it was proved on trial that the boy was hired out by his mother and she geting wages for him. this man young treats the boy wors than a dog out to [ought to be] treated. he neither feeds or cloths the boy he does not get half enougth to eat and no cloths but what his mother gives him.

Some time ago the boy left young and it was some weeks before he could find him but he found him at last. and on last Sunday young with two others found out where the boy was at and carred him home again and whiped him—the boy in an unhuman manner and still has him yet,. and I have stated in a former letter it is no use to appeal to the law here to have Justice done. in any Casese where a Colored person is to have or ought to have thre rights under the law. nor Can will it ever be any use as long as we have the officers . . . that we now have. I

sugusted in a former letter an establishment of a military court which is the only way that Justice can be done her now. as I before stated that the Colord people in this County. Can and would do very well if they Can hav what they ought to have. that is to get there children un bound. or restored to them and have the privilege of hireing them or working them themselvs. in order that they can help now to surport there parents in order that they may not be come a burthen upon the goverment. but if this state of thing is suffred to be Contued—some of them will be Compelled to leave ther native place for other quatrs and thus be come a burthen on the Goverment when they might be home here in native place and be a use to themselves and to a great many white people whou will hire them and gave them good wages. and so all would be benefited. the Colord people ask of me to say that they ask the favor to interfare in ther behalf or appoint some person to do so. in order that they may be settled and know what to do. It may be that some person have or may state that what is stated here by me is not so. but all I ask is an examination and you will find what I have stated is not as bad as it is. it is hoped that some thing will be done to have this matter investigated. . . .

I forgot to state that this woman rindy is now. held to bail for court to be trid in about tow weeks for persuading this boy to leave young. which she never did but I would not be surprised if she will be Convicted be cause she probly may not be able to have justice done her. when she is not even gilty of any offence so you may know how justice is adminsterd here in this den of treason yours truly

Joseph Hall

Please ansur this[273]

Young Carter Holmes was swept up in the Maryland apprenticeship system during the war and was still serving in this new kind of slavery three years later. In the letter written for him to a Freedmen's Bureau superintendent, Holmes indicates that he was promised food, clothing, and an education for his labor. He describes his employer as "kind" generally, but at the same time he provides a detailed description showing that kindness was a relative term.

Washington D.C. April 22nd 1867

Colonel: I respectfully make the following statement and request that such action may be taken by you in the premises as shall be deemed just.

About three years ago while at Mason's Island I was indentured or bound out by the person in charge there—Dr Nicholls I think—to James Suit living in Prince George County Md about 4 miles from Bladensburgh—who promised me to clothe me, feed and educate me, in compensation for services rendered by me to him—

Mr Suit has been kind to me generally but neither clothed me decently nor sent me to school Once—yes several times I have been whipped by Mr Suit without justification and by Mrs S. also—one time I was struck by her with a shovel—injuring my head very much because I could not fix a pot on a cook stove as she desired.

I have been so tired of not receiving any compensation for my services—no clothing, no chance for school—nothing but *whippings* that I determined to leave Mr Suit and arrived in this city yesterday—

Please don't let Mr Suit take me back for I have a mother and father (named Sylva and Abraham Holmes) who would care for me if they knew where I was. I think they are in this city. Respectfully Yours

his

Carter X Holmes

mark[274]

In the aftermath of the slave era, freedmen wielded power over their spouses that had been the sole prerogative of slaveholders during slavery. Freedmen Bureau agents, teachers, and missionaries cited several examples of domestic violence in the post-war period. This was evidently prevalent enough for black abolitionist poet and lecturer Frances E. W. Harper to preach against it after meeting with freedwomen throughout the South. The several examples of complaints sent to the Freedmen's Bureau probably represent a minority of the actual cases of spousal abuse.

Anderson District, South Carolina, August 23, 1866
Esther, a freedwoman being duly sworn deposes: I am the wife of a freedman named Joseph and have been living with him this year at Dr. Crumley's. He has frequently whipped me and otherwise maltreated me and has threatened to poison me. I fear bodily harm from him by reason of his menaces. I further swear that I do not make this complaint out of malice or for mere vexation.

Vicksburg, Mississippi, April 25, 1868
Julia Gibson (col) states that on Tuesday last her husband beat her over the head, and bit her hand. She has been laid up since till today. When she appr'd to make complaint, she showed a severe cut on her head and a very sore hand where he bit her. Her husband goes by the name of Willis Berkly and lives on Carters place.

Randolph County, Georgia, August 17, 1868
Julia Ray Complains that Alec who is her husband has beaten her badly & her appearance is such as to indicate a gross assault. Appeared and the assault acknowledged by dfdt, but as his wife had made up the quarrel she declined to prosecute. Ray said he did not before know that he could not whip his wife.[275]

Alec Ray's comment that he thought he had a right to whip his wife reflects the attitudes and laws concerning marital relations for both black and white families in the Reconstruction period. While wife abuse was certainly a factor in freedmen's family relationships, the dominant story is the degree to which former slaves focused on creating and protecting familial relations. A few family unifications crossed the color line. Angelina Grimke Weld and Sarah Grimke were sisters from a prominent slaveholding family who left the South to become noted abolitionist and feminist lecturers and writers. When they learned that they had nephews studying at Lincoln University, they promptly got in touch. Archibald and his younger brother Francis were the children of enslaved woman Nancy Weston and Sarah and Angelina's brother Henry W. Grimke. In the correspondence that follows, Angelina is trying to learn if Archibald is related to her. Her letter suggests that she is not at all surprised that she might have African American relatives.

Fairmont Febry 15 1868

Mr Grimke Sir

In a recent number of the Anti Slavery Standard I saw a notice of a meeting at Lincoln University of a Literary Society at which a young gentleman of the name of Grimke deliver'd an address. My maiden name was Grimke. I am the youngest sister of Dr John Grimke of So Carolina, & as this name is a very uncommon one it occurred to me that you had been probably the slave of one of my brothers & I feel a great desire to know all about you. My sister Sarah & myself have long been interested in the Anti Slavery cause, & left Charleston nearly 40 years ago, because we could not endure to live in the midst of the oppressions of Slavery. Will you therefore be so kind as to tell us who you are whether you have any brothers & sisters- who your parents were etc. etc

We rejoice to find you are enjoying the advantages of such an institution, & should be glad to know how you came introduc'd into it, & whatever you are willing to tell me about yourself

My husband Theodore D. Weld was one of the earliest Anti Slavery lecturers at the West.

Hoping to hear from you I remain Sir

Respectfully

Angelina Grimke Weld, Fairmount, Massachusetts

244

African American woman, ca. 1860–1870

Before his death, Henry Grimke willed Nancy Weston and their three sons to his eldest white son with the instructions that his and Nancy's children be treated as members of the family. Contrary to Grimke's wishes, they were treated as slaves and forced out of the home to survive on their own. Later Francis was sold and Archibald ran away. At the end of the war, the former slave family reunited. The three Grimke boys, Archibald, Francis, and John, attended freedmen's schools, and the two eldest graduated from Lincoln University in Pennsylvania, one of the nation's oldest black colleges. Archibald responds almost immediately to Angelina's letter, explaining the details of their relationship and his half-brother's brutal treatment of him, his brothers, and their mother.

Lincoln University Oxford Penna.

Feb. 20th. 1868

Mrs. A. G. Weld;

Dear Madam

I was some what surprised by receiving yours of the 15th—inst. I never expected to hear through the medium of a letter from "Miss Angelina Grimke" of Anti Slavery celebrity. I thank you madam for your kindness to me & concern for me. I shall proceed to give you a simple sketch of my history & of my connections.

I am the son of Henry Grimke a brother of Dr. John Grimke & therefore your brother. Of course you know more about my father than I do, suffice it to say he was a lawyer & was married to a Miss Simons the daughter of Wm Simons & she died leaving three children viz Henrietta, Montague, & Thomas. After her death he took my mother, who was his slave & his children's nurse; her name is Nancy Weston. I don't think you know her, but your sister Miss Ann Grimke knows her, I heard her speak of you ladies often, especially Miss Ann.

By my mother he had three children also, viz, Archibald which is my name, & Francis & John. He died about fifteen years ago, leaving my mother, with two children & in a pregnant state, for John was

born two mos. after he died, in the care of his son Mr. E. M. Grimke, in his own words, as I heard, "I leave Nancy & her two children to be treated as members of the family." He told my mother that he could not leave her free, i.e., he could not give her, her "free papers," because he favored a certain law, forbidding masters to leave their servants free, "but," said he, "I leave you better than free, because I leave you to be taken care of." His reasons for leaving us in the hands of his son, Montague is as follows: (in his words, speaking to mother) "I will not leave you in the hands of Henrietta for she might get married & her husband may [sell?] you, nor will I leave you in the hands of Tom, but I shall leave you in the hands of my son, in whom I can place confidence."

I am the oldest of the bros., was born 17th of Aug. 1849. Therefore my poor mother a defenceless woman, crippled in one arm, with no one to care for her in the world, for Mr. G. did not do as his father commanded, & three small children to provide for, was thrown upon the uncharitable world to struggle with its foaming billows alone. By dint of hard labor working her fingernails to their very quick she kept us from perishing by hunger & on some bleak Dec. day from the cold & sat by & nursed us when we were sick, yes, when at times it appeared that our immortal spirits were trembling on the verge of eternity ready to take his eternal flight to the land of spirits, she would untiringly sit by & nurse us until again we were in a convalescent, state. Thus she continued until 1860 when Mr. E. M. Grimke married a second time, his first wife having died four years previous to this period, & he wanted a boy to wait on him, he informed my mother that he wanted me & that she should send me to his house. His mandate was irresistible; it was a severe shock to my mother; it was unlooked for, unprovided for, she could indeed bear all the privations of this life & suffer, yea die for the sustenance of her children but to be deprived of them at a time when they were just becoming useful to her, & when she could just discern the fruits of her labor, was too shocking & heart rending & she gave way to agony of the separation.

But this was only the beginning of her sorrows, thus he kept on until she was rendered childless, earth became a blank she saw nothing, she

thought of no one but her sons, who were groaning from the severity of their hard task masters, & when she remonstrated at their unjust treatment she was thrown into a loathsome cell & kept there for six days eating nothing during her stay there, until at last sickness prostrated her in the dungeon then he was compelled to remove her by the express request of the Physician. I afterwards fled from my oppressor; Frank attempted to escape but was retaken, & sold, my little bro. was next taken away. Previous to this, the terrific contest begun, we were still struggling in the mighty grasp of the hideous monster, slavery. At last it received its death blow, it was buried in the grave of dishonor never more to smite the land with a curse & Freedom was proclaimed to all men: & again the disjointed members of our little family were united, & the quietude of the fireside returned; the public schools were flung open for all, I gladly embraced the opportunity & went to one of them where I got acquainted with Mrs. Pillsbury, the principal, a native of Mass. She was the principal of Winding Wave Boarding School, Ludlow, Mass, and the sister-in-law of Parker Pillsbury, Editor of the Anti Slavery Standard. Through her intercessions we (my self & Frank) were admitted here. I am supported by six young men, in Dr. Spring's Ch. N. Y. Squire F. W. Hotchkiss supports Frank, our clothes, books, & c, & c, not included in the support. My younger bro. is home with my mother he cannot get support, hence, he cannot come. Mother was well when I heard from her last, Dr. John Grimke died during the war, also Miss Mary Grimke, Miss Eliza Grimke went north after the war.

I hope dear Madam you will excuse this badly written epistle as it is about 12 o'clock P.M. perceiving your great desire to know about me, I sat down to write you as quick as possible. Perhaps you would like to see our picture, they are enclosed. I shall hope to hear from you soon.

Most respectfully yours

Archibald Henry Grimke.

P.S. I send you the history of the University, its catalogue & c &c.[276]

Young Archibald and Francis Grimke, late 1860s

Archibald Grimke later married a white woman, but their relationship ended soon after their wedding. Nevertheless, the sense of optimism, or perhaps naivete, evinced by black and white couples that racist attitudes would soon change was evident at the high point of Congressional Reconstruction, when a significant number of black men were elected to local, state, and federal positions. Soon after the repeal of Mississippi's law against interracial marriage, Northern white Mississippi legislator Albert T. Morgan and black schoolteacher Carrie Highgate were married and honeymooned in the North. Edmonia, Carrie's elder sister, wrote to Ann Smith, wife of the wealthy white abolitionist and friend Gerrit, about her sister's marriage. She asked if the newlyweds could visit the Smiths, probably recognizing that the couple would find it difficult to stay in most hotels and inns.

[McGrawville, New York]
September 2, 1870

My highly esteemed friend:

In July Mr. Smith very kindly invited me to visit you in this month. I write to ask permission to transfer the pleasure I would have in accepting the invitation to my sister—now Mrs. Col. A. T. Morgan. She has been married a month to one of the noblest gentlemen in the world. Most of that time they have spent boarding at a hotel in Cleveland O. They have their share of disagreeable things to contend with owning to the prejudice against the two races inter marrying. They are however so admirably suited to each other that they are happy. Col. Morgan is a noble type of abolitionist and is very desirous to meet Mr. Smith before his duties compel his return to Mississippi which will be in November. They have reason to apprehend considerable danger in Miss. But Col. Morgan is state senator and must brave what comes. They barely escaped being mobbed the night of their marriage.

Most respectfully yours,
Edmonia G. Highgate[277]

While marriages between blacks and whites were nearly impossible in this period, friendships across the color line were more successful, especially among former abolitionists and feminists. The deep friendship between Sarah Mapps Douglass and Sarah Grimke is revealed in their correspondence throughout Grimke's life. Even after Grimke's death in 1873, Douglass and the Grimke-Weld family continued to correspond. In the letter below, Douglass, now seventy-years-old, writes to Grimke's nephew, thirty-seven-year-old Charles Weld, son of Angelina Grimke and Theodore Dwight Weld, revealing not only her need to work in spite of her old age but also her great love of teaching and her affection for the Grimke-Weld family.

Philadelphia, June 1, 1876

Oh, dear Charley, what a comfort your letters would be to me if I could only read them! I have to study over your letter in order to find out all about Mr. Garrison and the memoirs. I thank you for the sweet pieces of poetry you were so kind as to send me. Surely, Charley, you are gifted with a *great* gift.

I suffer greatly from rheumatism, cannot do any house work not even sweep a room. Yet I go to school every day because my bread depends on it. I ride part of the way because it is so difficult for me to walk. I enjoy being in school. I love my work, God wills me to do it. It is sweet work.

Alas, Charley you cannot go with me to Quaker meeting. My health is so poor I do not get to meeting often. You would not know me, since my 60th year I look old. Silver lines are shining in my once dark hair.

My two brothers and myself make up the family. A woman comes on Saturdays and cleans up. My brothers help me a great deal. I do not know what I should do without them. I should be desolate indeed.

Thanks for telling me all about yourself. I always want to know how dear Aunt Sar's boy Charley is. Dear Father and Mother! I think I can see them in their loving beautiful old age. I am suffering severely today from pain in my hips but my heart is full of love to you, dear Charley. Fare thee well.

S. M. Douglass[278]

Sarah Mapps Douglass died six years later, in 1882. Similar to the deep friendship revealed in letters between Mapps Douglass and Sarah Grimke, Emma Brown and Emily Howland's close friendship is evident in their continued correspondence into the Reconstruction era. In her letter below, Brown, who taught in Washington, D.C., public schools until 1869 and later taught for a time in the Deep South, shares her views about the impact of the Congressional vote that gave black men the franchise in the District of Columbia. Now, it seemed to Brown, white men were catering to the interests of African Americans because of new black political power. Brown especially singles out Sayles J. Bowen, a white Washingtonian, who later ran for mayor.

Georgetown, [D.C.] March 23, 1867

My dear friend:

I believe I wrote you a dreadfully forlorn letter. I was very tired and had very nearly lost the small stock of sense I usually possess. . . .

A number of colored teachers, i.e. three, have recently been appointed by Mr. Bowen. Poor Rebecca Perry was the only one examined—she could not answer the questions asked her by the Rev. John Kimball. How I hate the wretch. I know he would gladly have all white teachers if he had the power to turn out colored ones. I forgot to state that Mr. Bowen's sudden preference for colored teachers is easily accounted for. Colored men can vote now. Mr. B. hopes to be Mayor so say folks. Colored men are now annoyed with bows, scrapes and hearty grasps of the hand from white men who did not know them a few weeks ago. Truly this is a strange world.

Are you really coming next month? Mother sends love

Very truly your friend

Emma[279]

In the letter below Emma Brown reveals the strength of her and Emily's friendship when she shares a very private matter concerning accusations against
her twenty-five-year-old brother, Richard Brown.

Georgetown, D.C., March 29, 1868

My dear friend:

I have wanted to write you before but have been too ill to do anything
after school hours. I have come home each day completely exhausted.
Now my head is aching severely—it has ached for three days. I sent
for a physician to-day. He told me what I knew before, that I am worn
out—that my liver is disordered.

We have been seriously disturbed. A bold, bad girl got into
trouble. She discovered that she would become a mother and accused
my brother of being her seducer. The girl's father has told Richard to
marry her, he refused and the man threatened to shoot him. The girl
is that Kate Barker who once accompanied me on a visit to you. I have
tried to save her from ruin but in vain. This girl got herself into trouble
with some white man—she could not force him to marry her—then she
tempted my brother. This he confessed to me with his face buried out
of sight. I felt for him—I blamed him—but I could not condemn him as
I did that wicked girl. We could have had the father put under bail to
keep the peace, but dreaded the publicity of the affair. My mother was
sick and almost worn out. She would start in her sleep and scream
out. I thought the best thing I could do would be to send my brother off
which I did. He is now in the West. He is looking for employment but
has not yet obtained work. I know it must be hard to be in a strange
place without work—but he has sinned and must expect to suffer. He
has been petted and spoiled I fear. I have felt almost hopeless over this.

I hope to be a better correspondent when my health is better.

Very sincerely yours,
E. V. Brown

Please burn this letter.[280]

Emma Brown worked in South Carolina and Mississippi during Congressional Reconstruction, when African American men briefly held important political positions in the South. She refers to three of these politicians. Francis L. Cardozo the son of a Jewish businessman and free black woman, was educated in Charleston and at the University of Glasgow, and served as South Carolina's secretary of state from 1868 to 1872 and then state treasurer from 1872 to 1876. Pennsylvania-born Jonathan J. Wright, like Cardozo, was well educated. He attended school in upstate New York, read for the bar, and served as a South Carolina supreme court justice from 1870 to 1877. Finally, James D. Lynch, the son of a white father and an enslaved woman, was educated in Maryland and served as Mississippi secretary of state from 1869 to 1872. In her letter, Brown briefly mentions former Confederate president Jefferson Davis, who had been recently released after serving two years in prison. Mainly, she reveals how much she was admired among many South Carolina politicians.

Jackson, Mississippi, May 27, 1870

My dear friend:

Your letter was handed me a day or two ago. It was sent from Charleston. I liked C. very much so far as company and gayety were concerned but I did not like the school. It was such a miserable affair—composed of ugly, impertinent, stupid scholars. In a fit of disgust I resigned and came to Jackson. I saw Mr. Cardozo Sec't'y of State of S.C. He is refined and polished—in fact, he is altogether splendid. Judge Wright is one of my best friends. I was introduced to all bright, particular stars of S.C. (colored ones I mean). I enjoyed life in Charleston and grew strong and healthy—but this climate does not seem to agree with me. I am not teaching but copying the Acts of Legislature. I have visited the Capitol. Both the Senate and House presented a very orderly appearance, but they do have some fighting and shooting. Jeff Davis was in town yesterday. He had not the courage to visit the Capitol and see colored men sitting there.

You know, I presume, that my friend, Rev. James Lynch is Sec't'y of State of Miss. I am at his house. His wife was very anxious for me to come here....

I have had about six love affairs on hand since I left home. Only this morning a letter containing an offer of marriage came from the most prominent member of the Lower House. Singular, is it not? He confessed that he is engaged to the most beautiful girl in Jackson (I have seen her). He calls himself a villain but says he will do anything—leave Miss., sacrifice the girl and everything else. Of course I shall decline the honor—but it does seem strange. I arrived here two weeks ago to-day. I wish I had remained in Charleston for the Negro men have annoyed me almost beyond endurance....

I have written very hurriedly because my head is aching terribly. I can scarcely sit up. This is a mean, dirty, dusty little city and I intend to go back to Charleston early in the fall. Direct to care of Hon. James Lynch.

Very sincerely your friend,
E. V. Brown[281]

Emma Brown returned to Washington, D.C., rather than to Charleston and eventually became principal of the prestigious Sumner School, where she thrived, though her headaches did not completely disappear.

Washington, [D.C.] January 25, 1875

My dear friend:

During the last two weeks I have been examining, promoting and grading. On Friday we finished and I went home ill. The severe labor brought on a nervous headache which has not entirely left me....

You will pardon my egotism if I inform you that this school is a success. I glory in it. It is just the field I like—wide enough for my ambition. It is *your* school for you incited or rather inspired me with zeal. With no talent—with nothing but energy I have I feel accomplished a little....

When are you coming to Washington? Do write soon—pardon egotism and everything else that is obnoxious in this letter.

Yours in love—
Emma V. Brown[282]

Mississippi senator Blanche K. Bruce, 1870s

Two months later, Emma Brown describes her friendship with two prominent black Mississippi politicians, both former slaves then serving in the United States Congress. Blanche K. Bruce, a Mississippi county tax collector, sheriff, and plantation owner, was elected to the U.S. Senate from 1875 to 1881. John R. Lynch, former speaker of the Mississippi state legislature, served in the U.S. House of Representatives from 1873 to 1877 and then again briefly in the early 1880s before Mississippi whites gained complete control over all congressional districts using tactics of terror and disfranchisement.

Washington [D.C.,] March 31, 1875

My dear Miss Howland:

I have waited for a letter from you but vainly. I have been worked almost to death this year; our teachers have been ill—one gave out and so much additional labor has been thrown on me. I get home exhausted.

I was escorted to a concert las night by Senator Bruce of Miss. The single ladies here rave over his good looks—he *is* good looking or rather very fine looking but I do not especially admire him. He is a great big good natured lump of fat. He wears the finest broadcloth, a lovely beaver the finest linen, diamond studs and his wellshaped hands are encased in the loveliest kids. He is gentlemanly and very jolly. Just the fellow to go around with. It is customary for Senator Bruce, Representative Lynch and myself to attend evening church, concerts &c in company. The beautiful ladies are quite disgusted and say in the hearing of the gentlemen "There goes that heartless Emma Brown, with no style and no beauty. What Bruce sees in her, or Lynch either it is difficult to imagine." The gentlemen are exceedingly amused at these comments and appear more devoted. These people do not know that a year ago Mr. Bruce stood above the grave of his betrothed. They do not know how his heart aches to-day. I know the story and as I do know it he knows that his friendly feeling toward me will not be mistaken. I knew both gentlemen in Miss.

My school is still flourishing. I am enjoying it. Do write soon.

Yours in love,

Emma[283]

258

Emma Brown eventually married another teacher, Henry Montgomery, with whom she worked at one of the Washington, D.C., schools. When she married in 1879, her teaching career ended. The District of Columbia forbade married women to teach, but she stayed involved in black education, reflecting African Americans' firm conviction that education was central to freedom.[284] Indeed, former slaves accelerated the process begun during the Civil War of creating their own educational institutions. Believing that an education was essential, illiterate and barely literate freedpeople built schools for their children after the war.[285] Sergeant John Sweeney, a free Kentucky man before the war, explains to Brigadier General Clinton B. Fisk his desire to open a school for black soldiers.

Nashville Tenn October 8th 1865

Sir I have the honor to call your attention To the necessity of having a school for The benefit of our regement We have never Had an institutiong of that sort and we Stand deeply inneed of instruction the majority of us having been slaves We Wish to have some benefit of education To make of ourselves capable of buisness In the future We have estableshed a literary Association which flourished previous to our March to Nashville We wish to become a People capable of self support as we are Capable of being soldiers my home is in Kentucky Where Prejudice reigns like the Mountain Oak and I do lack that cultivation of mind that would have an attendency To cast a cloud over my future life after have been in the United States service I had a leave of absence a few weeks a go on A furlough and it make my heart ache to see my race of people there neglected And ill treated on the account of the lack of Education being incapable of putting Thier complaints or applications in writing For the want of Education totally ignorant Of the Great Good Workings of the Government in our behalf We as soldiers Have our officers Who are our protection To teach how us to act and to do But Sir What we want is a general system of education In our regiment for our moral and literary elevation these being our motives We have the Honor of calling your very high Consideration Respectfully Submitted as Your Most humble servt

John Sweeney[286]

Fisk granted the soldier's request and eventually Sweeney became a teacher at a school in his hometown that included many wives and children of soldiers among its students.[287]

Another teacher, William M. Jennings, reports to the Christian Recorder on how eager former slaves are to get an education. His letter also reveals the lack of education among many white Southerners and their desire to learn.

June 30th, 1866

Mr Editor: As the freed people of this locality have been left entirely independent and free from Government support or patronage, a few facts about them may be of interest to your readers. A pleasant ride of about eight miles from the town of Portsmouth, Va., will bring you to the village of Deep Creek. Deep Creek is a small village with about three hundred inhabitants, two-thirds of which are freed people. . . . After entering the village, the first place that would attract the stranger's eye is an old romantic-looking building, which was formerly used as a hotel. But with a few nails and the work of several hours we converted it into quite a respectable looking school-house, which will accommodate two hundred scholars.

The people were eager to learn, and we soon had every seat filled with bright-looking, anxious pupils. They learn fast, faster than you would expect, and are thankful for the interest we take in them. They behave admirably in school, no where, with like advantages, could you find better order, and in many little acts do they express their appreciation of what the good friends are doing for them. There are some who walk five miles to school. An old lady came to me the other day and wished to know if I was the teacher. I told her yes. She then told me that she wanted to learn to read, so that she could read that good old Book, the Bible, but that she could neither see nor hear. These people have great faith in the Yankee teachers, and think they can do wonders. There has been a piece of ground given to the people, on which they intend building a school-house, and with a little help

from some of our good Northern friends they will be able to do so. All they want is encouragement.

Since I opened school the whites have found out that they, too, want the lamp of knowledge, and an education to fit them better to enjoy life, and have opened day and night school. It is a good thing they had the spirit to do so, for they need it. You in the North would be surprised to see the ignorance that exists among the whites. It is a rare thing to find a man that can write his own name. The colored people are two per cent ahead of them. . . .

Wm. M. Jennings[288]

The African Methodist Episcopal Church and other religious denominations were involved in establishing several schools and colleges in the post-war era. The letter to the *Christian Recorder* below illustrates the importance African Americans placed on having a black preparatory school for Wilberforce College, the African Methodist Episcopal Church institution established in Ohio in 1856.

September, 1869

The Kentucky Conference High School, Louisville Ky . . . [will be] established in accordance with a resolution passed at the Second Session of the Kentucky Conference of the A.M.E. Church held at Lexington, Aug. 21–29, and is intended to be a preparatory school to Wilberforce University. There will also be formed a Theological Class, which will afford rare advantages to young men having in view the Gospel Ministry. Competent assistance has been procured and no pains will be spared to make the school one of the best in the State. For further information or circulars address. R. G. Mortimer, Louisville, KY[289]

In 1870, black Virginia teacher R. A. Perkins writes to Freedmen's Bureau superintendent Ralza Manly asking for support.

Lynchburg June 2nd 1870

R. M. Manley

Dear Sir

I seat myself to address you a line or too in reference to my school. I have been teaching for the Pa Association since Oct last to the 27th . . . at which time the school closed, and now most of the larger boys and girls are at work in the tobacco factories, but there are a great many smaller children whose parents are anxious to continue sending them to school but they are not able to pay a sufficient tuition to support a teacher in behalf of this class of people and your honorable correspondent this letter is written. Can you not do something for us? The people are becoming interested in the education of the children and I hope you will aid them to some extent. If you can give something in support of myself that will enable me to carry on a school for two months it will be thankfully recd. Mr Yoder [wrote] to you before he went away; but as I never heard anything from his letter. I thought that I would write myself. You will please favor me with an early answer and do what you can for me.

No more at present
R. A. Perkins[290]

Freedmen's School on Edisto Island, South Carolina, ca. 1862–1865

Writing from New Orleans, black school principal Edmonia Highgate complains to the American Missionary Association's corresponding secretary that the Freedmen's Bureau withdrew its support for black education in New Orleans in early 1866, leaving thousands of children without access to an education. Highgate adds that the poor parents, some of whom were "Creole," free people of African and European ancestry, had been doubly negatively affected before the war and after because they were taxed to pay for an education for whites. She makes it clear that she is not referring to wealthy Creoles who had been slaveholders. Ironically, Highgate's school had once been a New Orleans slave pen.

New Orleans

Reverend M. E. Strieby   February 8, 1866

Dear Friend:

The schools of New Orleans have been sustained without aid from Northern Associations. But commencing with this month, the government has with-drawn its pecuniary assistance. While the Freedmen's Bureau still retains its supervision i.e. regulation of tuition fees, provision of school houses and school property, yet the colored people must compensate the teachers by making an advance installment of $1.50 per mo. for each child they send. This plan was proposed by Maj. Gen. Howard because the Bureau owes an arrearage on teachers salaries of four months standing. Consequently the number of teachers in the city which up to Feb'y 1st was 150 has been reduced to twenty-eight. I need scarcely inform you that something like 3000 children have been shut out of our schools because their widowed mothers are "too poor to pay." Their fathers being among the numbers "who made way for Liberty and died."

There is a class mostly Creoles, who have for years, paid an educational tax to support the schools of the whites, themselves deriving no benefit there from. They cannot afford to pay that tax and teachers also. I refer now to the poorer class of Creoles. Of course some of them are wealthy but do not feel in the least identified with the freed men or their interest. Nor need we wonder when we remember that many of them were formerly slaveholders. You know the peculiar institution cared little for the ethnology of its supporters.

The question is this dear sir, can the American Missionary Association pay several teachers under the F. Bureau's supervision? The people's fees will not warrant the salary of even the twenty eight teachers retained. The Fred. Douglass school of which I am principal, numbered 800 pupils, now it has but 127. Board and other expenses are exorbitant here. We still draw rations from the Government yet those who have to wait for so long for their salary are reduced to sad straits. It may perhaps amuse you to know that the building in which I teach was formerly a slave pen but now conveniently fitted up as a graded school.

Very truly yours,
Edmonia Highgate[291]

Black women from the North and South remained critical to the Southern educational effort, though they often experienced racism not only from white Northern teachers and superintendents but also from Southern whites hostile to black education. After whites rioted against black and white Union supporters who were holding a constitutional convention under Congressional Reconstruction policies, Highgate left New Orleans. She tells an A.M.A. official of her experiences in rural Louisiana, where Creole sharecroppers were able to include a 5 percent tax for their children's education in a sharecropping system that appears unusual in its planter and tenant conditions. In her lengthy letter, Highgate describes, too, her attempt to influence the morals of freedpeople in keeping the Sabbath and marriage. She ends her letter by describing the hard work and violence with which she and other teachers contended.

Lafayette Parish, Louisiana,
December 17th 1866

Rev. M. E. Strieby
Dear Friend:

After the horrible riot in New Orleans in July I found my health getting impaired, from hospital visiting and excitement so I came here to do what I could and to get stronger corporally. I have a very interesting and constantly

growing day school, a night school, and a glorious Sabbath School of near one hundred scholars. The school is under the auspices of the Freedmen's Bureau, yet it is wholly self supporting. The majority of my pupils come from plantations, three, four, and even eight miles distant. So anxious are they to learn that they walk these distances so early in the morning as never to be tardy. Every scholar buys his own book and slate &c. They, with but few exceptions are french Creoles. My little knowledge of French is put in constant use in order to instruct them in our language. They do learn rapidly. A class who did not understand any English came to school last Monday morning and at the close of the week they were reading "easy lessons." The only church of any kind here is Catholic and any of the people that incline to any belief are of that denomination.

There is but little actual want among these freed people. The corn, cotton and sugar crops have been abundant. Most of the women and larger children are hired by the year "on contract" upon the plantations of their former so called masters. One of the articles of agreements is that the planter shall pay "a five per cent tax" for the education of the children of his laborers. They get on amicably. The adjustment of relation between employer and former slaves would surprise our Northern politicians.

Most all of them are trying to buy a home of their own. Many of them own a little land on which they work nights and Sabbaths for themselves. They own cows and horses, besides raising poultry. The great sin of Sabbath breaking I am trying to make them see in its proper light. But they urge so strongly its absolute necessity in order to keep from suffering that I am almost discouraged of convincing them. They are given greatly to the sin of adultery. Out of three hundred I found but three couples legally married. This fault was largely the masters and it has grown upon the people till they cease to see the wickedness of it. There has never been a missionary here to open their eyes. I am doing what I can but my three schools take most of my time and strength. I am trying to carry on an Industrial School on Saturdays, for that I greatly need material. There are some aged ones here to whom I read the bible. But the distances are so great I must always hire conveyances and although I ride horseback I can seldom get a horse. There is more than work for two teachers yet I am all alone.

There has been much opposition to the School. Twice I have been shot at in my room. My night scholars have been shot but none killed. The rebels here threatened to burn down the school and house in which I board before the first month was passed yet they have not materially harmed us. The nearest military protection is two hundred miles distant at New Orleans. Even the F. M. Bau agt [Freedmen's Bureau agent] has been absent for near a month. But I trust fearlessly in God and am safe. Will you not send me a package of "The Freedmen" for my Sunday School? No matter how old they are for there has never been a Sunday School paper here.

Yours for Christ's poor
Edmonia Highgate[292]

Highgate returned to New Orleans and became an officer of the Louisiana Education Relief Association, an organization founded after the Freedmen's Bureau withdrew its support of black schools. The association, with Highgate's strong influence it seems, refused to support the New Orleans school board's decision to segregate schools. Though the association's initial efforts were in vain, continued pressure led to the school board's decision to desegregate its schools in January 1871, making it the only Southern city to have desegregated schools until the end of Reconstruction. Before then, however, Highgate had moved to eastern Mississippi, where she taught in a small town.[293] In a letter to the editor dated December 13, 1868, Highgate describes her work as teacher and missionary in Mississippi to the readers of the *Christian Recorder.* Baltimore free-born Reverend James D. Lynch, mentioned below, would soon become prominent in Mississippi politics.

Mr. Editor: Perhaps in none of the Southern States is the missionary work more interesting in its character than in Mississippi. Northern benevolence through various legitimate channels is accomplishing untold good here. There is a pressing need of more laborers in this harvest sure field. Laborers, who are willing to endure exposure to cold, inclement weather, to sacrifice all the luxuries and most of the comforts of Northern homes in order to patiently and

faithfully lay the foundation of a majesty State by their daily and nightly teaching in miserable dilapidated open unwarmed buildings. The hope of the South is in its youth. Therefore our missionaries make special efforts for them, not neglecting; however, to suggest reforms to the middle-aged and to cheer the way to the tomb for the old, by pointing them to the sure consolations of religion. Were we allotted time and space to refer at length to persons and work here, we would fill your columns with labors of your distinguished predecessor, Rev. James, Lynch, Presiding Elder of the Jackson District in the M.E. connection. Should we attempt the most unvarnished statement of the hundreds of miles he travels a month; the sermons he preaches in that time; the immense amount of miscellaneous ecclesiastical work he performs; to say nothing of what he does in the State interest or his editorial duties, and his valuable, regular correspondence with several popular journals, your readers would deem us guilty of fabricating. He combines the rare qualifications of an infuser of zeal and righteous emulation with a genuine nobleness that makes him proud of the privilege of himself, frequently performing dangerous and difficult noble acts. He is the great *L'Ouverture* in the missionary and reconstruction work in this State.

Fully appreciating the many and often fatal dangers that surround his paths he dashes on with Gen. Sherman like determination to the sea, which he will reach in a few years. He is emphatically the teachers' friend so also he claimed and most justly, by the most illiterate freedmen who even mutely appeals for his aid. Should any think we are tempted to dwell too long on Rev. James Lynch, let them remember it is impossible to fulfil the promise of the caption of this communication and do otherwise. We want all the encouragement, which each and every comfortably situated Northern family can so easily give by a little self-sacrificing effort. Our Sabbath schools need Bibles, Sabbath school papers and the religious literature. We teachers need a fund from which to draw to supply the necessities of the infirm sufferers we meet in our daily visitations. We want material for industrial schools in order that we may teach the girls and women to become good seamstresses and at the same time do much to reach glaring social

evils that exist unrebuked among them. Ours is a noble work transcending all sectarianism. It is most far-reaching in its scope and surprisingly thorough in its concentrative specialties. Aid us, then, as a high privilege. Remember that the teachers in the north are the rear guard of the grand army of the Republic. Do not think that an abiding peace is conquered. Take and see that your neighbors subscribe for "The Colored Citizen Monthly," the journal of the newly enfranchised in this State, published for one dollar a year, by Rev. James Lynch, at Jackson, Mississippi.

E. Goodelle Highgate[294]

As Highgate indicates, freedpeople insisted on the simultaneous establishment of schools and churches during and especially after the Civil War. Freedom meant establishing institutions that supported African American families in the present and for the future. In his letter to the *Christian Recorder*, U.S. Army Chaplain and African Methodist Episcopal Church minister Henry McNeal Turner reports on the swiftness with which former slaves in South Carolina formed their own churches.

January 20, 1866

Mr. Editor: In my last letter I stated that I would further inform you concerning Columbia, S.C., my former residence. I would remark that the colored people there are alive to their interests, as regards their churches. They have thrown off the slave-yoke of Southern Methodism, and united with the A.M.E. Church, and are standing in the full vigor of their God-given rights. Their places of worship at present are but temporary. They are preparing, however, to erect themselves a permanent edifice to worship God in. They are united to a man, as regards their efforts to elevate themselves; and one great reason is, Columbia is now blessed with men of large minds and comprehensive intellects. Such men as Revs. David Picket, Addison Richardson, Mr. William Simons, Mr. James Banfield, and other residents, are a host in themselves. They have also a firm man of God from Charleston, acting as their pastor, by appointment

of that inestimable hero of progression, Rev. R. H. Cain. His name is Rev. Brother Smith. I predict for that place great results of intelligence and social distinction.[295]

The *Christian Recorder* regularly reported on the growth of Southern black churches in the 1860s and 1870s among Methodists, Baptists, and Presbyterians.

Stalwarts of the abolition movement remained in touch throughout their lives, sharing news of family and friends. William Still, a former operator of the Underground Railroad and current co-owner of a coal delivery business, decided to compile the narratives of the fugitives whom he had aided in their escape to the North or to Canada. In his letter, he writes to journalist and former black nationalist Mary Ann Shadd Cary in Canada. Still describes his project and reports on the thrills of being a grandparent. "Blackstone" is a nineteenth-century reference to the study of law.

Apr. 13, 1871
William Still
Dealer of Lehigh and Schuylkill Coal
Yard, 1216, 1218, 1220 Washington Avenue, Philadelphia,
Mrs. M. A. S. Carry,
My Dear friend:
How have you been? I understand you are exploring Blackstone & teaching at the Same time. I have had you in my mind very often of late, thinking about writing to you but as usual my time has been all absorbed.

At last I am working day and night on my Underground Rail Road Book. And you may just beleive I have a "big job" of it. Many have been urging me to write and I have been putting it off from time to time in order to find suitable leisure for the work. But this Spring I came to the conclusion that I would let everything else go to grass, for 5 or 6 mos. any how while I give my undivided attention to the book. Well, my son-in-law can take care of my office at the yard (he is a first rate young man) and I will

Stick to my office at 244 South 12th St. and write like a Steamer running all the time. I have enough good live matter for two or three good vols. But I intend only to put in the cream and will craft it all in one vol. of about 700 pages. In it I shall have portraits & illustrations by the wholesale, and with regard to mechanical skill in every particular, it is to be first class. No black man's book. I have the material for a great book and I shall do what I can to meet the demand of the times in this direction. I will Say to you Confidentially there is not a man on this Continent I beleive who have the Narratives, letters & facts for a book such as I have. . . .

Now just listen- I am Grandpapa. What a Shame it is that even your own Children will help to make you seem old. Oldest daughter Carrie on the 26th of Dec. last brought forth a daughter. Some weeks afterwards the young Mother took cold and her case seemed very hopeless for a time, but after being confined to her bed 5 or 6 weeks, favorable systems began to appear and in a short-while she commenced to improve rapidly and is now pretty well again.

Letitia is quite stout- of course She will complain of rheumatism sometimes. She is this evening with Wilberforce & Frances Ellen at a Festival in the Central Ch.

How are your children doing? Have you them with you? I hope they are a comfort to you. Write me a long letter right away and let me hear from you. . . .

Why do you never come this way? Most happy would we be to have a visit from you. Mrs Still Sends her love to you.

> Yours truly
> William Still[296]

William Still's book, *The Underground Rail Road*, was first published in 1872 and has become an important resource for scholars. Mary Ann Shadd Cary taught in Washington, D.C., schools and earned a law degree in 1883 from Howard University at age sixty. Into old age, Shadd Cary continued to write for newspapers and advocate for women's suffrage.

Former fugitive Harriet Jacobs and her daughter, Louisa, finally settled in Cambridge, Massachusetts, in 1869. They opened a boarding house and remained active in African American causes after having spent the last four years doing relief work for the freedpeople in Washington, D.C.; Alexandria, Virginia; Savannah, Georgia; and Edenton, North Carolina. Harriet and Louisa had spent several months in England in 1868, raising funds for a Savannah project to aid freedpeople. Their efforts in the South were thwarted, because white supremacists used violence against anyone attempting to improve the lives of blacks. Writing from much less contentious surroundings, Louisa Jacobs expresses regret to Cordelia Downing, the daughter of northeastern businessman and abolitionist George T. Downing, that she is unable to attend Cordelia's upcoming wedding.

Cambridge, Trowbridge St.

May 16, 1870

My dear Miss Downing

Since I shall not have the pleasure of offering my personal congratulations on the 18th, I hope you will accept my next best self—that which comes from the heart through the pen.

May the life you are so soon to enter upon be one of great contentment and happiness. I do not say of cloudless happiness for I believe there is no such existence in this life. If we only hold and regulate the sunshine that lies within our reach, we shall not be deeply scarred by the cloud that will sometimes mar its brightness.

Aside from my friendship for you, there comes another and a longer one for Mr. De Mortie, and I can but ask God's best blessing on you both.— Mother joins me in kind wishes. Remember me to the family, And

Believe me Affectionately Yours

Louisa Jacobs[297]

Of course, courtship and marriage defined many African American relationships; creating families reflected a sense of possibility in this era. The Downing–De Mortie wedding was a major event in Washington, D.C., elite black society. According to the *New National Era*, "About 100 ladies and gentlemen, the elite of colored fashion and high life, were assembled" in the Downing's front parlor.

In the correspondence below, another couple, from Ohio, move from friendship to courtship when Nicey Bush declares her love to Harvey Moore.

Californian African American couple, ca. 1870s–1880s

Carthagena, Ohio
September 14, 1869

Dear Harvey,

I am well at present and hope these few lines may find you the same. There is something that compels me to write—yet something I have tried to keep which I cannot retain any longer that is love, yes I love you. You have stolen my heart. Now I know that I have treated you wrong you said I had but I never thought so before. I know that if you was to treat me now like I did you my heart would almost break. I would even receive letters from you and not answer them for a long time and some times not at all but I know that you are tender hearted and will forgive me for so doing. If I have wrote any thing wrong you will forgive me for it. Am in a hurry. I don't expect you can read this if you cant I will read it for you.

Nicey[298]

Based on Harvey's response, seen in the next two letters, it seems Nicey, though willing to declare her love, is not yet ready for marriage.

Coldwater, Ohio

October 26, 1869

Dear Nicey,

Your kind and affectionate letter of September 14th was received with much pleasure was read and reviewed more than once. I hope you will not be mad at me for my neglect. Pardon me if it be an offense. I would not knowingly wound your heart. [H]ow could I think that one whom I so ardently love. . . . My heart has bin stolen and I believe it's you that has in its possession. would you be willing to give me yours in return or would you refuse or persist in refusing to speak on this most solemn subject, subject of matrimony. I have no doubt you will censure me of forcing this question. I hope you will forgive me. You know I am weak minded and you say I am tender hearted but I don't think so. I fault my self for being hard hearted and always need to return evil for evil but I need not informe you, you know to much already, although if I had not such implicit confidence I could not divulge the secret emotions of my heart with such freedom. I have something I call a condisional proposition that I wish to make to you. If it is agreeable in reference to our future destiny you I must informe did not say any thing wrong in my view in your communication. I hope you will forgive me if I have said anything wrong now. I must bid you good night, happy dreams attend you

And I will be your most

Devoted Harvey

Carthagena Ohio
Dec. 20th 1869

Dear Nicey,

I must call you by that little name. A poem has elapsed since our correspondence began, but what motives were we prompted and to what purpose shall we concede I don't know why I can not cease to think of you, and to love you, you say I have stolen your heart. I can say this much you stole mine first and a fair exchange is no robery. I think it was down right [mean?] for you to keep from me your real centiment. If those hearts are blended and linked together by the ties of affection so let it be Never break or sever that vow, or promise you made in your last letter as there is something I have tryed to retain I find I can not so I will present you my heart and hand to accompany it provided you will accept of them in return for the one that was stolen from you as you have implicated me or rather charged me as the guilty one so you see at once I am generous.

Well Nicey when shall that happy day be, please decide the doubtful case, you may ask what day our wedding day, you must get your excuses ready, I shall be plain on this subject and short as I have not the talent to write a prolonged detail, think of this and tell me when I see you. Then I desire a private interview, then after I hear your decision, if you allow me I have something to tell you. I don't see how you could afforde to attach your self to one so limited in point of education circumstances and every other material consideration remember that notwithstanding I have commended my self to you, willing to shear all the joys and sorrows of life with you—Christmas gift dear and then a sweet kiss good bye as ever

Harvey

Nicey E. Bush and Harvey Moore were probably married during the Christmas season, if Harvey had his way. Some couples, like Amelia Loguen and Lewis Douglass, had an even longer courtship. After receiving a medical discharge from the army in 1864 because of a wound at the Battle of Fort Wagner that rendered him infertile, Sergeant-Major Henry Lewis Douglass regained his health and became a teacher. He quickly got involved in black politics in Washington, D.C., and Maryland, serving as a delegate to the Maryland Black State Convention and a claimant in a suit demanding that African Americans be given the right to testify in court. Lewis explains his political ventures to his fiancée, Amelia.

Ferry Neck, Jan. 7 1866

My Own Dear Amelia: I have just returned from the city of Baltimore where I have been to attend the colored State Convention. I was honored by being chosen temporary Chairman of the Convention, after which I was made chairman of the business committee. I also had the honor to prepare the address to the Legislature of the State which was received very flatteringly by the Convention. We had a rather stormy convention there being so many ignorant men as delegates, but on the whole the convention was a success and I feel morally certain will be productive of much good. We organized a State League and have taken measures to bring a suit against the State of Maryland for the purpose of making a test question as to the legality of refusing the colored man the right to give evidence in courts of justice against white as well as colored citizens of the United States living in Maryland. Mr. Wm. E. Matthews of Baltimore city and Lewis H. Douglass of Talbot County have been chosen by the Convention and the State League of Maryland to represent the colored people of the State in Washington during the present session of Congress. I will consequently spend the remainder of the winter in Washington or Baltimore. This I conceive to be the highest eminence that I have ever yet attained and places me still nearer that high mark to which I am aiming. And when I get up I can look back and say that I have come up not without trials and tribulations, but come up I will.

My holiday was work all the time. Christmas I was all day lost in the fog on the Chesapeake bay. All through Christmas week I was busy at the Convention. I am now preparing for my departure tomorrow for Washington. I will write you from Washington when I get there. Give my love to everybody and do not forget that I love you.

Yours Affectionately
Lewis H. Douglass[299]

The couple postponed their wedding until 1869. It seems Amelia had to come to terms with the idea of having a childless marriage. That year, Douglass was working for the U.S. Government Printing Office as a typesetter, a short-lived position because of the typesetter union's discrimination policy. As the letter indicates, the couple is trying to settle on the date of their marriage and who will serve in their wedding party. At the same time, they are contending with threats on Lewis's life, likely from white typesetters opposed to working with an African American. We also learn that Lewis chose Amelia's brother, Gerrit Loguen, for his best man.

Washington July 5 1869

My Dear Amelia,

I have been necessitated to allow your letter to go unanswered for a day or two, but I trust as Toots says "it's of no consequence." Now as to the day, so far as I am concerned, Saturday or any other day of the week would make no difference with me. I will tell you Amelia, I shall have you name the day, as custom has made it your prerogative so to do. I will not be able to leave here before the 24th October at any rate. I shall in all probability—go directly to Rochester, if I go by the way of New York City—shall call on you at Syracuse, but if I go by the direct road from Baltimore I can't of course call on my way, as time will be with me an important element. I may take the route through Pennsylvania home. But I think we have time enough left to settle definitely upon the day.

Helen Amelia
Loguen Douglass
and Lewis
Douglass,
ca. 1860–1880s

As to that threatening letter sent me do not be alarmed. The *New York Tribune* says in regard to it that "threatened men live long" and calls on the government to sustain me in my present position if it should be necessary to have a regiment of soldiers to guard me. Quite a stir for an insignificant human being like me to be kicking up.

Gerrit will stand up with me to keep me in courage when I promise to obey (?) you &c who will stand up with you when you promise to command me.

Amelia I don't know that I ever intimated to you that my preference is that the wedding or marriage should be conducted with least possible display: this, however, is only my preference, don't think that any arrangement you may make will meet with my disapprobation. To day the S. School with which I am connected is to hold a picnic, and I have been pretty busy for the last week. I sat down to write a good letter but am constantly bothered so must close.

> Love to all. Will write to Gerrit in a day or two.
> Your Affectionate
> Lewis[300]

Another letter from Lewis, written twelve days later, suggests that the couple has not yet settled on an exact date for the wedding but that his father, Frederick Douglass, agrees with Lewis's choice for a wife. Lewis had been living with his younger brother Charles and his wife but found it uncomfortable.

Washington, July 17, 1869

My Dear Amelia

Your letter of the 13th inst is received. I have been suffering with the tooth ache, for nearly a week, and am now happily over it. Because of a disposition of Charley's wife to be exceedingly disagreeable I have ceased to board with him, and am now boarding in the city of Washington. I hardly know yet whether I shall board this coming winter or keep house. I much prefer house keeping. Charles is the father of another soul.

I learn from father that he called on you a few days ago, and that he was much pleased, so much so that he congratulates me on my choice, and more than intimates that to Fred and myself . . . descanting quite fully on your many good points. What do you mean by saying that you come second in my love. I am utterly unable to understand you. Must I speak that I *love* you in the fullest meaning of that word. It may be however that in my last letter I did not express my self clearly which has led you to infer something harsh. Do not draw such inferences from any thing I may write, for my dear Amelia I am tortured daily by the confusion made by the printers. Now don't I pray you think of anything I say that seems harsh, for I love you sincerely, heartily.

I am to appear by shadow in the *Harper's Weekly* I suppose next week. By the way if you have any influence with that brother Gerrit of yours, have him hurry up those pictures I sent for.

Think only of the happiness in store for us, if we in love, constant and true to each other. Many temptations have been mine but I always think of you.

Your loving
Lewis
Gov't Printing Office[301]

In its October 10, 1869, issue, the *Christian Recorder* announced: "The marriage of a son of Frederick Douglass, to a daughter of Bishop Loguen." Quoting from the *Syracuse Journal*, the *Christian Recorder* reported that the young couple "flushed with the healthy glow and ruddy bloom of their ripening natures" and "assume the regal life of society that prepares them for future happiness, high responsibilities and sacred duties in their allotted circle, and bring joy to friends, happiness to themselves, and pleasure to all around them." According to the Syracuse paper, Lewis and Amelia were married Thursday, October 7, 1869, in her father's home. "Everything connected with the interesting ceremony was in keeping with the occasion, and many valuable, elegant and costly bridal presents were showered upon the bride, by warm friends and admirers from various parts of the state."[302] The couple lived in Anacostia, where Lewis soon joined his father as senior editor of the *New National Era Weekly*.

ACKNOWLEDGMENTS

This book began as a compilation of letters I often used when asked to tell the history of the African American experience to a number of diverse organizations outside the academy, including churches, libraries, sororities, and fraternities. Thus, my first thanks is to the several organizations, including "Couples Club" of Southern California, who helped me realize that even in this digital age, letters provide a more real and personal understanding of the past. I also wish to thank the librarians at the Massachusetts Historical Society, Boston Public Library, Boston Athenaeum, New-York Historical Society, New York Public Library, Pennsylvania Historical Society, the Library Company of Philadelphia, National Archives, Library of Congress, and especially at the Moorland-Spingarn Research Center at Howard University. An incredibly satisfying retreat from the archives was to sit at Walter and Linda Evans's dining-room table in Savannah, Georgia, to access the Walter O. Evans Collection of Frederick Douglass scrapbooks, letters, and photographs now housed in the Beinecke Rare Book & Manuscript Library at Yale University. Not only did Walter make his collection of Frederick Douglass materials available, but he and Linda were also perfect hosts during our stay in Savannah. A very special thanks to the remarkable historian, Ira Berlin (now deceased) and the many editors of *Freedom: A Documentary History of Emancipation, 1861–1867* for their compilation of documents selected from the holdings of the National Archives. I also wish to thank my two former students and research assistants, Rachel Ballard and Simrat Dugal, who early on in the project identified several letters in the archives and primary materials published in various texts. I also thank my friend and colleague, James Oakes who continues to give me unstinting support in reading and commenting on my various writing projects. Finally, thanks to Leslie Willis-Lowry for helping with the daunting task of identifying suitable images for the book, to Faith Childs of the Faith Childs Literary Agency, who unwaveringly shared my vision of making history more accessible to the general public, and to Mirabelle Korn and the rest of the team at Chronicle Books. As always, I am grateful to Terry for everything.

IMAGE CREDITS

Unidentified African American soldier in uniform with wife and two daughters. United States. [Between 1863 and 1865] Photograph. https://www.loc.gov/item/2010647216/.

Letter from John M. Washington to Annie E. Gordon: October 27, 1861. University of Virginia Library, Special Collections.

Position of Union and Rebel armies at Fredericksburg, Virginia. December 1, 1862. Robert Knox Sneden Diary. Virginia Museum of History and Culture.

Advertisement for the purchase of slaves, printed on July 2, 1853 by William F. Talbott of Lexington, Kentucky in Winston Coleman, Jr.'s *Slavery Times in Kentucky.* University of Kentucky.

African American slave families owned by Mrs. Barnwell. [Between 1860 and 1865] Photograph. https://www.loc.gov/item/2010651604/.

The Weekly Anglo-African. (New York [N.Y]) Vol. 1, No. 1 Ed. 1 Saturday, July 23, 1859. Texas Digital Newspaper Program. UNT Libraries.

Alexandria, Virginia, Slave pen. Interior view. United States. [Between 1861–1869] Photograph. https://www.loc.gov/item/2018670632

Alexandria, Virginia, Slave pen. Price, Birch & Co. dealers in slaves. United States. [Between 1861 and 1869] Photograph. https://www.loc.gov/item/2018670631/.

Dangerfield Newby. 1859. Courtesy of Kansas State Historical Society.

Contemporaries of John Brown–J.A. Copeland. [No Date Recorded on Caption Card] Photograph. https://www.loc.gov/item/2002736549/.

Emily Plummer photograph from Nellie A. Plummer, *Out of the Depths or The Triumph of the Cross* (1927), Charles Blockson Collection. Temple University Library.

Adam Plummer photograph from Nellie A. Plummer, *Out of the Depths or The Triumph of the* Cross (1927), Charles Blockson Collection. Temple University Library.

William Still. [Between 1870 and 1890] Friends Historical Library, Swarthmore College.

Barnard, George N. photographer. *The slave market, Atlanta, Ga.* United States Atlanta Georgia, 1864. [New York: E. & H. T. Anthony & Co., American and Foreign Stereoscopic Emporium, 501 Broadway, or earlier] Photograph. https://www.loc.gov/item/2011647092/.

New Orleans, LA old slave block in St. Louis Hotel. United States. Detroit Publishing Co [Between 1900 and 1910] Photograph. https://loc.gov/item/2016795470/.

J.A. Beard and May auction notice for Valuable Gang of Georgia and South Carolina field hands, The Historic New Orleans Collection 2014.03071.

Historic American Buildings Survey. Creator, and Orville W. Carroll, Boucher, Jack E. photographer. *Green Hill, Slave Auction Block. 378 Pannills Road (State Route 728), Long Island, Campbell County, VA.* Campbell County Virginia Long Island, 1933. Photograph. https://www.loc.gov/item/va0279/.

Barnard, George N., photographer. *"Auction and Negro Sales," Whitehall Street,* United States, Atlanta, Georgia. 1864 Photograph. https://www.loc.gov/item/201866988/.

New Orleans Slave Depot by J.W. Boazman, Natchez Trace Collection, ntc_0305a, The Dolph Briscoe Center for American History, The University of Texas at Austin.

$100 Reward! Ranaway from ... Ripley, Mo., ... 1860, a Negro Man [...] Photograph. https://www.loc.gov/item/98504563/.

Newspaper Clippings of Slave Runaway and Auction Notices, 1820s to 1850s. The Historic New Orleans Collection, 2014.0371.

William and Ellen Craft: ca. 1850s and 1860s. National Park Service taken from William Still's *Underground Rail Road* NPS William & Ellen Craft72a234fc-4e0a-4e3a-95f9-71aa2401000bOriginal.

Jermain W. Loguen, ca. 1850s and 1860s. Courtesy of the Onondaga Historical Association. Syracuse, New York.

James T. Rapier to John Rapier Jr., January 27, 1857. Courtesy of Moorland-Spingarn Research Center, Manuscripts Division, Howard University, Washington, D.C.

Frederick Douglass, ca. 1850s. National Portrait Gallery. Anna Murray Douglass, ca. 1850s. Charles Blockson Collection. Temple University Library.

Rosetta Douglass. Courtesy of the Moorland-Spingarn Research Center, Manuscript Division, Howard University, Washington, D.C.

Lewis H. Douglass. Courtesy of the Moorland-Spingarn Research Center, Manuscript Division, Howard University, Washington, D.C.

Charles R. Douglass. Courtesy of the Moorland-Spingarn Research Center, Manuscript Division, Howard University, Washington, D.C.

Frederick Douglass with daughter Annie Douglass, c. 1854. Daguerreotype. John B. Cade Library, Southern University and A&M College, Baton Rouge, LA.

Frederick Douglass, Jr. Frederick Douglass National Historic Site, National Park Service.

"I love a flower," ca. 1833. Library Company of Philadelphia.

Woodbury, D.B. photographer. *Arrival of Negro Family in the lines* United States, 1863. January 1. Photograph. https://www.loc.gov/item/2018671495/.

Soule, John P. photographer, *Contraband Camp-Harper's Ferry, Va.* Washington, D.C. United States, Washington, D.C., Harper's Ferry, West Virginia. 1862. Boston: Published by John P. Soule. 199 Washington Street. Photograph. https://lccn.loc.gov/2015647582

Smith, William Morris, photographer. *District of Columbia. Company E, 4th U.S. Colored Infantry at Fort Lincoln*: United States, Washington, D.C. [Between 1863 and 1866] Photograph. https://www.loc.gov/item/2018667050/ .

Mary S. Peake, ca. 1860s. Courtesy of Hampton University's Archival and Museum Collection.

Marriage Certificate for Rufus Wright and Elizabeth Turner, December 3, 1863. National Archives and Records Administration.

American, *Soldier and Companion*, between 1861 and 1865, tintype with brass mat and leather case. Detroit Institute of Arts, Founders Society Purchase, DeRoy Photographic Acquisition Endowment Fund and Coville Photographic Fund, 2001.133.

Letter of Union soldier Spotswood Rice to Kittey Diggs. 1864. National Archives and Records Administration.

Union soldier's mother to President Lincoln. 1863. CREDIT: Charles Blockson Collection. Temple University Library.

Rice photographers. *Portrait of Emma V. Brown / M.P. Rice, A. I. Rice, photographers. 1219 Penna. Avenue, Washington, D.C.* [Between 1874 and 1876] Photograph. https://www.loc.gov/item2018645037/ .

Union Army Surgeon Dr. John Rapier. 1864. Archives and Special Collections, Western Libraries, Western University, London, Canada.

John M. Washington. 1880. John Washington Papers, 1858–1865, Accession #15000, Special Collections, University of Virginia Library, Charlottesville, Va.

Anne Gordon Washington. 1880. John Washington Papers, 1858–1865, Accession #15000, Special Collections, University of Virginia Library, Charlottesville, Va.

Sergeant Major Lewis Douglass. 1863. Charles Blockson Collection. Temple University Library.

Helen Amelia Loguen. ca. 1860s. Courtesy of the Onondaga Historical Association. Syracuse, New York.

James Rapier with other African American Congressmen during Reconstruction1886. Collection of the U.S. House of Representatives (from James Blaine's *Twenty Years of Congress from Lincoln to Garfield*).

Unidentified African American Woman. [Between 1860 and 1870] Photograph. https://www.loc.gov/item2010648882/.

Shockley, J. R. photographer. *Two African American boys, full-length portrait, facing front/*, West Side of Main St., Hannibal, Mo. [Between 1860 and 1865] [Photograph. https://www.loc.gov/item/2010647915/ . 1860–1870 J.R.

Unidentified African American Woman., None. [United States, between 1860 and 1870] Photograph. https://www.loc.gov/item/2011649218/.

Young Archibald and Francis Grimke. Late 1860s. Presbyterian Historical Society.

Brady, Mathew B., photographer. *Sen. B.K. Bruce, Mississippi /* Brady, Washington, D.C. [Between 1863 and 1890] Photograph. https://www.loc.gov/item/2011649218/.

Cooley, Sam A. photographer. *Freedmen's school, Edisto Island S.C. Samuel A. Cooley, photographer, Savannah, Ga. Hilton Head S.C. Beaufort, S.C.* South Carolina United States Edisto Island. [Between 1862 and1865] Photograph. https://www.loc.gov/item/2010647918/.

California African American couple between 1870s and 1880s. Yale Collection of Western Americana, Beineke Rare Book and Manuscript Library.

Helen Amelia Loguen Douglass and Lewis Douglass between 1860 and 1880s. Frederick Douglass National Historic Site. National Park Service.

ENDNOTES

PROLOGUE

1 David W. Blight, ed., *A Slave No More: Two Men Who Escaped to Freedom, Including Their Own Narratives of Emancipation* (New York: Harcourt, Inc., 2007), 185–195.

2 Lawrence W. Levine, *Black Culture and Black Consciousness: Afro-American Folk Thought from Slavery to Freedom* (New York: Oxford University Press, 1977), xi.

3 James Oakes, *Slavery and Freedom: An Interpretation of the Old South* (New York: Alfred A. Knopf, Inc., 1990), 4.

4 Ibid.

5 Christopher Hager, *Word by Word: Emancipation and the Act of Writing* (Cambridge, MA: Harvard University Press, 2013), 3–5, 55–60.

PART ONE

6 David W. Blight, ed., *Narrative of Frederick Douglass, A Slave: Written by Himself* (Boston: Bedford/St. Martins, 1845, 1993), 1.

7 Walter Johnson, *River of Dark Dreams: Slavery and Empire in the Cotton Kingdom* (Cambridge, MA: Harvard University Press, 2013), 4–5, 10–11.

8 Henry Wiencek, "The Dark Side of Thomas Jefferson," *Smithsonian Magazine*, October 2012, 2–3; Wiencek, *Master of the Mountain: Thomas Jefferson and His Slaves* (New York: Farrar, Straus and Giroux, 2012), 8.

9 Wiencek, "Dark Side of Thomas Jefferson," 5-6.

10 Wiencek, "Dark Side of Thomas Jefferson," 2–4; Edward Baptist, *The Half Has Never Been Told: Slavery and the Making of American Capitalism* (New York: Basic Books, 2014), 33, 413.

11 Wiencek, "Dark Side of Thomas Jefferson," 5–6.

12 Tera W. Hunter, *Bound in Wedlock: Slave and Free Black Marriage in the Nineteenth Century* (Cambridge, MA: Harvard University Press, 2017), 4.

13 David Freedman, "African American Schooling in the South Prior to 1861," *Journal of African American History* 84 (Winter 1999):1–47; Edward E. Gordon and Elaine H. Gordon, Literacy in America (Westport, CT:Praeger Publishers, 2003).

14 For a recent history of slavery, see Brenda E. Stevenson, *What Is Slavery* (Malden, MA: Polity Press, 2015); see also John J. Zaborney, *Slaves for Hire: Renting Enslaved Laborers in Antebellum Virginia* (Baton Rouge: Louisiana State University Press, 2012) and for African American religious thought see Rita Roberts, *Evangelicalism and the Politics of Reform in Northern Black Thought, 1776–1863* (Baton Rouge: Louisiana State University Press, 2010), 41–43, 77–87, 199; and Albert J. Raboteau, Slave Religion: *The Invisible Institution in the Antebellum South* (New York: Oxford University Press, 1978).

15 Johnson, *River of Dark Dreams*, 5, 14; Stevenson, *What Is Slavery?*, 158.

16 Johnson, *River of Dark Dreams*, 9.

17 Steven Hahn, The Political Worlds of Slavery and Freedom (Cambridge, MA: Harvard University Press, 2009), 6.

18 Roberts, *Evangelicalism and the Politics of Reform*, 20; Robert W. Fogel and Stanley Engerman, "Philanthropy at Bargain Prices: Notes on the Economics of Gradual Emancipation," *Journal of Legal Studies* 3 (June 1974): 377–401.

19 James J. Gigantino, *The Ragged Road to Abolition: Slavery and Freedom in New Jersey, 1771–1865* (Philadelphia: University of Pennsylvania Press, 2015), 235–236.

20 Roberts, *Evangelicalism and the Politics of Reform*, 20–72.

21 Ibid., 63–66, 116–118.

22 Roberts, *Evangelicalism and the Politics of Reform*, 74, 185; for New York City, see Leslie Harris, *In the Shadow of Slavery: African Americans in New York City* (Chicago: University of Chicago Press, 2002), 96–133; Foner, *Gateway to Freedom: The Hidden History of the Underground Railroad* (New York: W.W. Norton & Company, 2015), 46–47.

23 Roberts, *Evangelicalism and Politics of Reform*, 176, 185.

24 See John G. Aiken, *A Digest of the Laws of the State of Alabama— 1833*. Alabama Department of Archives and History, Montgomery, Alabama. www.archives.alabama.gov 395-397; Arthur P. Bagby, et al., eds., *The Code of Alabama* (Montgomery. AL: Brittain and DeWold, 1852), 234–242.

25 Loren Schweninger, "John H. Rapier, Sr.: A Slave and Freedman in the Ante-Bellum South," *Civil War History* 20 (March 1974): 27–29; For a comprehensive study of free blacks in the antebellum South, see Ira Berlin, *Slaves Without Masters: The Free Negro in the Antebellum South* (New York: The New Press, 1974).

26 Michael P. Johnson and James L. Roark, *Black Masters: A Free Family of Color in the Old South* (New York: W.W. Norton & Company, 1984), 47–50.

27 Ibid., 42–50.

28 Ibid., 54–55.

29 Schweninger, "John H. Rapier, Sr.," 28–29; Johnson and Roark, Black Masters, 38–50.

30 Berlin, *Slaves Without Masters*, 197–198.

31 Johnson and Roark, *Black Masters*, 49–50.

32 Quoted in Deborah Gray White, Mia Bay, Waldo E. Martin Jr., *Freedom on My Mind: A History of African Americans with Documents* (Boston: Bedford/St. Martins, 2013), 176.

33 George Fredrickson, *Racism: A Short History* (Princeton, N.J.: Princeton University Press, 2002); for the U.S. role in the illegal transatlantic slave trade, see Leonardo Marques, *The United States and the Transatlantic Slave Trade to the Americas, 1776–1867* (New Haven, CT: Yale University Press, 2016).

34 C. Peter Ripley, ed., *Black Abolitionist Papers* (Chapel Hill: The University of North Carolina Press, 1992), 5:27–29.

35 Stanley Harrold, "Freeing the Weems Family: A New Look at the Underground Railroad," *Civil War History* 42 (December 1996): 293; For a fuller understanding of antebellum northern black activism, see Roberts, *Evangelicalism and Politics of Reform* and Patrick Rael, *Black Identity & Black Protest in the Antebellum North* (Chapel Hill: The University of North Carolina Press, 2002).

36 Robin Winks, *Blacks in Canada: A History* (New Haven, CT: Yale University Press, 1971), 142–177; Foner, *Gateway to Freedom*, 136, 142, 196.

37 Foner, *Gateway to Freedom*, 108-111.

38 Eric Foner, *Give Me Liberty! An American History* (New York: W.W. Norton & Company, 2011), 1:510–511 and Manisha Sinha, *The Slave's Cause: A History of Abolition* (New Haven, CT: Yale University Press, 2016), 390–391; for a thorough understanding of the 1850 Fugitive Slave Law and its impact, see R.J.M. Blackett, *The Captive's Quest for Freedom: Fugitive Slaves, the 1850 Fugitive Slave Law, and the Politics of Slavery* (Cambridge, MA: Cambridge University Press, 2018).

39 Ripley, *Black Abolitionist Papers*, 5:41.

40 Ibid., 5:48–49.

41 Berlin, *Slaves Without Masters*, 316–380.

42 Roberts, *Evangelicalism and the Politics of Reform*, 73–198, 74–77, 167–199.

43 Foner, *Gateway to Freedom*, 152.

CHAPTER ONE

44 E. Jennifer Monaghan, "Reading for the Enslaved, Writing for the Free: Reflections on Liberty and Literacy," *American Antiquarian Society* (2000), 339–341.

45 Barbara Jeanne Fields, *Slavery and Freedom on the Middle Ground: Maryland during the Nineteenth Century* (New Haven, CT: Yale University Press, 1985), 1–39.

46 Nellie A. Plummer, *Out of the Depths or The Triumph of the Cross* (Hyattsville, MD, 1927), 34. Digitized by Google: www.babel. hathitrust.org. See also, Christopher Hager, *Word by Word: Emancipation and the Act of Writing* (Cambridge, MA: Harvard University Press, 2013), 77–83.

47 Plummer, *Out of the Depths*, 7-43.; See also, Plummer Family, www.smithsonian.anacostia .

48 David Blight, *Frederick Douglass: Prophet of Freedom* (New York: Simon & Schuster, 2018), 79–192.

49 John Hope Franklin and Loren Schweninger, *In Search of the Promised Land: A Slave Family in the Old South* (New York: Oxford University Press, 2006), 11–47.

50 Michael P. Johnson and James L. Roark, Black Masters: *A Free Family of Color in the Old South* (New York: W.W. Norton & Company, 1984), 150.

51 Ibid., 220.

52 Ibid., xi–xiv; Michael P. Johnson and James L. Roark, *No Chariot Let Down: Charleston's Free People of Color on the Eve of the Civil War* (Chapel Hill: The University of North Carolina Press, 1984), 3–5, 89.

53 Dorothy Sterling, *We Are Your Sisters: Black Women in the Nineteenth Century* (New York: W.W. Norton & Company, 1984), 49.

54 Ibid., 48.

55 Ibid., 49–51.

56 Ibid., 45–46; Library of Virginia. www.lva.virginia.gov.

57 C. Peter Ripley, ed., *Black Abolitionist Papers* (Chapel Hill: The University of North Carolina Press, 1992), 5:43–50.

58 Plummer, *Out of the Depths*, 44–45; See also, Sterling, *We Are Your Sisters*, 46–47; Carter G. Woodson, *The Mind of the Negro as Reflected In His Letters During the Crisis, 1800–1860* (Washington, D.C.: The Association of Negro Life and History, 1926), 525.

59 Woodson, *Mind of the Negro*, 525.

60 Ibid., 526.

61 Ibid.

62 Ibid., 527.

63 Ibid.

64 Ripley, *Black Abolitionist Papers*, 4:331–334.

65 William Still, *The Underground Railroad: A Record of Facts, Authentic Narratives, Letters, &c.* (Medford, NJ: Plexus Publishing, Inc., 1872, 2005), 18–19.

66 Ibid., 233.

67 Ibid., 233.

68 Ibid., 19–20.

69 Ibid., 44–45.

70 Ibid., 237.

71 Ibid., 36.

72 Ibid., 194–195.

73 Ibid., 32.

74 Eric Foner, *Gateway to Freedom: The Hidden History of the Underground Railroad* (New York: W.W. Norton & Company, 2015), 152, 190; Still, *Underground Railroad*, 214–215.

75 Harrold, "Freeing the Weems Family: A New Look at the Underground Railroad," *Civil War History* 42 (December 1996): 293–304; Still, *The Underground Railroad*, 544.

76 *Liberator*, December 17, 1852.

77 For more fugitive slave letters to former masters, see Woodson, *Mind of the Negro*, 202–221; Ripley, B*lack Abolitionist Papers*, 4:87, 5:353.

78 Woodson, *Mind of the Negro*, 217–218.

79 Ripley, *Black Abolitionist Papers*, 4:87-88.

80 Woodson, *Mind of the Negro*, 217–218.

81 Loren Schweninger, "John H. Rapier, Sr.: A Slave and Freedman in the Ante-Bellum South." *Civil War History* 20 (March 1974): 23–29; Schweninger, "The Dilemma of a Free Negro in the Ante-Bellum South, with Documents," *Journal of Negro History* 62 (July 1977).

82 Schweninger, "The Dilemma of a Free Negro," 284–285.

83 Franklin and Schweninger, *In Search of the Promised Land*, 134–147.

84 The Rapier Family Papers. Moorland Spingarn Research Center. Howard University, Washington D. C., Folder 1.

85 Schweninger, "John H. Rapier, Sr.," 32.

86 Johnson and Roark, *No Chariot Let Down*, 29.

87 Ibid., 29–31.

88 Johnson and Roark, *No Chariot Let Down*, 85–87; Johnson and Roark, *Black Masters*, 173–184.

89 Johnson and Roark, *Black Masters*, 233–273.

90 Johnson and Roark, *No Chariot Let Down*, 128.

91 Johnson and Roark, *Black Masters*, 164–194; Foner, *Give Me Liberty! An American History* (New York: W.W. Norton & Company, 2011), 1:524–525.

92 The Frederick Douglass Papers. Digital Collection. Correspondence 1852–1863, 6–7.

93 David Blight, *Frederick Douglass: Prophet of Freedom* (New York: Simon & Schuster, 2018), 319.

94 Blight, *Frederick Douglass*, 266, 318–320.

95 Ibid., 8–9.

96 Sterling, *We Are Your Sisters*, 191–199.

97 Ibid., 131–132.

98 Ibid.

99 Erica L. Ball, *To Live an Antislavery Life: Personal Politics and the Antebellum Black Middle Class* (Athens: University of Georgia Press, 2012).

100 Frederick Douglass Family Papers. Walter O. Evans Collection of Frederick Douglass and Douglass Family Papers, Beinecke Rare Book & Manuscript Library, Yale University.

PART TWO

101 *Douglass' Monthly*, March 1863.

102 Ibid., 110–112.

103 Alexander H. Stephens, "Cornerstone Speech, delivered on March 21, 1861, in Savannah, Georgia. www.encyclopedia-virginia.org.

104 James Oakes, Freedom National: *The Destruction of Slavery in the United States, 1861–1865* (New York: W.W. Norton & Company, 2013), 73–83.

105 Letter from Hannibal Guards to General James S. Negley, *Pittsburgh Gazette*, April 18, 1861, quoted in James M. McPherson, *The Negro's Civil War: How American Negroes Felt and Acted during the War for the Union* (New York: Pantheon, 1965), 19–20.

106 Ibid. 22.

107 *Montreal Witness*, September 1862, in Black Abolitionist Archive, University of Detroit Mercy, research.udmercy.edu/find/special_collections/digital/baa/ Document 10260.

108 *Weekly Anglo-African*, April 27, 1861.

109 Oakes, *Freedom National*, 274–293. Oakes questions the idea that Lincoln's interest in emancipation was hindered by his concern to keep the Border States from leaving the Union. He suggests it may be that "emancipation made keeping the Border States from seceding more difficult. . . . Lincoln was struggling to keep them in the Union while at the same time he was pressuring them to abolish slavery."

110 Ira Berlin, Barbara J. Fields, Steven F. Miller, Joseph P. Reidy, and Leslie Rowland, eds. *Free at Last: A Documentary History of Slavery, Freedom, and the Civil War* (New York: The New Press, 1992), xxix.

111 McPherson, *Negro's Civil War*, 44–45.

112 Berlin, et al. *Free at Last*, 3.

113 Donald Yacovone, ed. *A Voice of Thunder: A Black Soldier's Civil War* (Urbana: University of Illinois Press, 1998), 144.

114 Oakes, *Freedom National*, 136-144, 226–239; James McPherson, *Battle Cry of Freedom: The Civil War Era* (New York: Oxford University Press, 1988), 353–356, 499–502. For the full text of both acts, see the Freedmen and Southern Society Project online: www.freedmen.umd.edu.

115 McPherson, Battle Cry, 371; Thomas Holt, Cassandra Smith-Parker, and Rosalyn Terborg-Penn, "A Special Mission: The Story of the Freedmen's Hospital, 1862–1962" (Washington, D.C.: Academic Affairs Division, Howard University, 1975).

116 For a timeline of events and excerpts of the Confiscation Acts see Berlin et al. *Free at Last*, vii-xxviii; C. Peter Ripley, ed. *Black Abolitionist Papers* (Chapel Hill: The University of North Carolina Press, 1992), 5:152; Michael Vorenberg, "Abraham Lincoln and the Politics of Black Colonization," *Journal of the Abraham Lincoln Association* 14 (Summer 1993), 22–45.

117 Oakes, *Freedom National*, 341; see also, McPherson, *Negro's Civil War*, 28, 41, 48, 296.

118 *Christian Recorder*, January 10, 1863.

119 Rita Roberts, *Evangelicalism and the Politics of Reform in Northern Black Thought, 1776–1863* (Baton Rouge: Louisiana State University, 2010), 198–199.

120 *Douglass' Monthly*, January 1863.

121 Yacovone, *A Voice of Thunder*, 15.

122 *Douglass' Monthly*, August 1863.

123 Berlin et al., *Free at Last*, 436–437.

124 McPherson, *The Negro's Civil War*, 161–239.

125 Yacovone, *Voice of Thunder*, 19; Virginia M. Adams, ed., *On the Altar of Freedom: A Black Soldier's Civil War Letters from the Front* (Amherst: University of Massachusetts Press, 1991), xxxiv.

126 McPherson, *Negro's Civil War*, 193.

127 Ira Berlin, ed., *Freedom: A Documentary History of Emancipation, 1961–1867. The Black Military Experience* (Cambridge, MA: Cambridge University Press, 1982) Series II (Book 2), 362–368.

128 See McPherson, *Negro's Civil War*, 193–203; Berlin et al, *Free at Last*, 473–477.

129 Ira Berlin, ed., *Freedom: A Documentary History of Emancipation, 1861–1867. The Black Military Experience* (Cambridge, MA: Cambridge University Press, 1982) Series II (Book I), 409.

130 Ibid., 433–434.

131 Ibid., 433–436.

132 Berlin, *Freedom: The Black Military Experience* Ser. II (Bk1), 438.

133 Ibid., 408–409.

134 Berlin et al., *Free at Last*, 437–438; McPherson, *Negro's Civil War*, 238–239.

135 Berlin et al., *Free at Last*, 447; James M. McPherson, *Battle Cry of Freedom: The Civil War Era* (New York: Oxford University Press, 1988), 566.

136 McPherson, *Battle Cry of Freedom*, 566.

137 Berlin et al., *Free at Last*, 448.

138 McPherson, *Battle Cry of Freedom*, 748; McPherson, *Negro's Civil War*, 216–221; *Christian Recorder*, April 23, 1864.

139 McPherson, *Negro's Civil War*, 216, 234–237.

140 Iver Bernstein, *The New York City Draft Riots: Their Significance for American Society and Politics in the Age of the Civil War.* (New York: Oxford University Press, 1990), 17-192; McPherson, *Negro's Civil War*, 193-203; Ripley, Black Abolitionist Papers, 5:229.

141 McPherson, *Negro's Civil War*, 249–254.

142 McPherson, *Negro's Civil War*, 136–138.

143 Ripley, *Black Abolitionist Papers*, 5:40–141.

144 Berlin et al., *Free at Last*, 140–142.

145 Ibid., 144–145.

146 Ibid., 161; John Hope Franklin and Evelyn Brooks Higginbotham, *From Slavery to Freedom: A History of African Americans* (New York: McGraw Hill, 2011), 230–231.

147 Berlin et al., *Free at Last*, 268–269.

148 McPherson, *Battle Cry of Freedom*, 841–842; Eric Foner, *Reconstruction: America's Unfinished Revolution, 1863–1877* (New York: Harper & Row, 1988), 70–72.

149 Oakes, *Freedom National*, 439.

150 Ibid., 439–442.

151 Ibid., 480.

152 Ibid., 392, 434–488.

153 McPherson, *Negro's Civil War*, 237; Ripley, *Black Abolitionist Papers*, 5:179.

154 Berlin et al., *Free at Last*, 164–165.

CHAPTER TWO

155 Plummer, *Out of the Depths*, 83.

156 Plummer, *Out of the Depths*.

157 Henry L. Swint, *Dear Ones at Home: Letters from the Contraband Camps* (Nashville, TN: Vanderbilt University Press, 1966), 41.

158 Elizabeth Botume, *First Days Amongst the Contrabands* (First printed: Boston: Lee and Shepard Publishers, 1893. Available in Internet Archive, 2010 archive.org.), 154.

159 Sterling, *We Are Your Sisters: Black Women in the Nineteenth Century* (New York: W.W. Norton & Company, 1984), 191–202, 286.

160 John Hope Franklin and Loren Schweninger, *In Search of the Promised Land: A Slave Family in the Old South* (New York: Oxford University Press, 2006), 135–140, 180–208.

161 Franklin and Schweninger, *In Search of the Promised Land*, 211–218.

162 Johnson and Roark, *Black Masters*, 262–263.

164 *Liberator*, September 5, 1862.

165 Sterling, *We Are Your Sisters*, 265.

166 Woodson, *Mind of the Negro*, 527–528.

167 Plummer, *Out of the Depths*, 76.

168 Ibid., 16, 76–77.

169 Ira Berlin, Barbara J. Fields, Steven F. Miller, Joseph P. Reidy, and Leslie Rowland, eds. *Free at Last: A Documentary History of Slavery, Freedom, and the Civil War* (New York: The New Press, 1992), 29–30.

170 Ripley, *Black Abolitionist Papers*, 5:187–192.

171 *Douglass' Monthly*, August 1863.

172 Ira Berlin, ed., *Freedom: A Documentary History of Emancipation, 1961–1867. The Black Military Experience* (Cambridge, MA: Cambridge University Press, 1982) Series II (Book 2), 661–664.

173 Frederick Douglass Papers. Library of Congress. Correspondence: Digital Collection. 1864 Mixed Materials, 51–53.

174 Berlin, *Freedom: The Black Military Experience*, Ser. II (Book 2), 686–688.

175 Swint, *Dear Ones at Home*, 41–42.

176 Ibid., 107.

177 Ibid., 18, 83–84.

178 Elizabeth H. Botume, *First Days Amongst the Contrabands*, 153–156.

179 Ibid., 148–150; See also, James M. McPherson, *Battle Cry of Freedom: The Civil War Era* (New York: Oxford University Press, 1988), 807-830.

180 Randolph B. Campbell and Donald K. Pickens, " 'My Dear Husband': A Texas Slave's Love Letter, 1862," *Journal of Negro History* 65 (Autumn 1980): 361–364. See Query XIV, Thomas Jefferson, *Notes on Virginia.* https://docsouth.unc.edu/southlit/jefferson/jefferson.html.

181 Sterling, *We Are Your Sisters*, 241.

182 Berlin, *Freedom: The Black Military Experience*, Ser. II (Book 2), 689.

183 Ibid., 690.

184 Ira Berlin, Barbara J. Fields, Thavolia Glymph, Joseph P. Reidy, Leslie S. Rowland, eds. *Freedom: A Documentary History of Emancipation, 1861–1867. The Destruction of Slavery.* Series I, Volume I (New York: Cambridge University Press, 1985), 365.

185 Berlin, ed., *Freedom: The Black Military Experience*, Series II (Book 2), 680.

186 Berlin et al., *Free at Last*, 450–451.

187 Berlin, *Freedom: Black Military Experience*, Ser. II (Bk 2), 664–665.

188 Ibid., 665.

189 Johnson and Roark, *No Chariot Let Down*, 150.

190 Johnson and Roark, *No Chariot Let Down*, 152.

191 Sterling, *We Are Your Sisters*, 201–202.

192 Ibid., 285–287.

193 *The Christian Recorder*, February 17, 1864.

194 William McFeely, Frederick Douglass (New York: W.W. Norton & Company, 1991), 219–221; See also Sterling, *We Are Your Sisters*, 138–139.

195 Frederick Douglass Papers. Digital Collection. 1862 Correspondence, 16–21.

196 McFeely, *Frederick Douglass*, 220–221; See Rosetta Douglass, *My Mother As I Recall Her* for an understanding of the resourcefulness of Anna Murray Douglass. Frederick Douglass Papers. Digital Collection.

197 Frederick Douglass Papers. Digital Collection. 1862 Correspondence, 42–48.

198 Ibid., 48–53.

199 Jacob C. White Papers. Moorland Spingarn Research Center. Howard University, Washington D.C.

200 Rapier Family Papers. Moorland Spingarn Research Center. Howard University, Washington D.C., Folder 76.

201 Botume, *First Days Amongst the Contrabands*, 147.

202 Ibid., 148.

203 John M. Washington Papers, 1858-1865. Special Collections, University of Virginia Library, Charlottesville, Va., Box 2, Folder 1.

204 Frederick Douglass Family Papers. Walter O. Evans Collection of Frederick Douglass and Douglass Family Papers, Beinecke Rare Book & Manuscript Library, Yale University.

205 Ibid.

206 Woodson, *The Mind of the Negro*, 540–544. Regarding Wendell Phillips, see *New York Times*, March 25, 1862.

207 Frederick Douglass Papers. Digital Collection. Correspondence 1852–1863 Mixed Materials, 10–13. For a comprehensive and lively account of the 54th and 55th Colored Infantry and the 5th Calvary, see Douglas R. Egerton, *Thunder at the Gates: The Black Civil War Regiments that Redeemed America* (New York: Basic Books, 2016).

208 Woodson, *The Mind of the Negro*, 540–544.

209 Egerton, *Thunder at the Gates*, 157–158.

PART THREE

210 David W. Blight, ed., *Narrative of the Life of Fredrick Douglass: An American Slave* (Boston: Bedford/St. Martin, 1993), 2.

211 Steven Hahn, Steven F. Miller, Susan E. O'Donovan, John C. Rodrigue, and Leslie Rowland, eds., *Freedom: A Documentary History of Emancipation, 1861-1867, Land and Labor, 1865*. Series 3: Volume 1 (Chapel Hill: The University of North Carolina Press, 2008), xi.

212 John W. Blassingame and John R. McKivigan, eds., *The Frederick Douglass Papers: Speeches, Debates, and Interviews*. Series One, Volume 4, 1864–80 (New Haven: Yale University Press, 1991), 74–79.

213 Ibid., 600–601; John Hope Franklin and Evelyn Brooks Higginbotham, *From Slavery to Freedom: A History of the African Americans* (New York: McGraw Hill, 2011), 220.

214 Hahn et al., *Freedom: Land and Labor*, Ser. 3, Vol. I, 603.

215 Ibid., 90–95.

216 Eric Foner, *Reconstruction: America's Unfinished Revolution, 1863–1877* (New York: Harper & Row, 1988), 15, 17, 68–70, 96–98, 596; Hahn et al., *Freedom: Land and Labor*, Ser. 3, Vol. I, 600.

217 Hahn et al., *Freedom: Land and Labor*, Ser. 3, Vol. I, 602.

218 Susan Benson, "Injurious Names: Naming, Disavowal, and the Recuperation in Context of Slavery and Emancipation," in *The Anthropology of Names and Naming*, eds. Gabriele vom Bruck and Barbara Bodenhorn (New York: Cambridge University Press, 2006) 178–199; Leon Litwack, *Been In the Storm So Long: The Aftermath of Slavery* (New York: Vintage Books, 1979), 247–251.

219 Jacqueline Jones, *Labor of Love, Labor of Sorrow: Black Women, Work, and the Family from Slavery to the Present* (New York: Basic Books, 1985), 43–48.

220 Hahn et al., *Freedom: Land and Labor*, Ser. 3, Vol. I, 747.

221 Speech of the Hon. T. Stevens of Pennsylvania delivered in the House of Representatives, March 19, 1867: on the Bill H.R. no. 20 https://archive.org/details/speechofhonstev01stev.

222 Foner, *Reconstruction*, 51.

223 Ibid.; Ira Berlin, Thavolia Glymph, Steven F. Miller, Joseph P. Reidy, Leslie S. Rowland, and Julie Saville, eds., *Freedom: A Documentary History of Emancipation, 1861–1867. The Wartime Genesis of Free Labor: The Lower South* Series I, Volume III (New York: Cambridge University Press, 1990), 9.

224 Hahn et al., *Freedom: Land and Labor*. Ser. 3, Vol. I, 689.

225 Ibid., 687–688.

226 James D. Anderson, *The Education of Blacks in the South, 1860–1935* (Chapel Hill: The University of North Carolina Press, 1988), 5.

227 Ibid., 5–7; Swint, *Dear Ones at Home Contraband Camps*, 176; Anderson, *Education of Blacks*, 5; Dale J. Cohen, Sheida White, and Steffaney B. Cohen, "Mind the Gap: The Black-White Literacy Gap in the National Assessment of Adult Literacy and Its Implications," Journal of Literacy Research 44 (2012), 125.

228 Foner, *Reconstruction*, 97–101, 144; Anderson, *Education of Blacks*, 4–20.

229 Foner, *Reconstruction*, 95–102.

230 Ibid. 291, 27.

231 Ibid., 35-37, 190–198.

232 Douglas A. Blackmon, *Slavery by Another Name: The Re-Enslavement of Black Americans from the Civil War to World War II* (New York: Anchor Books, 2008).

233 Foner, Reconstruction, 198.

234 Ibid.

235 Ibid., 198–200.

236 Ibid., 200–203.

237 Ibid.

238 Quoted in Hahn et al., *Freedom: Land and Labor*, Ser. 3, Vol. I, 974.

239 Ibid.

240 Ira Berlin, ed., *Freedom: A Documentary History of Emancipation, 1861–1867: The Black Military Experience* Series II (Book 1), (New York: Cambridge University Press, 1982), 32.

[241] Foner, *Reconstruction*, 243.

[242] Ibid. 256, 267–277.

[243] Eric Foner, *The Story of American Freedom* (New York: W.W. Norton & Company, 1998), 105.

[244] Ibid., 281–307; White et al., *Freedom on My Mind*, 393.

[245] White et al., *Freedom on My Mind*, 395–396.

[246] Foner, *Reconstruction*, 271–278.

[247] Ibid. 110, 316–333; Hahn et al., *Freedom: Land and Labor.* Ser. 3, Vol. I, 799–800.

[248] Foner, *Reconstruction*, 102, 351–352, 545–547.

[249] Ibid., 279; See also, 512–612.

[250] Ibid., 587–598; See also, W.E.B. DuBois, *Black Reconstruction in America, 1860–1880* (New York: Atheneum, 1935, 1992), 431–524.

CHAPTER THREE

[251] Nellie A. Plummer, *Out of the Depths*, 106.

[252] Ibid.

[253] For Emilie Davis's Diary, see Judith Giesberg, ed., Emilie *Davis's Civil War: The Diaries of a Free Black Woman in Philadelphia, 1863–1865*; Plummer, *Out of the Depths*, 92–107.

[254] Reva B. Siegel, "The Rule of Love: Wife Beating as Prerogative and Privacy," (1996). Faculty Scholarship Series. Paper 1092 http://digitalcommons.law.yale.edu/fss_papers/1092.

[255] Ibid., 304–305; Angela Morgan Papers, http://quod.lib.umich.edu/b/bhlead/umich-bhl-8629?view=text.

[256] Steven Hahn, Steven F. Miller, Susan E. O'Donovan, John C. Rodrigue, and Leslie Rowland, eds., *Freedom: A Documentary History of Emancipation, 1861–1867, Land and Labor, 1865*. Series 3: Vol I (Chapel Hill: The University of North Carolina Press, 2008), 262–264.

[257] Ibid., 699–700.

[258] *New York Daily Tribune*, August 22, 1865.

[259] Ira Berlin, ed., *Freedom: A Documentary History of Emancipation, 1861–1867: The Black Military Experience*. Series II (Book 2) (New York: Cambridge University Press, 1982),703–705.

[260] Ibid., 705–706.

[261] Ibid., 706.

[262] Ibid., 698.

[263] Ibid., 697–698.

[264] Sterling, *We Are Your Sisters*, 316.

[265] Swint, *Dear Ones at Home*, 242–243.

[266] *Christian Recorder*, 1866 & 1868 passim.

[267] Leon F. Litwack, *Been in the Storm So Long: The Aftermath of Slavery* (New York: Vintage Books, 1980), 232.

[268] Ira Berlin, Steven F. Miller, Joseph P. Reidy, and Leslie S. Rowland, eds., *Freedom: A Documentary History of Emancipation, 1861–1867, The Wartime Genesis of Free Labor: The Upper South* Series I, Volume II (New York: Cambridge University Press, 1992), 462–463.

[269] Ibid., 543–544.

[270] Hahn et al. *Land and Freedom*, Series 3: Vol. 1, 973–974.

[271] Sterling, *We Are Your Sisters*, 315.

[272] Ibid.

[273] Berlin et al., eds., *Freedom: The Wartime Genesis of Free Labor*, Series I, Vol. II, 544–545.

[274] Ibid., 346.

[275] Sterling, *We Are Your Sisters*, 338–340.

[276] Archibald Grimke Papers, Moorland Spingarn Research Center, Howard University. Washington D. C., Series B and C.

[277] Sterling, *We Are Your Sisters*, 302–303.

[278] Ibid., 133.

[279] Ibid., 289.

[280] Ibid., 289–290.

[281] Ibid., 290–291; Emily Howland Papers. #2681 Cornell University Library. Ithaca, New York.

[282] Ibid., 292.

[283] Ibid., 293.

[284] Ibid., 293–294; See also Harrold Stanley, *Subversives: Antislavery Community in Washington, D.C., 1828–1865* (Baton Rouge: Louisiana State University Press), 171–174, 192, 200, 232–233.

[285] James D. Anderson, *The Education of Blacks in the South, 1860–1935* (Chapel Hill: The University of North Carolina Press, 1988), 3–32.

[286] Ira Berlin, ed., *Freedom: The Black Military Experience*, Series II (Book 2), 615.

[287] Foner, *Reconstruction*, 96–97.

[288] *Christian Recorder*, July 14, 1866.

[289] Ibid., December 18, 1869.

[290] Records of the Freedmen's Bureau: Virginia 1870.

[291] Sterling, *We Are Your Sisters*, 297–298.

[292] Ibid., 298–299.

[293] Ibid., 299–302.

[294] *Christian Recorder*, January 16, 1869.

[295] *Christian Recorder*, January 20, 1866.

[296] Mary Ann Shadd Cary Papers, Moorland Spingarn Research Center, Howard University. Washington D. C. Folder 6.

[297] George T. Downing Papers, Moorland Spingarn Research Center, Howard University. Washington D. C., Box 152-2, Folder 16.

[298] Jesse Moorland Papers, Moorland Spingarn Research Center, Howard University. Washington D.C., Box 126-1 & 2.

[299] Frederick Douglass Family Papers. Walter O. Evans Collection of Frederick Douglass and Douglass Family Papers, Beinecke Rare Book & Manuscript Library, Yale University.

[300] Ibid.

[301] Ibid.

[302] *Christian Recorder*, October 10, 1869.

INDEX

letter writing guides, 9
Levine, Lawrence, 8
Liberator, 27, 76, 77, 127
Lincoln, Abraham
    captured black soldiers and, 114
    colonization and, 104, 106
    death of, 199–200
    Emancipation Proclamation and, 106, 140
    letters to, 161–65
    mob rule and, 21
    pardon policy of, for former rebels, 206
    as presidential candidate, 96
    secession and, 102
    slavery and, 101, 102, 104, 106, 119, 201
Lincoln, Mary Todd, 116
Lincoln University, 205, 244, 246
literacy, 8, 15–16, 33–35, 204–5
Lockwood, Lewis, 130
Logue, Sarah, 78–81
Loguen, Amelia. *See* Douglass, Amelia Loguen
Loguen, Gerrit, 277, 278
Loguen, Jermain, 27, 42, 76, 78–81, 99, 187
Louisiana Education Relief Association, 267
Louisiana Native Guard, 107
Lynch, James D., 254, 255, 267, 268, 269
Lynch, John R., 212, 258

M

Maimi, Meunomennie L., 138–40
Manly, Ralza, 262
marriage
    certificate, 144
    courtship and, 97–99, 126, 183–84, 186–90, 193–97, 273–80
    domestic violence and, 217, 243–44
    importance of, 273
    interracial, 218, 250–51
    slavery and, 8–9, 15, 17, 151–55, 217
McCune Smith, James, 26, 115, 197
McKim, J. Miller, 70
Miner, Myrtilla, 41
Mitchell, Alice, 233
Montgomery, Henry, 259
Moore, Harvey, 273–76
Moore, Mariah, 68
Morgan, Albert T., 218, 250
Mortimer, R. G., 261
Mount Rose, 217
Murray, Anna. *See* Douglass, Anna Murray
Murray, Elizabeth, 174
Murray, Perry, 174

N

names, 179, 202
National Convention of Colored Men, 115
National Equal Rights League, 115
Newby, Dangerfield, 30, 48–51
Newby, Harriet, 48–50
New England Freedmen's Aid Society, 124
newspapers, 26
New York African Free School, 20–21
Nicholson, Sarah, 58

O

Oakes, James, 8, 102, 119
Oberlin College, 21, 96, 124, 168, 171
O'Neall, John B., 22
Owens, Caddy, 154
Owens, Peggy, 154
Ozanne, Urbain, 235

P

Peake, Mary S., 116, 130–31
Pennington, James W. C., 102, 107
Pennsylvania Abolition Society, 116
Perkins, Frances W., 124
Perkins, R. A., 262
Philbrick, Edward, 118
Phillips, Wendell, 193, 194
Picquet, Louisa, 47
Pillsbury, Frank, 94, 250
Plummer, Adam, 34–37, 55–60, 122, 134–36, 216–17
Plummer, Elias, 36, 56, 57
Plummer, Emily Saunders, 34–37, 55–56, 58–60, 122, 134–36, 217
Plummer, Henry, 35, 56, 122, 216
Plummer, Julia Ann, 35
Plummer, Margaret Jane, 36, 58
Plummer, Marjory Ellen Rose, 36
Plummer, Nellie, 36, 37, 60, 122, 216
Plummer, Nicholas Saunders, 35, 58
Plummer, Robert, 37, 60
Plummer, Sarah Miranda, 35, 36, 37, 56, 57, 58, 122, 133–35, 216
political officeholders, 211, 213, 254, 258
Pollard, Elizabeth, 239

R

racism, 8, 21–24, 38, 40–41, 102, 108–9, 112–14, 138, 168, 201, 206–10, 217–18, 265, 272. *See also* white supremacy
Ramsey, Elizabeth, 47
Rapier, Henry, 39, 82
Rapier, James, 39, 82, 83, 85, 113, 212
Rapier, John, Jr., 39, 82, 83, 85, 113, 124–25, 179–82
Rapier, John, Sr., 38–39, 82–83, 85, 124
Rapier, Richard, 39, 82
Ray, Alec, 243–44
Ray, Julia, 243
Reconstruction
    African American men as officeholders during, 211, 213, 254, 258
    end of, 214–15
    former slaves' view of, 216
    land ownership and, 203–4
    legacy of, 218
    legislation for, 211
Reed, Sarah, 228–29
refugee camps, 105, 121, 130, 148, 156, 200–201, 231
Revels, Hiram, 212, 213
Reynolds, Lucinda, 233
Rice, Spotswood, 157–59
Riley, Catherine, 222–24, 226–27
Riley, George, 222–24, 226
Riley, James, 226–27
Riley, Norman, 222–24, 226
Roark, James, 40

but they did not go. I went but sat outside and smoked and talked all the time. I did not speak to a lady the whole night for I did not know but one and that slightly. I played non (e) or admired non (e) that was my first party this year and will be my last – certainly for I do not like partys where you are not.

Susan did really promise to come to Richmond to live and I made her believe I would come back next year to live too. Please don't tell her this. I can gas any body but you. Between you and me there is and must ever be sincerity & truth. You tell me of unhappy hours for me. I beseech you to be easy and assured that the memory of thee ever admonishes me to be careful. Oh, my own sweet Annie I know you love me and I am so proud of it and it sends a thrill to my heart when I think of it. My heart tells me when you are unhappy and then I become so